Palgrave Studies in Agricultural Economics and Food Policy

Series Editor
Christopher Barrett
Cornell University
Ithaca, NY, USA

Agricultural and food policy lies at the heart of many pressing societal issues today and economic analysis occupies a privileged place in contemporary policy debates. The global food price crises of 2008 and 2010 underscored the mounting challenge of meeting rapidly increasing food demand in the face of increasingly scarce land and water resources. The twin scourges of poverty and hunger quickly resurfaced as high-level policy concerns, partly because of food price riots and mounting insurgencies fomented by contestation over rural resources. Meanwhile, agriculture's heavy footprint on natural resources motivates heated environmental debates about climate change, water and land use, biodiversity conservation and chemical pollution. Agricultural technological change, especially associated with the introduction of genetically modified organisms, also introduces unprecedented questions surrounding intellectual property rights and consumer preferences regarding credence (i.e., unobservable by consumers) characteristics. Similar new agricultural commodity consumer behavior issues have emerged around issues such as local foods, organic agriculture and fair trade, even motivating broader social movements. Public health issues related to obesity, food safety, and zoonotic diseases such as avian or swine flu also have roots deep in agricultural and food policy. And agriculture has become inextricably linked to energy policy through biofuels production. Meanwhile, the agricultural and food economy is changing rapidly throughout the world, marked by continued consolidation at both farm production and retail distribution levels, elongating value chains, expanding international trade, and growing reliance on immigrant labor and information and communications technologies. In summary, a vast range of topics of widespread popular and scholarly interest revolve around agricultural and food policy and economics. The extensive list of prospective authors, titles and topics offers a partial, illustrative listing. Thus a series of topical volumes, featuring cutting-edge economic analysis by leading scholars has considerable prospect for both attracting attention and garnering sales. This series will feature leading global experts writing accessible summaries of the best current economics and related research on topics of widespread interest to both scholarly and lay audiences.

More information about this series at
http://www.palgrave.com/gp/series/14651

Johan Swinnen

The Political Economy of Agricultural and Food Policies

palgrave
macmillan

Johan Swinnen
LICOS Centre for Institutions and Economic Performance
University of Leuven
Leuven, Belgium

Palgrave Studies in Agricultural Economics and Food Policy
ISBN 978-1-137-50101-1   ISBN 978-1-137-50102-8   (eBook)
https://doi.org/10.1057/978-1-137-50102-8

Library of Congress Control Number: 2018938172

© The Editor(s) (if applicable) and The Author(s) 2018
This work is subject to copyright. All rights are solely and exclusively licensed by the
Publisher, whether the whole or part of the material is concerned, specifically the rights of
translation, reprinting, reuse of illustrations, recitation, broadcasting, reproduction on
microfilms or in any other physical way, and transmission or information storage and retrieval,
electronic adaptation, computer software, or by similar or dissimilar methodology now
known or hereafter developed.
The use of general descriptive names, registered names, trademarks, service marks, etc. in this
publication does not imply, even in the absence of a specific statement, that such names are
exempt from the relevant protective laws and regulations and therefore free for general use.
The publisher, the authors, and the editors are safe to assume that the advice and information
in this book are believed to be true and accurate at the date of publication. Neither the publisher
nor the authors or the editors give a warranty, express or implied, with respect to the material
contained herein or for any errors or omissions that may have been made. The publisher remains
neutral with regard to jurisdictional claims in published maps and institutional affiliations.

Cover image © Granger Historical Picture Archive / Alamy Stock Photo
Cover design by Tom Howey

Printed on acid-free paper

This Palgrave Macmillan imprint is published by the registered company Nature America,
Inc. part of Springer Nature.
The registered company address is: 1 New York Plaza, New York, NY 10004, U.S.A.

Foreword

Agricultural and food policy is intensely political everywhere in the world. As a result, agriculture and the post-harvest food value chain are among the most distorted sectors in the global economy. This is perhaps most obvious in high-income countries, where rice policy in Japan, the European Union's Common Agricultural Policy, and various farm programs in the USA attract massive subsidies grossly out of proportion to their share of national output. It is not mere coincidence that the American presidential electoral process begins in Iowa, the quintessential agricultural state, compelling serious candidates to genuflect before farm interests as they commence their campaign for leadership of the world's largest economy. And this dynamic extends into middle- and low-income countries as well. China, now the world's second largest economy, has rapidly transitioned from significant net taxation of agriculture just a generation ago to massive subsidization of the sector today. In low-income countries too, food price and agricultural land tenure policy are among the most sensitive matters under government control.

A solid understanding of the processes and interests that guide agricultural and food policy is therefore essential to any serious student of agricultural economics and food policy. First principles from welfare economics provide essential building blocks for understanding not just aggregate welfare effects but, even more importantly, who wins and who loses from which policies, and thus what coalitions might form in favor of or against particular policies, as well as how those coalitions might evolve with the emergence of new technologies (such as genetically modified foods) and markets (e.g. for biofuels). But a firm analytical grasp of these material interests' principles must also be blended with a nuanced understanding of key institutions and of how ideology and information—including that increasingly provided through mass and social media—drive political economy in ways commonly overlooked in the simplest economic models of policy choice.

Professor Jo Swinnen is perhaps uniquely positioned to blend these various insights to deliver a compelling compact treatise on the political economy of agricultural and food policy. Over the past 20-some years, he has generated a steady stream of seminal articles that have established him as one of the world's most sophisticated and knowledgeable scholars in this domain. In this engaging volume Professor Swinnen draws together various threads from his own and others' writings into an impressive tapestry that proves a compact, elegant, and accessible introduction to the subject. He starts by laying out the conceptual underpinnings of modern political economy in admirably clear, non-technical terms. He then goes on to describe what a sprawling empirical literature on the political economy of food and agricultural policies tells us about the key determinants of different policy regimes. He unpacks the complex stories of agricultural policy evolution in the transition economies of Asia and Europe, the coalition of interests that lead to the structure of the Farm Bills enacted in the USA every five or so years, and how the march of economic development naturally shifts the pressures governments face around food and agricultural policy. As he skillfully explains, some policies have the potential to create significant aggregate welfare gains, as is the case with publically funded agricultural research and extension, and yet struggle to find adequate political support. The challenge is how to design mechanisms that credibly commit governments to compensate those who might be adversely affected by policies that would unquestionably improve aggregate welfare. The significant transactions costs involved in the policy-making process also exert a major influence over policy design and the political economy of policy choice, in ways that superficial observers commonly miss but Swinnen explains lucidly.

We stand at an unusual moment in time when the political economy of food and agriculture is shifting at a pace never before seen. Over the past generation we have witnessed the dramatic liberalization of previously state-controlled agricultural sectors across much of Europe, Asia, and Africa. Middle-income countries such as Brazil, China, and India have become global leaders in agricultural research, turning them into aggressive commercial competitors in the global marketplace, in part due to strategic interventions by their governments. The global institutions designed to manage global markets, most notably the World Trade Organization (WTO), have proved increasingly irrelevant as global value chains employing private standards increasingly drive exchange, and as non-tariff barriers addressing environmental, labor, and food safety concerns play an ever larger role in trade policy. Moreover, global food prices have trended upward since hitting their inflation-adjusted all-time low in December 1999, with price spikes in the late 2000s and early 2010s suddenly turning trade policy issues upside down. Where the WTO and its predecessor arrangements were organized around combatting import restrictions and dumping of exports, suddenly export restrictions became the policy tool of greatest concern in global dialogues. Remarkably, distortions in the global agricultural economy have nonetheless been falling over this time. At a time of rapid and dramatic change, a firm grasp of the political economy of agricultural and food policy is more essential than ever.

The powerful insights Professor Swinnen offers in this volume are too numerous to capture adequately in a foreword. In clear prose it lays out the central issues in accessible terms and compactly summarizes a deep and complex literature with remarkable precision and rigor. Suffice to say, serious students of the political economy of agricultural and food policies need to read this volume.

It is a great pleasure to include Jo Swinnen's outstanding book in the Palgrave Studies in Agricultural Economics and Food Policy series. It will prove an essential reference to anyone striving to understand the origins and evolution of agricultural and food policy in modern society.

Cornell University
Ithaca, NY, USA

Christopher Barrett

PREFACE

The background picture on the cover is an illustration of *the Women's March on Versailles* in October 1789. Food security was uncertain and food shortages common in those years in France, except in the palaces of Versailles near Paris where the King and his entourage resided. The women's march started with riots of poor women in Paris faced with high prices and scarcity of bread. Their protests and demands for food policy reforms quickly turned into a broader call for political reforms. Supported by those who were seeking liberal political reforms, the women and their allies ransacked the city armory for weapons and marched to the King's palace of Versailles. The confrontation resulted in significant policy changes and proved to be a defining moment of the French Revolution which not only removed the French King from power but eventually inspired revolutions and political institutions across the world.

The story illustrates the interaction between food, economics, and politics. Food security is influenced by economic policies which are in turn determined by political systems and decision-making. Yet, inversely, political decisions and even political institutions are or can be influenced by the production and consumption of food. The interaction between these economic and political forces and institutions is at the heart of political economy and the focus of this book.

My research in political economy started as a PhD student in Cornell University when professor Harry de Gorter encouraged me to use the data which the World Bank had just assembled on agricultural price distortions to empirically test some of the existing political economy theories for a paper in a course. Before starting running regressions he suggested to read

Anthony Downs' *An Economic Theory of Democracy*, Mancur Olson's *The Logic of Collective Action*, and classic articles by Gary Becker and so on, and not to be easily satisfied with existing theories or explanations. The term paper turned into a full PhD and, in a way, "the rest was history", as they say.

By the time I finished my PhD, the Berlin Wall had fallen, and a whole new research area was opening up, both geographically and conceptually with a new focus on institutions. It became quickly clear that there was no way to study the economic changes properly without (explicitly) integrating politics and institutions in theoretical models and empirical analyses.

Over the past 25 years, the political economy of institutional change and policy reform have been major research areas for myself and my institute, the LICOS Centre for Institutions and Economic Performance at the University of Leuven. In between I learned about practical applications of political economy "from the inside" as I worked in various capacities as advisor to governments and to international institutions. I spent time several years working at the European Commission and at the World Bank. In all of these cases I learned about how politics is constraining economic decision-making, and therefore essential to take into account when designing policy advice, but also that the interaction is often both ways and that reforms "can happen" if well timed and well integrated in the political economy environment.

A few years ago, Chris Barrett approached me, as the editor of this book series, to write a book on political economy for his series. Chris deserves credit or blame (depending on whether you like what's in front of you) for having convinced me to undertake writing this book while all indicators said I had no time given all my other commitments. In his usual friendly yet determined style, he succeeded in keeping me sufficiently on track to get it ultimately finished and published. He also reviewed an earlier version of the manuscript and gave excellent comments that improved the book.

This book draws on contributions of many people and many collaborations with colleagues and students from which I learned so much. There are too many to mention all of them, but I should mention a few (apologies to those who I did not mention). Harry de Gorter's drive to come up with better explanations, to think outside the box, and to relate complex models to intuitive explanations was crucial in my early development as a researcher. Our trips to Berkeley, where I learned from Gordon Rausser, David Zilberman, Alain de Janvry, and others, were major steps for me, which resulted later in several joint projects. I benefited tremendously from research collaborations on political economy with my former students Pavel Ciaian, Koen Deconinck, Erik Mathijs, Giulia Meloni, Hannah Pieters, Jan Pokrivcak, Thijs Vandemoortele, Kristine Van Herck, and others, both in developing theory and in empirical work.

Alessandro Olper reviewed an earlier version of this manuscript and gave great comments. But his contribution is much larger as I have learned much from him and enjoyed collaborating on various political economy projects with him, often combined with excellent wine (his recommendations in Italy) or beer (my recommendations in Belgium). Jill McCluskey has been my long-time and much appreciated partner in analyzing the political economy of media and information. Vibrant exchanges with Julian Alston, on and off Rosarito Beach, stimulated my thinking on the political economy of public goods. I've learned much from Kym Anderson, initially from reading his papers and later from working with him. Scott Rozelle provided enthusiastic insights on the political economy of one country only but (as he never forgets to remind me) it's the equivalent of "more than a thousand Belgiums". David Orden, Wally Falcon, Roz Naylor, Harry de Gorter, and Jikun Huang gave input on and/or reviewed specific parts of the book, which greatly improved these parts.

The process took so long that editors changed and the publishing company changed names more than once in the meantime. I sincerely thank Allison Neuberger, Sarah Lawrence, and Elisabeth Graber from Palgrave Macmillan/Springer/Nature for handling the many delays, postponements of deadlines, adjustments of contracts, and so on and for staying with me in the process. I presume they are very happy that the book is finished.

As always, Elfriede Lecossois was fantastic in figuring out my notes and writings, keeping track of the many chapter versions, and staying upbeat throughout the numerous revisions. Liz Ignowski did a wonderful job in assisting me with the data and figures and with editorial assistance. Giulia Meloni provided many suggestions using her unique knowledge of languages and historical political economy, including the illustration of the Women's March on Versailles. I also thank Scott Rozelle, Wally Falcon, and Roz Naylor for hosting me regularly in Stanford University at the Center for Food Security and the Environment. These times away from the home office are always very productive and were great in terms of making progress on this book. That said, my ultimate thanks go to LICOS Centre for Institutions and Economic Performance and its students, faculty, and staff for providing a wonderful research atmosphere and being a stimulating place full of bright minds and creative ideas, and to the generous funding from the University of Leuven, which helps turning abstract ideas into something more tangible.

Leuven, Belgium   Johan Swinnen
January 2018

CONTENTS

Part I		1
1	Introduction	3
2	Political Coalitions in Agricultural and Food Policies	13
3	Factors Influencing Policy Choices	35
Part II		67
4	The Development Paradox	69
5	Anti-Trade Bias and the Political Economy of Instrument Choice	87
6	Development Paradox and Anti-Trade Bias Revisited?	95
7	Policy Reform in History: Europe, the USA, and China	109

xiii

xiv CONTENTS

Part III   135

8 Food Price Volatility   137

9 Crises, Media, and Agricultural Development Policy   151

10 Food Standards   169

11 Public Investments in Agricultural and Food Research   189

12 Land and Institutional Reforms   199

13 Policy Interactions   225

Index   241

LIST OF FIGURES

Fig. 2.1	A simple value chain model. (*Landowners, rural credit organizations, insurance companies, companies processing seeds, fertilizers, agrochemicals, etc)	15
Fig. 2.2	Equity and efficiency impact of an import tariff in a small open economy	16
Fig. 2.3	Subsidies, land markets, and political coalitions	21
Fig. 4.1	Nominal rates of assistance to agriculture (NRAs), 1960s–1980s (%). (Source: Anderson 2009; Anderson and Nelgen 2012)	70
Fig. 4.2	Share of agriculture in employment in the USA, France, and Germany (%), 1900–2010. (Source: European Commission, Eurostat, NBER, ILO and Swinnen 2009, 2017)	72
Fig. 4.3	Share of food in consumption expenditures (%) in the UK, France, and Germany, 1900–2010. (Source: European Commission, Eurostat, NBER, ILO and Swinnen 2009, 2017)	73
Fig. 4.4	Agricultural subsidies (NRA %) and public agricultural R&D expenditures in Belgium, 1880–1980. (Source: Data from Swinnen 1992, 2009, 2017)	81
Fig. 4.5	Agricultural subsidies (PSE %) and public agricultural R&D expenditures in China, 1960–2010. (Source: Data from OECD 2017; Pardey, P.G., et al. 2016)	81
Fig. 5.1	NRAs to exportable and import-competing agricultural products, 1960s–1980s (%). (Source: Anderson 2009, 2016; Anderson and Nelgen 2012)	88
Fig. 6.1	Nominal rates of assistance to agriculture (NRAs), 1960s–2010s (%). (Source: Anderson 2009; Anderson and Nelgen 2012)	96

xvi   LIST OF FIGURES

Fig. 6.2   NRAs to exportable and import-competing agricultural products, 1960s–2000s(%). (a) Poor Countries; (b) Rich Countries. (Source: Anderson 2009; Anderson and Nelgen 2012)   97

Fig. 6.3   Share of agriculture in GDP (%) in Brazil, China, and India (1970–2015). (Source: World Bank)   98

Fig. 6.4   Agricultural policy instruments in OECD countries (coupled and decoupled PSE as % of total), 1990–2009. (Source: Based on Swinnen et al. 2010 using data from OECD)   99

Fig. 7.1   Average NRA (%) for Belgium, the Netherlands, Germany, France, and the UK, 1910–1969. (Source: Swinnen 2009, 2017)   111

Fig. 7.2   Transport costs and wheat prices in England, 1870–1895 (index 1870=0). (Source: Own calculations based on Tracy 1989)   113

Fig. 7.3   Agricultural support in the EU (PSE-total and PSE-coupled), 1985–2015. (Source: OECD)   115

Fig. 7.4   Agricultural support in the USA (NRA/PSE-total and NRA/PSE-coupled), 1955–2016. (Source: 1955–1985: NRA from Anderson 2009 and Gardner 2009; 1986–2016: PSE from OECD)   121

Fig. 7.5   Agricultural support in China (PSE), 2000–2016. (Source: OECD)   129

Fig. 7.6   Income and agricultural support in China (NRA/PSE %) 1980–2015. (Note: NRA % until 2005 and PSE % from 2006 onward; Source: OECD and Anderson and Nelgen 2012)   130

Fig. 7.7   Urban/rural income ratio in China, 1978–2015. (Source: Huang and Yang 2017; NBSC data)   130

Fig. 8.1   Global food price index, 1990–2017. (*2002–2004=100 index Source: FAO)   138

Fig. 8.2   Distortions from price stabilization   140

Fig. 8.3   Socially and politically optimal prices with global price volatility   143

Fig. 8.4   Rice prices in China and on world markets (2006–2013). (Source: Pieters and Swinnen (2016), based on FAO data)   143

Fig. 8.5   Wheat prices in Pakistan and on world markets (2006–2013). (Source: Pieters and Swinnen (2016), based on FAO data)   144

Fig. 9.1   Food prices and mass media coverage of agriculture and food security, 2000–2012. (Source: Guariso et al. (2014))   158

Fig. 9.2   Mass media coverage and development policy priorities* on agricultural development and food security 2000–2012. (*Indices of media coverage and WB-IMF development committee coverage of agriculture and food security Source: Guariso et al. (2014))   159

LIST OF FIGURES   xvii

Fig. 9.3 Agricultural development funding, 1996–2012. (**a**) Overseas Development Aid (ODA) to Agriculture (% of total ODA commitments); (**b**) FAO funding as % of UN agencies total. (Source: Guariso et al. (2014) based on data from OECD and the Global Policy Forum)   160

Fig. 9.4 Global poverty and hunger, 1996–2012. (Source: Guariso et al. (2014))   162

Fig. 10.1 The growth of food standards: SPS notifications to WTO (total number). (Source: Own calculations based on data from WTO)   170

Fig. 10.2 Impact of standards in closed economy   173

Fig. 11.1 Welfare and distributional effects of public research in a closed economy   191

Fig. 11.2 Welfare and distributional effects of public research in a small open economy   195

Fig. 12.1 Importance of land renting in Western Europe. (Source: Ciaian et al. (2015), based on FADN data)   201

Fig. 13.1 Joint welfare and distributional effects of public research and price interventions in a closed economy   229

LIST OF TABLES

Table 4.1	The role of food and agriculture in economic development	71
Table 4.2	History of taxation and subsidization of agriculture under communist political regimes in the Soviet Union and China	73
Table 12.1	Voting rights reforms and landowners' parliamentary power in England	204
Table 12.2	Political and economic conditions for agricultural reforms under communism	212

PART I

CHAPTER 1

Introduction

Food and agriculture have been subject to heavy-handed government interventions throughout much of the history and across the globe, both in developing and in developed countries. Today more than 500 billion (half a trillion) US dollars are spent by some governments to support farmers while at the same time some governments impose regulations and taxes that hurt farmers. Political considerations are crucial to understand these policies since almost all agricultural and food policies have redistributive effects and are therefore subject to lobbying and pressure from interest groups and are used by decision-makers to influence society for both economic and political reasons.

Some policies, such as import tariffs or export taxes, have clear distributional objectives and reduce total welfare by introducing distortions in the economy. Other policies, such as food standards, land reforms, or public investments in agricultural research, often increase total welfare but at the same time also have distributional effects. These distributional effects will influence the preferences of different interest groups and thus trigger political action and influence policy decisions.

The inherent interlinkage between efficiency and equity issues in policy-making made that for much of history, economics and politics were closely related disciplines and often written about by the same authors, as reflected in the works of the original architects of the economics discipline, such as Adam Smith, John Stuart Mill, David Ricardo, and so on. In the late

© The Author(s) 2018
J. Swinnen, *The Political Economy of Agricultural and Food Policies*,
Palgrave Studies in Agricultural Economics and Food Policy,
https://doi.org/10.1057/978-1-137-50102-8_1

4   J. SWINNEN

nineteenth century the economics discipline started separated itself from the "political economy" framework.[1]

The revival (or return) of political economy started in the 1950s and 1960s and was referred to as "neoclassical political economy" or "new political economy", as economists started using their economic tools to analyze political processes and to study how policy prescriptions were influenced by a variety of factors before they became public policy (or not) (see, e.g. Weingast et al. 1981). Economists started modeling how incentives of political agents and constraints of political institutions influenced political decision-making—and the effectiveness of various types of agents in influencing the outcome of that decision-making.

The start of this field is often associated with publications such as Anthony Downs' 1957 book, *An Economic Theory of Democracy*, Mancur Olson's 1965 book *The Logic of Collective Action* and James Buchanan and Gordon Tullock's *The Calculus of Consent* in 1962. In the following years important articles were written on "rent-seeking", including classic papers by Tullock (1967), Krueger (1974), and Bhagwati (1982). George Stigler's (1971) *The Theory of Economic Regulation* and contributions by Sam Peltzman (1976) and Gary Becker (1983) formed the basis of the (new) "Chicago school of political economy". Related to the growth of the neoclassical political economy was the growth of the "new institutional economics" based on the work of Ronald Coase (1960), Douglas North (1981, 1990), and Oliver Williamson (1975, 1985).

---

[1] According to Wikipedia and The Palgrave Dictionary of Economics, *political economy* originated in moral philosophy. It was developed in the eighteenth century as the study of the economies of states, or *polities*, hence the term *political* economy. Originally, *political economy* meant the study of the conditions under which production or consumption within limited parameters was organized in nation-states. In that way, political economy expanded the emphasis of economics, which comes from the Greek *oikos* (meaning "home") and *nomos* (meaning "law" or "order"). Thus, political economy was meant to express the laws of production of wealth at the state level, just as economics was the ordering of the home. The French physiocrats, along with Adam Smith, John Stuart Mill, David Ricardo, Henry George, Thomas Malthus, and Karl Marx were some of the exponents of political economy. In the late nineteenth century, the term *economics* came to replace *political economy*, coinciding with the publication of *Principles of Economics*, an influential textbook by Alfred Marshall (1890). Earlier, Jevons (1879), a proponent of mathematical methods applied to the subject, advocated *economics* for brevity and with the hope of the term becoming the recognized name of science, despite calling his book *The Theory of Political Economy*. In fact, one of the oldest and most prestigious economics journals today is the *Journal of Political Economy*, which "has since 1892 presented significant research and scholarship in economic theory and practice (JPE website).

These theories and insights have been used to study public policies generally, and have been applied to analyze food and agricultural policies. The 1980s and the first half of the 1990s were a very active period in the field of political economy of agricultural policy. This research was not only triggered by the emerging general theories of "new political economy", coming from Downs, Olson, Stigler, Becker, and so on but also by the puzzling question: *why was agriculture subsidized in rich countries and taxed in poor countries?* New data, and in particular those collected as part of the World Bank study organized by Krueger et al. (1991), showed that in countries where farmers were the majority of the population, they were taxed, while in countries where they were the minority, farmers received subsidies: the so-called *development paradox* (an issue I will address in Chaps. 4 and 6). The combination of an intriguing question, a rich set of new general theories to apply, and fascinating data induced a rich and vast literature on the political economy of agricultural trade and distortions in the 1980s and the first part of the 1990s.[2]

The past 15 years saw a revival of interest in the political economy of agricultural policies, sparked by a similar combination of factors as in the 1980s: new data, new theories, and new intriguing questions (Swinnen 2009, 2010). First, there were important new general insights and political economy models with important implications for the political economy of agricultural policy distortions. Contributions in the late twentieth century and early twenty-first century (a) often focused on the role of institutions (political and other) and their interactions with economic policies (e.g. Acemoglu (2003) and Persson and Tabellini (2000, 2003)) and (b) tried to move beyond the structural economic factors on which most of the earlier research concentrated. These studies provided better microfoundations for analyzing political-economic decision-making by establishing stronger links between theory and empirics. This includes, for example, Grossman and Helpman's menu-auctions approach (1994; 1995) and their applications, studies by Acemoglu and Robinson (2001, 2008) on the interactions between institutions and policy-making, and applications of Baron and Ferejohn's (1989) model of decision-making rules and the role of agenda-setting.[3] An important new research area was

---

[2] A survey of this literature is in de Gorter and Swinnen (2002).

[3] In this book I will not attempt to provide a comprehensive review of the general literature. I refer to Rausser et al. (2011) who identify broadly six "schools" in the political economy literature. Other relatively recent surveys of the political-economic literature include Dewan

in the economics of (mass) media and what it implied for public policy-making (McCluskey and Swinnen 2010; Mullainathan and Shleifer 2005; Strömberg 2004).

Second, new datasets on institutional and political variables and on agricultural and food policies have been particularly important. An important contribution was the World Bank's project on measuring distortions to agricultural incentives, coordinated by Kym Anderson. This project created a much richer dataset on agricultural policies than had been available before (Anderson 2009, 2016). One of the important contributions of the dataset is that it provides evidence of important changes in the global distribution of policy distortions. Key findings are that taxation of farmers has fallen in many developing countries, including in the poorest countries of Asia and Africa, and that at the same time trade-distorting farm subsidies in rich countries have fallen as well—suggesting important new political economy questions (issues addressed in Chaps. 5 and 6).

The third reason of new interest was important new questions to be addressed. One key question was how major institutional and political reforms in the 1980s and the 1990s had affected agricultural policy and policy reforms. Over the past 30 years major regulatory inefficiencies have been removed and important policy reforms have been implemented contributing to much more liberal agricultural and food markets than in the previous decades (Anderson 2009; Rozelle and Swinnen 2004). This includes the shift of a large share of the emerging and developing countries from state-controlled to market-based governance of agricultural and food systems. These dramatic political and economic changes raised many interesting and fascinating political economy questions, such as "Why did the Communist Party introduced major economic reforms in China but not in the Soviet Union?" (Rozelle and Swinnen 2009; Swinnen and Rozelle 2006). The most well-known (and dramatic) shifts occurred in China and the former "Eastern Bloc" (i.e. the Soviet Union and Eastern Europe), but similar changes also occurred in other parts of Asia, Latin America, and Africa (Swinnen et al. 2010). Agriculture and food security were major issues in these countries, and there were very important policy questions related to the food policies and agricultural reforms (issues which will be addressed in Chaps. 6, 7 and 12).

and Shepsle (2008a, b), Mueller (2003), and Weingast and Whitman (2006). More specific reviews are: for trade policy Grossman and Helpman (2001, 2002) and Rodrik (1995); for fiscal and monetary policy Persson and Tabellini (2000); for the relationship between governance structures and fiscal and growth-promoting policies Persson and Tabellini (2003).

Another question related to the impact of changes in international organizations and international trade agreements on the political economy of agricultural policies. Examples are the Uruguay Round Agreement on Agriculture (URAA), the establishment of the WTO, the North American Free Trade Agreement (NAFTA), the enlargement of the EU with ten new member states, and the rapid growth of preferential and bilateral trade agreements in recent years. The failure to reach agreement in the Doha Round trade negotiations of the World Trade Organization (WTO) has, again, brought to the forefront the important role that political considerations continue to play in agricultural policy and in international trade and relations. Despite a strong decline of the agricultural sector in terms of employment and output in rich countries, agriculture and agricultural policy remains disproportionately important for rich countries in their trade negotiations.

The turnaround in global agricultural and food markets in the second half of the 2000s also induced new economic and political debates on agricultural and food policies. Instead of export subsidies and import tariffs, export barriers and price ceilings were introduced to prevent food prices from rising. The political economy questions were about how and why policies (and governments) responded in such a way to changes in global agricultural markets, and to new global challenges related to food price volatility (issues addressed in Chap. 8) and the failure of governments and donors to stimulate investment and productivity growth in agriculture (see Chaps. 9, 11 and 13).

Another hot issue in the political economy of agricultural and food policy relates to food standards and the shift from traditional trade barriers (such as import tariffs) to so-called non-tariff measures. This was triggered by two separate developments: a rapid growth in public and private standards in global agri-food chains and a concern that with binding WTO constraints on tariffs, governments were looking for other instruments to protect their domestic interest groups (see Chap. 10).

In summary, political considerations are crucial to an understanding of the agricultural and food policies of the developing and developed countries, their trade negotiations position, the constraints on the ability to reform unilaterally or to reform as part of a broader reform strategy, or to understand suboptimal public investments and regulations in food and agriculture.

1.1 Themes, Approach and Structure of the Book

This book integrates key insights of both the older and the new literature and provide a comprehensive review of the political economy of agricultural and food policies.

1.1.1 Methodology and Approach

The book uses insights from theoretical and empirical studies. However I refrain from using advanced technical methodologies. In some sections I explain theoretical arguments but I do not use mathematical models. Mostly I use words and an occasional graph. For the empirical discussions I mostly discuss the results of statistical and econometric studies and occasionally present some summary tables. Throughout the book I include references to articles or books which provide a more technical explanation of the theories and to the detailed econometric studies. I hope this makes the book accessible for people who are less technically skilled in economic theory and econometrics, while at the same time providing value for those who are also interested in the more technical and advanced theoretical and empirical aspects.

As this book is addressing global political economy issues and policies, unavoidably a selection needs to be made in terms of which policies will be covered, and in how much detail. In this book I focus mostly on structural changes in policies, using average numbers and "stylized facts" to represent global or regional or historical observations and developments. However, in a few chapters I go into more detail into the policy process, explaining the role of specific institutions and in some cases specific people or vested interests. I believe that both are important. The (statistical) analysis of averages (using quantitative indicators) and a more qualitative approach of case studies of policies and reforms and the role played by specific institutions and vested interests are both valuable and yield complementary insights.

1.1.2 Structure and Themes

The book is organized in three parts. Chaps. 2 and 3 in Part I present key insights from the theoretical and empirical literature on factors that affect agricultural and food policy and the political economy mechanisms behind them. This includes an analysis of the role of inequality and structural changes in the economy, the role of political institutions and ideology, the impact of crises, and the political economy of information and the role of the mass media.

Chapters in Parts II and III of the book will use these and other insights to provide explanations for specific empirical observations. This book covers the political economy of various aspects and forms of "agricultural and food policies". While the size constraints of a book are obviously less restrictive than those of an article, still not everything can be covered within this book and a selection of topics and specific policies needed to be made.

Part II focuses on policies which are extensively motivated by redistributing income (or rents) between different groups in society. A large part of the literature has studied price and trade interventions in agricultural and food markets. This includes the explanation of agricultural protection in the twentieth and twenty-first centuries, why there has been a turn-around in the past 30 years and subsidization in rich countries has declined at the same time when agricultural taxation of poor countries has declined. Besides understanding at what level the policy interventions are set, the book will also discuss the nature of the agricultural and food policy instruments that are used to distribute income in the economy.

Part III covers a variety of other "agricultural and food policies" which may create economic benefits (by stimulating growth or reducing externalities, imperfections, etc.) but redistribute income at the same time. For example, in recent years various types of standards have become increasingly important in food markets and value chains with important implications for trade, agricultural production, and poverty. Also policies to reduce price volatility, investments in public goods (such as public research) and agricultural development, and property rights regulations and their reforms are analyzed. The last chapter discusses how these various policies may interact, through economic and political mechanisms.

REFERENCES

Acemoglu, D. 2003. Why Not a Political Coase Theorem? Social Conflict, Commitment, and Politics. *Journal of Comparative Economics* 31: 620–652.

Acemoglu, D., and J.A. Robinson. 2001. A Theory of Political Transitions. *American Economic Review* 91: 938–963.

———. 2008. Persistence of Power, Elites, and Institutions. *American Economic Review* 98: 267–293.

Anderson, K. 2009. *Distortions to Agricultural Incentives: A Global Perspective, 1955–2007.* London/Washington, DC: Palgrave Macmillan and the World Bank.

———. 2016. Agriculture Trade, Policy Reforms, and Global Food Security. Springer.

Baron, D.P., and J.A. Ferejohn. 1989. Bargaining in Legislatures. *American Political Science Review* 83: 1181–1206.

Becker, G.S. 1983. A Theory of Competition Among Pressure Groups for Political Influence. *Quarterly Journal of Economics* 98: 371–400.

Bhagwati, J.N. 1982. Directly Unproductive Profit Seeking Activities: A Welfare Theoretic Synthesis and Generalization. *Journal of Political Economy* 90: 988–1002.

Buchanan, J.M., and G. Tullock. 1962. *The Calculus of Consent.* Ann Arbor: University of Michigan Press.

Coase, R.H. 1960. The Problem of Social Cost. *Journal of Law and Economics* 3: 1–44.

de Gorter, H., and J. Swinnen. 2002. Political Economy of Agricultural Policies. In *The Handbook of Agricultural Economics,* ed. B. Gardner and G.C. Rausser, vol. 2, 2073–2123. Amsterdam: Elsevier Science.

Dewan, T., and K.A. Shepsle. 2008a. Recent Economic Perspectives on Political Economy, Part I. *British Journal of Political Science* 38: 362–382.

———. 2008b. Recent Economic Perspectives on Political Economy, Part II. *British Journal of Political Science* 38: 543–564.

Downs, A. 1957. *An Economic Theory of Democracy.* Newyork: Harper.

Grossman, G.M., and E. Helpman. 1994. Protection for Sale. *American Economic Review* 84 (4): 833–850.

———. 1995. Trade Wars and Trade Talks. *Journal of Political Economy* 103 (4): 675–708.

———. 2001. *Special Interest Politics.* Cambridge, MA: MIT Press.

———. 2002. *Interest Groups and Trade Policy.* Princeton: Princeton University Press.

Jevons, W.S. 1879. *The Theory of Political Economy.* 2nd ed. London: Macmillan.

Krueger, A.O. 1974. The Political Economy of the Rent Seeking Society. *American Economic Review* 64: 291–303.

Krueger, A.O., M. Schiff, and A. Valdés. 1991. *The Political Economy of Agricultural Pricing Policy.* London: Johns Hopkins University Press for the World Bank.

Marshall, A. 1890. *Principles of Political Economy.* New York: Maxmillan.

McCluskey, J.J., and J.F.M. Swinnen. 2010. Media Economics and the Political Economy of Information. In *The Oxford Handbook of Government and Business,* ed. D. Coen, W. Grant, and G. Wilson. Oxford: Oxford University Press.

Mueller, D.C. 2003. *Public Choice III.* Cambridge/New York: Cambridge University Press.

Mullainathan, S., and A. Shleifer. 2005. The Market for News. *American Economic Review* 95: 1031–1053.

North, D.C. 1981. *Structure and Change in Economic History*. New York: W.W. Norton and Co.

———. 1990. A Transaction Cost Theory of Politics. *Journal of Theoretical Politics* 2: 355–357.

Olson, M. 1965. *Logic of Collective Action: Public Goods and the Theory of Groups*, Harvard Economic Studies, vol. 124. Cambridge, MA: Harvard University Press.

Peltzman, S. 1976. Towards a More General Theory of Regulation. *Journal of Law and Economics* 19 (2): 211–240.

Persson, T., and G. Tabellini. 2000. *Political Economics: Explaining Economic Policy*. Cambridge, MA: MIT Press.

———. 2003. *The Economic Effects of Constitutions*. Cambridge, MA: MIT Press.

Rausser, G., J. Swinnen, and P. Zusman. 2011. *Political Power and Economic Policy: Theory, Analysis, and Empirical Applications*. Cambridge: Cambridge University Press.

Rodrik, D. 1995. The Political Economy of Trade Policy. In *Handbook of International Economics*, ed. G. Grossman and K. Rogoff, vol. 3. North-Holland/Amsterdam: Elsevier.

Rozelle, S., and J. Swinnen. 2004. Success and Failure of Reforms: Insights from Transition Agriculture. *Journal of Economic Literature* XLII: 404–456.

———. 2009. Why Did the Communist Party Reform in China, But Not in the Soviet Union? The Political Economy of Agricultural Transition. *China Economic Review* 20 (2): 275–287.

Stigler, G.J. 1971. The Theory of Economic Regulation. *Bell Journal of Economics and Management Science* 2: 3–21.

Strömberg, D. 2004. Mass Media Competition, Political Competition, and Public Policy. *Review of Economic Studies* 71: 265–284.

Swinnen, J. 2009. The Growth of Agricultural Protection in Europe in the 19th and 20th Centuries? *The World Economy* 32 (11): 1499–1537.

———. 2010. Political Economy of Agricultural Distortions: The Literature to Date. Chap. 3 in *The Political Economy of Agricultural Price Distortions*, ed. K. Anderson. Cambridge/New York: Cambridge University Press.

Swinnen, J., and S. Rozelle. 2006. *From Marx and Mao to the Market: The Economics and Politics of Agricultural Transition*. Oxford: Oxford University Press.

Swinnen, J., A. Vandeplas, and M. Maertens. 2010. Liberalization, Endogenous Institutions, and Growth. A Comparative Analysis of Agricultural Reforms in Africa, Asia, and Europe. *The World Bank Economic Review* 24 (3): 412–445.

Tullock, G. 1967. The Welfare Cost of Tariffs, Monopolies, and Theft. *The Western Economic Journal* 5: 224–232.

Weingast, B.R., and D. Wittman, eds. 2006. *The Oxford Handbook of Political Economy*. Oxford: Oxford University Press.

Weingast, B.R., K.A. Shepsle, and C. Johnsen. 1981. The Political Economy of Benefits and Costs: A Neoclassical Approach to Distributive Politics. *General Political Economy* 89: 642–664.

Williamson, O.E. 1975. *Markets and Hierarchies: Analysis and Antitrust Implications*. New York: The Free Press.

———. 1985. *The Economic Institutions of Capitalism*. New York: Free Press.

CHAPTER 2

Political Coalitions in Agricultural and Food Policies

2.1 Introduction

Political economy models of agricultural and food policy often consider "producers", "consumers", and "taxpayers" as the main agents to study the impacts of policies, the political incentives, and the impact on policy outcomes. One (theoretical) reason is its didactic use, that is, to avoid unnecessary complications in deriving policy effects and identify equilibria. Another (empirical) reason is the absence of disaggregated information of policy impacts on various agents within (or outside) the value chain.

It is, of course, well known that in reality many more agents are affected—and also play a role in lobbying governments to introduce or remove certain policies. In agricultural and food policies "other agents" include input suppliers (such as landowners, seed and agro-chemical companies, or banks), traders, food processors, retail companies, environmental and food advocacy groups, and so on. These agents may be differently affected by policies, depending on the nature of the policy (e.g. whether the policy is targeted to the (raw) agricultural commodity or to a processed commodity)—or whether farm subsidies affect land or other production factors. As a consequence, these different agents have sometimes joined forces ("political coalitions") with farmers or with final consumers to influence policy-makers in setting public policies. In other cases they have opposed each other on policy issues.

© The Author(s) 2018
J. Swinnen, *The Political Economy of Agricultural and Food Policies*,
Palgrave Studies in Agricultural Economics and Food Policy,
https://doi.org/10.1057/978-1-137-50102-8_2

These coalitions are not static. There are several reasons why political coalitions may change: traditional power structures within value chains may change with some (sub)sectors growing and others declining with economic development, new technologies may bring new players into the value chains, new policy instruments may be introduced (or considered), and so on. New players have emerged for a variety of reasons. Growing awareness of environmental issues increased lobbying by environmental organizations. Technological advances, such as biotechnology and genetically modified (GM) crops, created new vested interests—and changed these of others. In the 1970s there was no pro- or anti-GM lobby since there was no GM. Biofuels have emerged as an important factor in agricultural markets and food policy with oil prices rising and with the search for renewable energy sources. The growth of policies such as crop insurance subsidies has brought new sectors, such as insurance companies, into the lobbying game for farm support programs. With income growth and globalization, interest in local products has taken on a new form. Consumers are interested in local foods, while farm groups see it as a potential way of marketing and protecting their products. At the policy front this has, for example, resulted in regulations on geographical indications (GI)—an issue which has created tensions in trade negotiations (Josling 2006; Meloni and Swinnen 2018).

In this section I illustrate and discuss a series of such political coalitions in agricultural and food policies.

2.2   Value Chains and Political Coalitions

The nature of public policies influences the structure of the political game by determining the possible coalitions—and vice versa. Consider a simple value chain as illustrated in Fig. 2.1. While this value chain is more elaborate than the producer-consumer dichotomy, it still ignores many potential other value chain issues, such as competition between feed and food (and thus livestock versus crops), between food and fuel use, "environmental interests", and so on. Yet, despite its simplicity it is useful to illustrate potential coalitions.

Agricultural and food policies typically intervene in specific parts of the value chain. The type of instrument used and the "location" of intervention has a major impact on the possible political coalitions. The nature of the policy instrument will determine whether the interests of farmers and

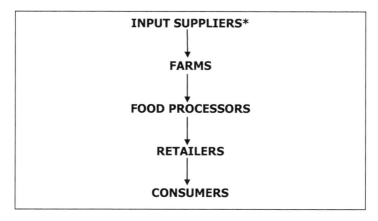

Fig. 2.1 A simple value chain model. (*Landowners, rural credit organizations, insurance companies, companies processing seeds, fertilizers, agrochemicals, etc)

processors or other agents are aligned or not (i.e. whether they have opposing or conflicting interests in setting public policy interventions).[1]

Consider trade and price interventions, such as import tariffs and price support measures, which have been and still are the dominant form of agricultural and food policies (see Chaps. 4, 5 and 6). The use of tariffs goes back centuries. Price support measures, combined with import tariffs and export subsidies, were key component of many countries' agricultural and food policies. Figure 2.2 illustrates the impact of such import tariffs on the efficiency (distortions) in agri-food markets and the income distributional (equity) effects. With an upward sloping supply function representing producers and a downward sloping demand function representing consumers, it is well known that import tariffs benefit producers (the impact on their welfare is area A) and hurts consumers (their welfare declines by areas A + B + C + D). The government or taxpayers benefit as well since taxes equivalent to area C are raised by the import tariff. Total welfare is lower by areas B + D as gains to producers and taxpayers are lower than the losses for consumers. The same analysis can be made for countries keeping food prices low by taxing farmers.

---

[1] Not surprisingly, this makes the choice of the policy instrument the subject of lobbying itself. I discuss the endogeneity of instrument choice in agricultural and food policy in Chap. 5.

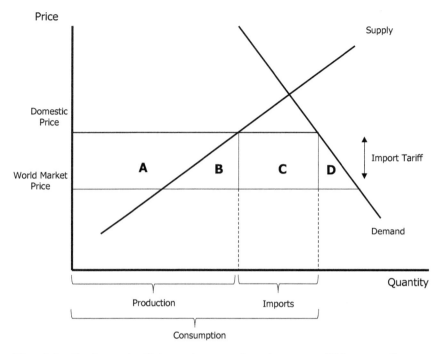

Fig. 2.2 Equity and efficiency impact of an import tariff in a small open economy

But who are these "producers" and "consumers"? Import tariffs may be imposed on processed food products (e.g. pasta or specific cheeses) or on (raw) agricultural products (e.g. cereals or milk). In case import tariff and price interventions are at the level of the agricultural commodities, the food processors (buyers of cereals or milk) may have opposing interests to the farmers, since they are "the consumers"—even if they can pass part of the increased costs on to "final consumers".

However, "agricultural policies" (such as tariffs, import quota, or price interventions) often do not apply to the raw agricultural products as they are sold by the farmers, but to products which have undergone a certain level of processing or marketing. For example, it is typically not the raw milk or the sugar beets that are traded or purchased by government agencies but processed products such as milk powder, cheese, or sugar. Hence, interests of food-processing companies involved in early stage processing will often be aligned with those of farmers, while those of further processing may be opposite.[2]

Take the case of sugar: the "production side" includes sugar processing companies and the farmers producing sugar cane or sugar beet (and other agents, such as landowners and agribusinesses supplying inputs to the farmers). The "consumer side" also includes food companies. Some sugar is "consumed" directly by households, but most is sold to the food industry, which uses the sugar in various products sold to retailers and only then households consume the sugar. This separation is well illustrated by the debate on the ending of the sugar production quotas in the EU in recent years. The EU's beverage and confection industries and sweetener companies have lined up to lobby the EU decision-makers against the extension of the EU sugar quota, while the sugar processing companies are lobbying in favor.

In Briones Alonso and Swinnen (2016), we try to account for this by presenting a methodology to measure the policy effects along the value chain. We apply this methodology to the wheat-flour chain in Pakistan and find important impacts for all agents, including grain traders and milling companies.[3] Also in other countries grain traders (which can be multinational companies) and large processing companies are affected by "agricultural policies" and will actively lobby for or against them.

2.2.1 Consumers

"Consumers" can refer to a multitude of agents who can form a coalition. History provides many examples of the importance of political coalitions. For example, the often heralded period of free trade in the nineteenth century comes to an end when cheap grain imports hit the West European

---

[2] The growth of agricultural protection in many OECD countries was associated with the growth of cooperative agribusiness and food-processing companies. The growth and concentration of agribusinesses and food-processing companies created a strong political coalition with farm interests in lobbying for agricultural policies (Anderson 1995). Farm-related cooperatives and business organizations in the agri-food sector became important interest groups, with, for example, agricultural credit cooperatives, dairy and sugar processing companies joining farm unions in actively lobbying for government support and import protection for their sectors. Since farm lobbies and agribusiness interests were increasingly well capitalized and concentrated, they became an important force in orchestrating public policies that benefited their interests (Gawande and Hoekman 2006; López 2008).

[3] Other examples are Ivanova et al. (1995) and Swinnen (1996) who disaggregate policy impacts among many agents along the wheat-bread value chains in Bulgaria.

markets after 1875. As we document in Chap. 7, reactions of governments in Europe differ because of different political coalitions. The governments of France and Germany introduced import tariffs to protect their grain farms. France and Germany were characterized by a large agricultural population, little industrialization, and a large crop sector. In contrast, countries such as the UK and Belgium did not impose import tariffs for grain. Belgium and the UK were already quite industrialized, and grain tariffs were opposed by a coalition of workers and industrial capital (who benefited from low food prices (and thus low wages) with cheap grain imports); the transport industry and the coal mines (where horse power (and thus cheap grain) was important); the brewing industry (using grain as raw material); the harbors, opposed to any tariffs that would limit the trade volume; and livestock farmers who benefited through low feed prices.

Interests and power relations on the consumer side of the value chains have changed over time. The growth of food-processing and marketing companies created new powerful, often international players with strong vested interests. More recently, growing concentration in the retail sector have made the retail sector a more powerful sector in the value chain (Swinnen and Vandeplas 2010). This may benefit consumers since for many agricultural policy issues consumer and retailer interests are aligned and their political coalition may be reinforced by growing retail concentration.[4]

Consumer interests changed over time. In the post-war years, especially in countries which had faced food shortages during war times the argument of sufficient food through stimulating local production touched a nerve among consumers. Politicians who had to address the nation's basic concerns and consumers who faced hunger and food shortages during times when food imports and long-distance food supplies were interrupted were sympathetic to the call for supporting domestic food production.

While poor food consumers are obviously still very much concerned about food prices today (as was very clear during the 2007–2011 price spikes (see Chap. 8)), in the twenty-first century, consumers are arguably more concerned about the safety and quality of food and with environmental

---

[4] In response to concerns on abuse of market power and unfair practices in the food supply chain emerged in the EU, the European Commission establishment the *High Level Forum for a Better Functioning Food Supply Chain*, which includes different stakeholders from the food supply chain. The Forum agreed on a set of principles of good practices in vertical relationships and launched a voluntary framework for implementing the principles of good practice (the Supply Chain Initiative). However, regulations differ significantly between EU member states (Swinnen and Vandevelde 2017).

and ethical standards of their food. All developed countries have introduced important food safety regulations to protect consumers, often triggered by crises. Two major food safety crises with global implications occurred in Europe, one in the mid-nineteenth century and one in the late twentieth century. The first was when new technological innovations allowed scientists to test food ingredients—several of which were cheap substitutes and some even poisonous, triggering strong public reactions against and regulations imposed on the food industry (Meloni and Swinnen 2015). The second was in the late 1990s which triggered traceability requirements and private sector initiatives in value chains (see also Chap. 10).[5] Also in China an important food safety scandal in the 2000s triggered major changes in its food safety regulations (Mo et al. 2012).

This does not only apply to policies affecting the downstream value chain but also upstream. For example, regulations which affect input prices (such as fertilizer subsidies or land regulations) may involve very different political coalitions than policies where there are important leakages to (benefits for) the owners or producers of farm inputs (such as price support or direct payments which increase land prices). In some of these regulations, interests of input suppliers and farmers will be aligned, in others they will conflict.

2.2.2   *Landowners*

Landowners and farmers have always had a complex relationship. In countries where farmers own most of their land, their interests mostly coincide. However, in many parts of the world, farmers rent a considerable part of their land (either through sharecropping or cash rent contracts)—and there have been considerable changes on this through history (Swinnen et al. 2014). In Europe, a hundred years ago, land was at the center of agricultural policy reflecting major economic and political conflicts between landowners and farmers. At the end of the nineteenth century and early twentieth century, landowners and tenant farmers fought over land rental

---

[5] Food scares that plagued the EU in the 1990s resulted in major legislative changes such as the Basic Food Law Regulation, including the creation of the European Food Safety Authority (EFSA). Consumers' quality and safety concerns also triggered strong reactions from the food processors and retailers. This included both the introduction of private standards to address concerns that were/are not addressed by public regulations, the pre-empting of public regulations by private standards, and their lobbying to influence the nature of public food regulations (Winfree and McCluskey 2005; Vandemoortele and Deconinck 2014).

conditions. These conflicts resulted in a series of land regulations (Swinnen 2002)—see also Chap. 12.

In recent decades political relations between landowners and farmers in Western countries are very different. They join forces in lobbying for agricultural subsidies. Farm subsidies, either linked to production or to land use, have spilled over into high land prices and rents creating a coalition between farmers and landowners. Studies in the USA and Canada have demonstrated significant increases in land prices as a consequence of farm payments (Barnard et al. 1997; Goodwin et al. 2003; Kirwan 2009; Roberts et al. 2003; Vyn et al. 2012). In recent EU policy discussions, landowners have not opposed moving from trade-distorting price support toward non-trade-distorting decoupled farm payments, since the payments are still linked to land use and thus keep land prices high (Ciaian and Swinnen 2009; Ciaian et al. 2010, 2014; Salhofer and Schmid 2004).

The reason is explained in Fig. 2.3. The horizontal axis represents all land (L) with L^A land used for farming and L^N land used for other purposes. D_0^A represents the demand for land by farmers and D^N the demand for land for other purposes. L_0^A and r_0^A are the equilibrium land allocation and land rent, respectively. Now consider how the land market changes when agricultural production gets subsidized. Subsidies for grain or other crops will increase the demand for land. This is represented by the shift in the land demand function from D_0^A to D_s^A.[6] The result of the increased farmers' demand for land is an increase in the price of land (from r_0^A to r_s^A) and an increase in the use of land for agriculture from L_0^A to L_s^A. Fig. 2.3 also allows to identify the impacts of the agricultural subsidies in the land market. Users of the land for other purposes than farming lose because they pay a higher price and can use less land: their losses are equal to area C in Fig. 2.3. Farmers gain from the subsidy. Their gross benefits are represented by the sum of areas A and B. However, because the subsidies drive up the demand for land, part of the benefits are passed on to landowners with land prices increasing from r_0^A to r_s^A. In fact, landowners gain area B and the net gains for farmers is area A. Figure 2.3 suggests that a significant part of the subsidies targeted to farmers end up with landowners. The size of this will depend on the shape of the land demand functions. However, empirical studies do show that the benefits for landowners can be very significant. Studies vary from 20% to 90%, depending

---

[6] Formally D^A represents the value marginal product of agricultural production which shifts up with the per unit subsidy level (see Ciaian and Swinnen 2006, 2009).

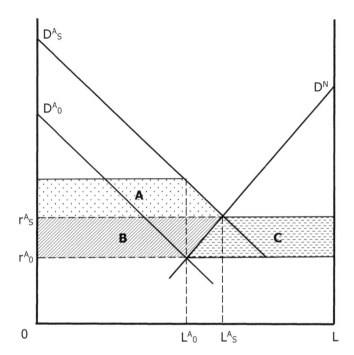

Fig. 2.3 Subsidies, land markets, and political coalitions

on the implementation and the nature of the subsidies and the functioning of the land market. In fact, very recent estimates by Ciaian et al. (2016) suggest that no less than 70% of agricultural subsidies in the EU end up with landowners.

Hence, not surprisingly, landowners are active lobbyists in favor of farm subsidies in these situations. It should be clear that a similar analysis could be applied to other farm inputs, such as agricultural machinery, fertilizer,[7] seeds, water (rights),[8] and so on. Agribusiness and input owners have lots of stake, even indirectly, in agricultural policy.

[7] For an analysis of the political economy of fertilizer subsidies in Africa, see Mason et al. (2017).
[8] Political economy issues are important in optimal water allocation and (clean) water rights distributions in many countries in the world (see, e.g. special issues of *Choices Magazine* in 2017 edited by Madhu Khanna and David Zilberman).

2.2.3 Environmental Concerns

Environmental organizations have emerged as an important lobby group in agricultural policy discussions. Conservation has a long history in US agricultural policy dating back to the Dust Bowl era of the 1930s (Gardner 2002)—see also Chap. 7. Environmental concerns took on new prominence in the 1985 and 1990 Farm Bill: the latter was entitled the "Food, Agriculture, Conservation and Trade Act." Farm groups seeking to limit agricultural production—thereby raising prices—joined a political coalition with environmentalists to establish a Conservation Reserve Program (CRP) for the protection of erodible land (Orden et al. 1999). Farmers can place their land in the CRP in exchange for CRP payments. In 2012, 27 million acres of US cropland, involving nearly 400,000 farms, were in the CRP. With higher commodity prices after 2005, CRP payments became less competitive, and fewer farmers were interested in CRP (Cuellar et al. 2014).

In the EU, environmental organizations did not have a major impact on agricultural policy until the 2000s. Hopes were high among the environmental organizations that, given the need to address climate change and other environmental concerns, important further changes could be made in the CAP reform to enhance the environmental impact of CAP subsidies. Policy discussions focused on how to reform the farm payments, as increased pressure from taxpayers and demands from environmental groups challenge the current payment structures. One key element was greening of the payments as farm support would be better linked to environmental objectives.

Farm organizations lobbied to secure the payments. They were supported in these efforts by landowners, who are benefiting from spillover effects of the land-based payments. Farm associations formed a strategic coalition with environmental groups to lobby for as a large a CAP budget as possible during the economic and financial crisis. However, as soon as the budget for the 2014–2020 CAP was fixed, the coalition fell apart as farm groups started lobbying to remove or weaken environmental constraints on the payments (Hart 2015; Matthews 2015). In the end, environmentalists were very disappointed with an outcome which some have described as a "green wash" instead of "greening" (Erjavec et al. 2015; Hart 2015).

A crucial factor in the successful lobbying of farmers in the EU against more environmental constraints and the recent fall in interest of US farmers in the CRP are the rising agricultural and food prices in the late 2000s.

The rising food prices caused concern among poor consumers, many of whom were already suffering from the most severe economic crisis since the 1930s. Producing and securing food suddenly re-emerged as an important policy concern. Environmental concerns gave way to food security and production objectives in political coalitions, and high prices made CRP less attractive to farmers.

2.2.4   International Interests

So far, we discussed mostly domestic interests, but obviously foreign companies and international organizations may try to influence domestic policies. For example, when OECD agricultural policies with high import tariffs and export subsidies in the second half of the twentieth century were distorting international agricultural markets in the 1970s and 1980s, international pressure increased on their policy-makers to reduce the distortions. This was very clear in countries such as the EU which had previously been a major net importer of agricultural and food products, and where agricultural subsidies caused a reduction in imports and growth of subsidized exports. Important outside pressure came from exporting nations, such as the USA and Australia, and developing countries, NGOs, and international organizations which accused the EU of causing poverty and hunger in poor rural households.[9] This contributed to significant reforms in the 1990s as part of the GATT[10] "Uruguay Round Agreement on Agriculture" (URAA), which was later integrated in the WTO (see Chap. 5).

Another example of international pressure on domestic agricultural and food policies are the so-called structural-adjustment programs (SAPs). They were introduced in many developing countries in the 1980s and 1990s under pressure from international institutions, such as the IMF and the World Bank, and had major impact on agricultural policies—see Chap. 6.

---

[9] For example, organizations such as the OECD and the World Bank emphasized how the EU (and other countries including the USA) was hurting the world's poor by contributing to low agricultural and food prices through their agricultural subsidies. Non-governmental organizations (NGOs) took the same position. See Swinnen (2011) for details.

[10] General Agreement on Tariffs and Trade.

2.2.5 Globalization of Value Chains and New International Coalitions

In our discussion so far, we distinguished between "domestic interests" and "foreign interests". This distinction is consistent with the analysis in traditional trade and political economy models. However, in today's world of global value chains this distinction is not that clear anymore, and these global value chains may need to be integrated explicitly in useful analytical approaches for political economy studies (Olper 2017). For example, if companies are sourcing inputs from foreign subsidiaries or contracting with foreign farms or companies for their raw materials, the interests of these (domestic) companies are closely aligned with their (foreign) input suppliers.

Traditional trade models do not accurately capture these effects since they (implicitly) assume costless switching between different producers and consumers if prices or costs change. However, in a world with extensive and elaborate product and process standards, such switching can imply significant transaction costs. For this reason trading is increasingly integrated in global value chains with elaborate and sophisticated forms of vertical coordination (Antras 2015; Nunn 2007; Sexton 2012; Swinnen and Vandeplas 2011; Swinnen et al. 2015).

The spread of such global value chains has thus implications for the political economy of agricultural and food policies as it changes the incentives of various agents in the value chains to lobby for or against import protection and integration in international trade agreements (Blanchard and Matschke 2015; Olper 2017). Blanchard et al. (2016) show that trade protection is lower when the domestic content of foreign produced final goods is higher and (vice versa) for foreign content of domestically produced goods. In other words, the integration of economies and companies in global value chains tends to dampen the incentives for policies that hurt trade. Other recent studies show that more intensive global value chain integrations are associated with deeper trade agreements (Ruta 2017).

2.2.6 GM Regulations and Agribusiness

One of the most controversial recent policy issues is related to a new technology: genetically modified (GM) agricultural products (Paarlberg 2001; Pinstrup-Andersen and Schioler 2003). One of the most striking observations is the difference in GM regulation between countries such as the USA and the EU (Qaim 2009, 2016).

While the USA (and several other countries such as Canada, Brazil, and China) has approved the use of GM in agriculture, the EU has followed a precautionary approach in establishing new legislation to regulate GM technology. For some time this led to a de facto EU moratorium on the approval of GM products both for imports and for domestic production. The restrictions on imports have been reduced since 2003, but the staunch opposition of consumers and anti-GM activist groups in combination with the institutional set-up of the EU's decision-making procedure on genetically modified organisms (GMOs) have led to something like a regulatory gridlock on GM production in the EU (Swinnen and Vandemoortele 2011a, b). This has continued until today.

A crucial element was the differential role played by various interest groups in the EU and the USA.[11] Various groups have tried to influence policy-making on GM: activist groups, farmers, biotech innovators, competing input suppliers (chemical companies), and so on. Graff et al. (2009) argue that the US agribusiness industry has been a much more pro-GM lobbying force than the EU agribusiness industry. Some of the most important GM products are effectively competing with traditional agribusiness products. This applies especially to GM traits which substitute for pesticides and insecticides. As a result many of the large agro-pharmaceutical companies, such as Bayer and BASF, were uncertain what side to take in the debate. GM opened up new avenues for profit and commercial avenues in the future, but at the same time potentially undermined their traditional profits.

In the USA some of the key companies, both the new GM start-ups—most of whom developed in the USA—and large traditional agribusiness companies, in particular Monsanto, went all out lobbying for GMO. This created a very different political coalition in the USA than in the EU, contributing to a different regulatory outcome. Later in the process some of the European agribusiness companies seem to have changed their mind, with BASF introducing some new GM products and Bayer trying to take over Monsanto. However by that time the EU decision process was stuck

---

[11] Another key difference between the EU and the USA was the regulatory environments and attitudes. When GM emerged as a major policy issue the regulatory environment in Washington DC was dominated by the Reagan-era anti-regulation philosophy (Charles 2001). In contrast, in the EU, the GM policy issues became most important when food safety crises of the 1990s contributed to a great weariness about new food technologies, including genetic modification (Swinnen et al. 2011). As explained in Chap. 10, the food safety crises led to several policy initiatives to regulate the food chain.

in a policy gridlock. As a result, BASF and other European companies have moved much of their GM research capacity and product development to non-EU countries, including the USA.

2.2.7   An Iron Triangle of Food Aid

Another interesting case of coalition politics is the peculiar constellation of interests that have historically aligned to generate food aid programs from donor countries. This has been observed in many donor countries but is especially powerful (and best documented) in the US Chris Barrett's and Dan Maxwell's (2007) book, *Food Aid After Fifty Years*. They document how influential NGOs, however well intended their objectives, have come to depend on food aid as a resource for their operations, and this dependence has affected their lobby activities.[12] American millers and processors have benefited handsomely from the food aid program due to procurement modalities, and US shipping companies have benefited from legal requirements that most food aid has to be transported by US (private) ships.

This coalition of NGOs, agribusiness and maritime transport businesses has resulted in highly suboptimal (food) aid policies that have persisted for more than 60 years because the coalition is sufficiently powerful to let the system continue; and this is also a major reason why food aid has not fully migrated from USDA to USAID, unlike in other donor countries where food aid has been placed wholly under the control of international development agencies rather than ministries of agriculture (Barrett and Maxwell 2007).

2.2.8   Food, Feed, and Fuel

The late 2000s have witnessed a dramatic introduction of biofuels in agricultural and food markets and policy. The political and policy background to biofuels in the 1990s and early 2000s was very different than today's. With large crop surpluses and low agricultural prices, policy-makers were looking for ways to support farmers without the burden of huge subsidies. Using crops for alternative uses was one method of removing such surpluses and boosting prices. At the same time, the Gulf War served as a reminder that countries needed to wean themselves from foreign crude oil sources.

---

[12] See also Chap. 9 on how fundraising incentives interact with policy objectives for NGOs and international organizations and Swinnen et al. (2011) for a formal model of this.

Increased recognition of climate change stemming from greenhouse gas emissions presented yet another rationale for moving away from fossil fuels. As a result, both the EU and the USA stimulated the development of biofuels. The growth of biofuels was much stronger in the USA (mostly corn-based ethanol) than in the EU (mostly biodiesel).[13]

After 2007, the policy climate on biofuel changed. The turnaround was triggered by two developments. First, while there is disagreement on the size of the impact, biofuels generally have been an important driver of increasing food prices, which spiked in 2007 and 2008 (de Gorter et al. 2013). Second, biofuels were originally thought of as environmentally friendly fuels, due to their decreased carbon impact relative to fossil fuels. However, indirect effects on land use change (e.g. deforestation) may lead to an increase—rather than a decrease—in greenhouse gas emissions (GHGE). These factors transformed the debate on biofuels, triggering what the biofuels industry has described as a policy U-turn.[14]

However lobbying by various organizations with vested interest in biofuels have led to a postponement of the decision. In general the growth of biofuels has created new political alliances. As biofuels contributed to grain price spikes in the late 2000s, this stimulated the creation of political coalitions of grain farmers and biofuel industries, versus livestock farmers, consumers and other sectors hurt by rising feed and food costs (de Gorter et al. 2015).

2.2.9 Insuring Crops or the Insurance Industry?

Agriculture has always been a risky business as a consequence of uncertain weather, prices, diseases, and pests. Since 1998, US agricultural policy has gradually increased subsidies to use insurance instruments to help combat

---

[13] The US biofuels legislation was built on a history of tax exemptions and tariffs (taxes on imports), but the fundamental policy shift was the introduction of mandates for the use of biofuels in transportation—the Renewable Fuel Standard (RFS) in 2005 (de Gorter et al. 2015; Lobell et al. 2014; Naylor 2012). The impacts of the US biofuels legislation were large. From 2004 to 2012, the amount of corn used for ethanol increased from about 1.2 billion bushels to about 5 billion bushels. Over 40% of US corn use now goes to ethanol.

[14] In the EU, from encouraging this sector through production targets and blending mandates, the EC is now backtracking and seeks to minimize the use of food-crop based biofuels. The new biofuel sustainability requirements of the 2009 Renewable Energy Directive try to limit the impact of biofuels on rising food prices (European Commission 2009). In 2012, the EC published a proposal limiting the use of food-crop-based biofuels at 5% of consumption of energy for transport in 2020.

those risks (Glauber 2004). The crop insurance program is a public-private partnership, in which the government pays part of the insurance premiums of farmers, and agrees also to underwrite some costs of the private insurance companies. Between 2005 and 2012, government budget costs for crop insurance rose sharply, and in 2012, about 90% of US cropland was covered by the Federal Crop Insurance Program (FCIP). In addition to yield coverage, farmers can also purchase revenue-based insurance, which covers several dimensions of price variability.

Not surprisingly, the insurance industry has now become an active participant in the discussions on the US Farm Bill as crop insurance programs have become the largest expenditure item on recent Farm bills. During the 2013 legislative process the insurance industry lobbied senators aggressively and outmaneuvered the advocates for reform, effectively maintaining support for the crop insurance program in the 2014 Farm Bill (Coble et al. 2013; Cuellar et al. 2014). Their successful lobbying was also due to the fact that the combination of increased budgetary transparency and high agricultural prices in the late 2000s and early 2010s has caused a shift (back) from direct payments toward more coupled programs, such as crop insurance payments (Coble et al. 2013; de Gorter et al. 2015; Goodwin and Smith 2013).

Interestingly, the EU Commission also considered proposing an insurance policy for including in the new CAP. They launched several studies on the issue but concluded that too much of the subsidies would end up with the insurance companies rather than farmers. In addition, the risk of creating new vested interest in future CAP policies through this new instrument reduced their enthusiasm for an agricultural insurance policy.

2.2.10   *Consumer-Farmer Coalitions*

So far in all the examples "(final) consumers" and "(agricultural) producers" have conflicting interests. However, there are also cases where they may join together in lobbying. This can be the case when food standards are set and their interests align with consumers benefiting from protection against unhealthy or low-quality products and producers from protection against foreign competition (see Chap. 10). Another case is when they both benefit from subsidies paid by taxpayers.

Food policy to address consumer concerns can be very differently organized depending on the nature of the welfare system. This is well illustrated by the difference between Europe and the USA. In Europe, government support for poor consumers in the EU now occurs mostly through social spending, not through food market regulations. Social groups that are particularly vulnerable to food costs, such as the elderly, the unemployed and the poor, can draw on social security programs.

This is very different in the USA where the coalition between consumers' and producers' interest in agricultural policy is much more direct (Orden et al. 1999). The Supplemental Nutrition Assistance Program (SNAP, earlier known as *food stamps*) is a major item of the US' "Farm Bill". SNAP payments go to families with net-incomes less than the poverty line. In 2012, some 47 million Americans—about 15% of the entire nation—received SNAP payments, and the $112 billion consumer package is now the core of USDA's budget Cueller et al. (2014).

This huge safety-net consumer program is located within the USDA's budget rather than within the Department of Health and Human Services, the home for virtually all other welfare programs, for historical and political reasons. The food stamp program was originally designed to distribute surplus agricultural commodities to assist poor and needy families in the 1930s and later became a part of President Kennedy's "War on Poverty". Because the 1930s food stamp program was within the USDA, due to strong links with agricultural political interests, it remained there. Cuellar et al.'s (2014) claim is "arguably the most prominent example of coalition politics in American food and agriculture policy", that is, the cooperative dynamic between supporters of domestic nutrition assistance and supporters of domestic farm subsidies to pass the Farm Bill. This entails an informal understanding whereby members of Congress who support domestic nutrition assistance either vote in favor of, or remain silent on, proposals to subsidize farmers, as long as domestic nutrition assistance programs are also funded adequately. The Farm Bill thus requires the support of both sides.[15]

2.3   Conclusions

Political coalitions have changed over the past decades (and centuries) as economic development implies the relative decline of some sectors in the value chain and the (relative) growth of others. New technologies and

---

[15] What makes this piece of legislation particularly interesting is that the provision of nutritional assistance provides a safety net for low-income consumers, particularly in times of high or volatile food prices caused in part by agricultural policies like the corn-ethanol program. The convergence of special interests creates a peculiar equilibrium in US food and agricultural policy that is extremely difficult to disrupt.

globalization have introduced new players into the value chains and new policy instruments have provided incentives for others to join the lobbying game.

This chapter discussed reasons why such changes may affect the political coalitions and the resulting policy equilibria, and a series of changes in political coalitions that have affected policy outcomes. This includes historical changes in agricultural protection, the impact of changes in consumer interests in recent decades, changes in concentration in the downstream sectors of the value chains, the growth of environmental interests and emergence of new (bio)technologies, the growth of biofuels, and new policy instruments such as crop insurance subsidies. In general each of these changes has had (sometimes very profound) impacts on agricultural and food policy decisions.

REFERENCES

Anderson, K. 1995. Lobbying Incentives and the Pattern of Protection in Rich and Poor Countries. *Economic Development and Cultural Change* 43 (2): 401–423.

Antras, P. 2015. *Global Production: Firms, Contracts, and Trade Structure.* Princeton: Princeton University Press.

Barnard, C.H., G. Whittaker, D. Westenbarger, and M. Ahearn. 1997. Evidence of Capitalization of Direct Government Payments into U.S. Cropland Values. *American Journal of Agricultural Economics* 79 (5): 1642–1650.

Barrett, C.B., and D. Maxwell. 2007. *Food Aid After Fifty Years: Recasting Its Role.* Abingdon/New York: Routledge.

Blanchard, E., and X. Matschke. 2015. US Multinationals and Preferential Market Access. *Review of Economics and Statistics* 97 (4): 839–854.

Blanchard, E.J., C.P. Bown, and R.C. Johnson. 2016. *Global Supply Chains and Trade Policy* (No. w21883). National Bureau of Economic Research.

Briones, Alonso E., and J. Swinnen. 2016. Who Are the Producers and Consumers? Value Chains and Food Policy Effects in the Wheat Sector in Pakistan. *Food Policy* 61: 40–58.

Charles, D. 2001. *Lords of the Harvest. Biotech, Big Money, and the Future of Food.* New York: Basic Books.

Ciaian, P., and J. Swinnen. 2006. Land Market Imperfections and Agricultural Policy Impacts in the New EU Member States: A Partial Equilibrium Analysis. *American Journal of Agricultural Economics* 88 (4): 799–815.

———. 2009. Credit Market Imperfections and the Distribution of Policy Rents. *American Journal of Agricultural Economics* 91 (4): 1124–1139.

Ciaian, P., D. Kancs, and J. Swinnen. 2010. *EU Land Markets and the Common Agricultural Policy*. Brussels: CEPS Publications.

———. 2014. The Impact of the 2013 CAP Reform on Land Capitalization. *Applied Economic Perspectives and Policy* 36 (4): 643–673.

Ciaian, P., Kancs, D.A. and Espinosa, M., 2016. The Impact of the 2013 CAP Reform on the Decoupled Payments' Capitalisation into Land Values. Journal of Agricultural Economics. Forthcoming.

Coble, K., B. Barnett, and J. Riley. 2013. *Challenging Belief in the Law of Small Numbers*. In Agricultural and Applied Economics Association 2013 Crop Insurance and the Farm Bill Symposium, Louisville, October/September.

Cuellar, M., D. Lazarus, W.P. Falcon, and R.L. Naylor. 2014. Institutions, Interests, and Incentives in American Food and Agriculture Policy. In *The Evolving Sphere of Food Security*, ed. R.L. Naylor, 87–121. Oxford: Oxford University Press.

De Gorter, H., D. Drabik, and D.R. Just. 2013. Biofuel Policies and Food Grain Commodity Prices 2006–2012: All Boom and No Bust? *AgBioforum* 16 (1): 1–13.

———. 2015. *The Economics of Biofuel Policies*, Palgrave Studies on Agricultural Economics and Food Policies. New York: Springer.

Erjavec, E., M. Lovec, and K. Erjavec. 2015. Greening or Green Wash ? Drivers and Discourses of the 2013 CAP reforms. In *The Political Economy of the 2014–2020 Common Agricultural Policy*, ed. J. Swinnen. Brussels: CEPS Publications.

Gardner, B.L. 2002. *American Agriculture in the Twentieth Century*. Cambridge, MA: Harvard University Press.

Gawande, K., and B. Hoekman. 2006. Lobbying and Agricultural Trade Policy in the United States. *International Organization* 60: 527–561.

Glauber, J.W. 2004. Crop Insurance Reconsidered. *American Journal of Agricultural Economics* 86 (5): 1179–1195.

Goodwin, B.K., and V. Smith. 2013. What Harm Is Done by Subsidizing Crop Insurance? *American Journal of Agricultural Economics* 95 (2): 489–497.

Goodwin, B.K., A.K. Mishra, and F.N. Ortalo-Magné. 2003. What's Wrong with Our Models of Agricultural Land value? *American Journal of Agricultural Economics* 85: 744–752.

Graff, G.D., G. Hochman, and D. Zilberman. 2009. The Political Economy of Agricultural Biotechnology Policies. *AgBioforum* 12 (1): 34–46.

Hart, K. 2015. The Fate of Green Direct Payments in the CAP Reform Negotiations: The Role of the European Parliament. In *The Political Economy of the 2014–2020 Common Agricultural Policy*, ed. J. Swinnen. Brussels: CEPS Publications.

Ivanova, N., J. Lingard, A. Buckwell, and A. Burrell. 1995. Impact of Changes in Agricultural Policy on the Agro-Food Chain in Bulgaria. *European Review of Agricultural Economics* 22 (3): 354–371.

Josling, Tim. 2006. The War on Terroir: Geographical Indications as a Transatlantic Trade Conflict. *Journal of Agricultural Economics* 57: 337–363.

Kirwan, B. 2009. The Incidence of US Agricultural Subsidies on Farmland Rental Rates. *Journal of Political Economy* 177 (1): 138–164.

Lobell, D.B., R.L. Naylor, and C.B. Field. 2014. Food, Energy, and Climate Connections in a Global Economy. In *The Evolving Sphere of Food Security*, ed. R.L. Naylor, 238–268. Oxford: Oxford University Press.

López, R.A. 2008. Does 'Protection for Sale' Apply to the US Food Industries? *Journal of Agricultural Economics* 9 (1): 25–40.

Mason, Nicole M., Thomas S. Jayne, and Nicolas van de Walle. 2017. The Political Economy of Fertilizer Subsidy Programs in Africa: Evidence from Zambia. *American Journal of Agricultural Economics* 99 (3): 705–731.

Matthews, A. 2015. The Multi-Annual Financial Framework and the 2013 CAP reform. In *The Political Economy of the 2014–2020 Common Agricultural Policy*, ed. J. Swinnen. Brussels: CEPS Publications.

Meloni, G., and J. Swinnen. 2015. Chocolate Regulations. In *The Economics of Chocolate*, ed. M. Squicciarini and J. Swinnen, 268–303. Oxford: Oxford University Press.

———. 2018. *Trade and Terroir. The Political Economy of the World's First Geographical Indications.* Mimeo. Leuven: LICOS Discussion Paper.

Mo, D., J. Huang, X. Jia, H. Luan, S. Rozelle, and J. Swinnen. 2012. Checking into China's Cow Hotels: Have Policies Following the Milk Scandal Changed the Structure of the Dairy Sector? *Journal of Dairy Science* 95 (5): 2282–2298.

Naylor, R.L. 2012. Biofuels, Rural Development, and the Changing Structure of Agricultural Demand. In *Frontiers in Food Policy: Perspectives on Sub-Saharan Africa*, ed. W. Falcon and R.L. Naylor. Stanford: Stanford Center on Food Security and the Environment (Printed by CreateSpace).

Nunn, N. 2007. Relationship-Specificity, Incomplete Contracts, and the Pattern of Trade. *The Quarterly Journal of Economics* 122 (2): 569–600.

Olper, A. 2017. The Political Economy of Trade-Related Regulatory Policy: Environment and Global Value Chain. *Bio-based and Applied Economics* 5 (3): 287–324.

Orden, D., R. Paarlberg, and T. Roe. 1999. *Policy Reform in American Agriculture: Analysis and Prognosis.* Chicago: University of Chicago Press.

Paarlberg, R.L. 2001. *The Politics of Precaution: Genetically Modified Crops in Developing Countries.* Washington, DC: International Food Policy Research Institute.

Pinstrup-Andersen, P., and E. Schioler. 2003. *Seeds of Contention: World Hunger and the Global Controversy Over GM Crops.* Baltimore/London: International Food Policy Research Institute.

Qaim, M. 2009. The Economics of Genetically Modified Crops. *Annual Review of Resource Economics* 1 (1): 665–694.

———. 2016. *Genetically Modified Crops and Agricultural Development.* New York: Springer.

Roberts, M.J., B. Kirwan, and J. Hopkins. 2003. The Incidence of Government Program Payments on Land Rents: The Challenges of Identification. *American Journal of Agricultural Economics* 85: 762–769.

Ruta, Michele. 2017. *Preferential Trade Agreements and Global Value Chains: Theory, Evidence, and Open Questions (English),* Policy Research Working Paper No. WPS 8190. World Bank Group, Washington, DC.

Salhofer, K., and E. Schmid. 2004. Distributive Leakages of Agricultural Support: Some Empirical Evidence. *Agricultural Economics* 30 (1): 51–63.

Sexton, R.J. 2012. Market Power, Misconceptions, and Modern Agricultural Markets. *American Journal of Agricultural Economics* 95 (2): 209–219.

Swinnen, J. 1996. Endogenous Price and Trade Policy Developments in Central European Agricultrue. *European Review of Agricultural Economics* 23 (2): 133–160.

———. 2002. Political Reforms, Rural Crises, and Land Tenure in Western Europe. *Food Policy* 27 (4): 371–394.

———. 2011. The Right Price of Food. *Development Policy Review* 29 (6): 667–688.

Swinnen, J., and T. Vandemoortele. 2011a. Policy Gridlock or Future Change? The Political Economy Dynamics of EU Biotechnology Regulation. *AgBioforum* 13 (4): 291–296.

———. 2011b. Trade and the Political Economy of Food Standards. *Journal of Agricultural Economics* 62 (2): 259–280.

Swinnen, J., and A. Vandeplas. 2010. Market Power and Rents in Global Supply Chains. *Agricultural Economics* 41 (s1): 109–120.

———. 2011. Rich Consumers and Poor Producers: Quality and Rent Distribution in Global Value Chains. *Journal of Globalization and Development* 2 (2): 1–28.

Swinnen, J., and S. Vandevelde. 2017. 5. Unfair Trading Practices—The Way Forward. Unfair Trading Practices in the Food Supply Chain, p.60.

Swinnen, J., P. Squicciarini, and T. Vandemoortele. 2011. The Food Crisis, Mass Media and the Political Economy of Policy Analysis and Communication. *European Review of Agricultural Economics* 38 (3): 409–426.

Swinnen, J., L. Knops, and K. van Herck. 2014. Food Price Volatility and EU Policies. In *Food Price Policy in an Era of Market Instability. A Political Economy Analysis,* ed. P. Pinstrup-Andersen. Oxford: Oxford University Press.

Swinnen, J., K. Deconinck, T. Vandemoortele, and A. Vandeplas. 2015. *Quality Standards, Value Chains, and International Development.* Cambridge: Cambridge University Press.

Vandemoortele, T., and K. Deconinck. 2014. When Are Private Standards More Stringent than Public Standards? *American Journal of Agricultural Economics* 96 (1): 154–171.

Vyn, Richard J., Zahoor Ul Haq, Jeevika Weerahewa, and Karl D. Meilke. 2012. The Influence of Market Returns and Government Payments on Canadian Farmland Values. *Journal of Agricultural and Resource Economics* 37 (2): 199–212.

Winfree, J.A., and J.J. McCluskey. 2005. Collective Reputation and Quality. *American Journal of Agricultural Economics* 87 (1): 206–213.

CHAPTER 3

Factors Influencing Policy Choices

Various schools of thought in political economy research (see Chap. 1), and many applications to agricultural and food policies, have shown how a variety of factors influence policy decisions and their implementation. These factors are income distribution, economic structure, governance structures (including domestic political institutions and international organizations), ideology, costs of information, transaction costs, and so on. This chapter explains how these factors influence policies. The rest of the book will draw upon insights explained here to discuss the political economy of specific agricultural and food policies and the governments' choices.

3.1 Income Distribution

Agricultural and food policies are often designed to alter the resulting distribution of income from what would otherwise emerge under undistorted market outcomes. That "without-policy" income distribution, therefore, plays a major role in policy decisions. Several elements of income distribution affect agricultural and food policies. First, overall economic development is typically associated with some sectors growing (and some declining) faster than others. Growth and decline of specific sectors thus affects the inter-sectoral distribution of income. As an economy develops, incomes in other sectors typically grow faster than in agriculture. Second,

© The Author(s) 2018   35
J. Swinnen, *The Political Economy of Agricultural and Food Policies*,
Palgrave Studies in Agricultural Economics and Food Policy,
https://doi.org/10.1057/978-1-137-50102-8_3

sectors are differentially affected by trade liberalization according to their comparative advantage and the pre-reform structure of protection. Third, historically, agricultural markets and food prices have fluctuated, thereby causing important short-term changes in income distribution. Fourth, large differences in income distribution and wealth may exist not only between agriculture and the rest of the economy, but also within the agricultural sector. All of these elements play a role in setting policy for food and agriculture.

3.1.1 *Relative Income and Loss Aversion*

As income distribution changes, this creates political incentives—both on the demand (e.g. farmers' or consumers') side and the supply (politicians') side—to exchange government transfers for political support. When farm incomes from the agricultural market decline relative to other sectors, farmers look for non-market sources of income, such as government support, either because the return to investment is greater from lobbying activities than from market activities, or because the willingness to vote for and support politicians grows as the political rents that are generated increase. For similar reasons, governments are more likely to support sectors with a comparative disadvantage than sectors with a comparative advantage. Since benefits from market returns are lower in sectors with a comparative disadvantage, those sectors' incentives to seek income from government support are relatively higher.

The nature of the mechanism through which these changing political incentives operate has been modeled in various ways. For example, Swinnen and de Gorter (1993) and Swinnen (1994) have used a politician-voter interaction model, in which differences in marginal utility drive the result.[1] In their models, the political gains from supporting low income groups are larger than the political losses from taxing high income groups because the marginal utility gains in the low income group are larger than the marginal utility losses in the high income group. However, this mechanism does generally not lead to full compensation of the income gap or an egalitarian income distribution as the marginal political costs rise with increased taxation and the marginal political benefits fall with increased subsidization. The political equilibration is reached before policies fully compensate for changing market conditions, or before incomes are equalized.

---

[1] These models are related to earlier work on conservative social welfare functions (Corden 1997), senescent industry support (Hillman 1982) and ideas in de Gorter and Tsur (1991).

Others, such as Freund and Özden (2008) and Tovar (2009), focus on the importance of aversion to loss in determining political reactions in order to explain why declining sectors, such as agriculture, receive support.[2] As people react stronger to losses than to gains, they prefer policies that avoid (or mitigate) losses over those that create gains. Through the political system governments and politicians react to these differences in policy preferences of the electorate and introduce policies that mitigate economic declines.

Both models (political support driven by differences in marginal utility changes and loss aversion) can explain why governments alter their trade restrictions in response to volatility in international prices of farm products. When market prices fall, governments often increase import tariffs and producer subsidies or reduce export taxes. When market prices rise, governments often lower tariffs or raise export taxes. This results in "countercyclical policies".[3]

Still others focus on interest groups' unequal ability to appropriate the benefits of lobbying (Baldwin and Robert-Nicoud 2007). In an expanding industry with low barriers to entry, policy-created rents attract new entries that erode those rents. In declining industries, this is not the case. Since the sunk costs of market-entry create quasi-rents, profits in declining industries can be raised without attracting entry, as long as the level of quasi-rents does not rise above a normal rate of return on the sunk capital. The result is that losers invest more resources in lobbying activities.

As already mentioned, income distribution may change for structural or cyclical reasons. For example, overall economic development is typically associated with some sectors growing and some declining faster than others. Growth and decline of specific sectors affect the inter-sectoral distribution of income. In addition, agricultural markets and food prices fluctuate around longer-term trends, causing important short-term changes in income and welfare distribution. Historically, this has induced governments to intervene in order to (partially) offset these market developments (as we explain and document in several chapters in this book). In particular,

---

[2] Tovar's (2009) empirical estimates of loss-aversion parameters are very close to earlier general loss-aversion estimates obtained by Kahneman and Tversky (1979) with experimental data.

[3] In some countries such countercyclical policy objectives are quite explicit. For example, the USA has several policies in place which are dependent on or triggered by low agricultural prices, including so-called countercyclical payments. Also in the EU, part of the agricultural policy budget is earmarked to be used when market conditions create "crisis situations" for farmers.

governments continue to intervene in order to insulate their domestic agricultural markets from international price fluctuations. This tendency involves increasing import tariffs or export subsidies when market prices decline and suspending import tariffs or export subsidies (or increasing export taxes) when market prices rise. The persistence of such policy responses was particularly evident when international prices for staple foods spiked recently (see Chap. 8). At such times, both exporting and importing nations altered their trade taxes, but in opposite directions (Anderson and Nelgen 2012; Ivanic and Martin 2014).

3.1.2   Inequality and Ideology

A related but somewhat different argument focuses on asset inequality. Asset inequality may influence policy directly and indirectly, through its effect on political institutions. Dutt and Mitra (2002) find that a rise in asset inequality is likely to have quite different effects in a labor-abundant economy compared to a capital-abundant one; these findings appear robust in both cross-sectional and time-series analyses. Olper (2007) finds that agricultural protection is, on average, negatively related with inequality, but the inequality effect is conditional on the ideology of the ruling government. Although left-wing governments usually support agriculture less, they also tend to support farmers more in unequal societies (see also Sect. 3.5).

Acemoglu and Robinson (2001, 2006) demonstrate both theoretically and empirically that economic inequality, the form of government, and redistributive policies interact dynamically. Societies with highly unequal distributions of assets (such as land) tend to be politically unstable, moving back and forward between (left-wing) revolutionary pressure exerted by the poor, who try to redistribute wealth through political change and land reforms, and (right-wing) dictators, who try to protect the concentrated resources of the rich. In more equal societies, redistribution can occur within a more stable democratic setting. Hence, these studies indicate that asset inequality affects redistribution not only directly, but also indirectly, through the political system (see also Sect. 3.4).

Finally, it may be useful to emphasize again that while inequality may result in political pressures and policies to reduce this inequality, this will ultimately not (necessarily) result in equality—as is obvious when looking at the real world. This can also be explained by different models. The Swinnen (1994) model (which keeps the political regime fixed) shows that countercyclical policies will be implemented but do not fully offset the initial inequality. At some point the opposition from "the rich" to further increasing taxes will be politically stronger than the political support from "the poor" in response to higher transfers. This point will arrive before full equality is reached. The Acemoglu-Robinson dynamic model which endogenizes political institutions implies that if inequality is large and pressure for substantial redistribution very high, revolutions and political coups to change the political regime may result rather than redistributive policies.

3.2 ECONOMIC STRUCTURE

Economic structural factors other than income distribution or asset inequalities also affect political incentives in setting agricultural policies. Several theoretical studies explain how differences (or changes) in structural conditions coincide with economic development, or are associated with different commodities for a given level of development. Market structures affect the costs and benefits of policy distortions and thus the incentives for political activities undertaken in order to influence governments (Anderson 1995; Swinnen 1994). Hence, the structure of the economy affects the distribution and the size of political costs and rents generated by agricultural policies. These costs and benefits, in turn, determine the government's political incentives. They can thus contribute to explaining why agricultural and food policies may be correlated with economic development and specific commodities.

Several forces drive the relationship between policies and economic development. A key element is that the income-distributional effects of policies are different in a poor agrarian economy than in a rich industrial economy. In a poorer economy, most workers spend a large share of their income on food. Any policy that increases the cost of food will be strongly opposed by workers and by industrial capitalists who want to keep wages low. They will support policies that keep food prices (and the pressure on wages) low. By contrast, in a rich economy, in which workers spend a smaller share of their income on food, a rise in the relative price of farm products benefits farm households proportionately more than it harms non-farm households and industrialists (Anderson 1995). The per unit political cost of increasing farm incomes by policies that increase prices thus falls as the economy becomes richer. Even though the share of farmers in the voting population declines, when there are few farmers, less opposition to protecting them arises. Swinnen (1994) has shown that, under plausible assumptions, the second of those two effects dominates.

Ample empirical evidence confirms these theoretical predictions. It shows that support to food consumers, agriculture, and specific agricultural commodities is correlated with structural factors.[4] These factors include the share of food in consumer expenditures, the share of agricultural employment in the economy, indicators of comparative advantage, and supply and demand elasticities.

3.3 Deadweight Costs and Transaction Costs

Demand and supply elasticities affect the distortions and benefits of policy and thus the choices of policy-makers. (Gardner 1983, 1987; de Gorter et al. 1992). The distortions (deadweight costs) and transfer costs of policy intervention typically increase with higher supply elasticities and the commodity's trade balance (i.e. when its net exports increase). Because of the inherent changes in the distribution of costs and benefits of policies and the associated political incentives, political economy theories predict that exports will be subsidized less (or taxed more) than imports and that commodity support is negatively correlated with the supply elasticity.

Deadweight costs not only affect the total transfer but also the policy instrument choice. Competition in the political marketplace, whether between interest groups, political parties, or both, induces governments to choose policy instruments that minimize market distortions (Becker 1983; Wittman 1989; Rausser and Foster 1990; Besley et al. 2010). Swinnen et al. (2016) show that for a wide range of countries, the share of market-distorting instruments in total transfers is negatively correlated with the export share. This negative correlation suggests that when exports are large, countries use non- or less-distortionary instruments more often than border measures (see Chap. 5).

Deadweight costs are not the only costs that matter in policy choice. Correct policy analyses should explicitly account for costs involved in the implementation, administration, and enforcement of the policies (Coase 1960, 1988; North 1990). Coase (1988) refers to economic analyses that exclude transaction and administration costs as "blackboard economics" that are meaningful only in the classroom but not in the real world. From

---

[4] See, for example, Anderson, Hayami, and colleagues (1986), Rausser and de Gorter (1989), Gardner (1987), and Swinnen et al. (2001), and (c) recent empirical studies using new datasets (including Gawande and Hoekman 2006, 2010; López and Matschke 2006; Masters and Garcia 2010; Olper and Raimondi 2010, 2013).

the standpoint of public policy, taking into account real-world transaction costs and constraints may change the evaluation of the relative efficiency of particular policy and instruments (Dixit 1996).

Interestingly, the existence of transaction costs has been used both to defend and to criticize the use of government policies. Coase (1988) argues that by ignoring transaction costs, most studies underestimate the costs of government policy and that existing policies are even more inefficient than is usually argued. In contrast, Munk (1989, 1994) argues that including transaction costs in the analysis leads to the conclusion that agricultural policies such as import tariffs are more efficient than is often claimed, since their transaction costs are low compared to the costs of other policies (such as lump-sum transfers). Similarly, Vatn (2002) suggests that the profession's preference for decoupled and better-targeted policies over price support policy, based on deadweight cost arguments, may be incorrect when transaction costs are taken into account. Still, Corden (1997) argued that rarely are these factors sufficient to make trade policy the most efficient instrument for achieving domestic social objectives.

While the transaction costs argument on public policy is conceptually clear and intuitively appealing, empirical evidence is very limited. The size of transaction costs of different policies is only rarely measured (North 1990; OECD 2007; Rørstad et al. 2007).

3.4 Political Institutions

The importance of political institutions for public policy has long been recognized (e.g. in the seminal work by Buchanan and Tullock 1962). A growing body of economic literature has emerged in the past few decades that analyzes the role political regimes on policy-making.[5] To relate some of these insights to agricultural and food policies, it is useful to examine the literature that considers the political regime (or "constitutional choice", in the framework of Aghion et al. 2004) as providing a degree of insulation for policy-makers. The political regime determines to what extent the government, once appointed, can rule without ex post control, what type of majorities the government needs in order to ensure its ability to pass legislation, and whether some groups have veto power.

Various institutional mechanisms affect how preferences of citizens influence the choice options and incentives of government, and, hence, on policies. These mechanisms relate to the differential effects of democracy

---

[5] See Rausser et al. (2011) for a review of this literature.

42   J. SWINNEN

versus autocratic regimes (Acemoglu and Robinson 2006; North et al. 2009); to the effect of different electoral systems (Persson and Tabellini 2003), including systems based on proportional or majoritarian electoral structures (Roelfsema 2004; Rogowski and Kayser 2002); and to the effect on the selection and implementation of public policies of autonomy given to bureaucrats and implementing institutions (Prendergast 2007).

3.4.1   Political Regimes

Several models predict the effect of political regimes (autocracies versus democracies) on public policies. Models based on the median-voter theorem predict that democracies tend to redistribute from the rich to the poor. In democracies, this is expected because the distribution of political power (measured by votes) is typically more equal than the distribution of income and wealth. This effect will increase as income becomes more unequal, since in that situation, the middle class has greater incentive to form coalitions with the poor (Alesina and Rodrik 1994; Persson and Tabellini 1994). Similarly, democratic regimes could lead to economic policy reforms if these reforms created more winners than losers (Giavazzi and Tabellini 2005). Further, McGuire and Olson (1996) argue that democracies tend to tax less and spend more on public goods than autocracies because the autocrat sets tax rates to maximize resources for his private rents.

A series of empirical studies have investigated these effects related to trade policy. Overall, they suggest that democracy positively affects economic (trade) liberalization (e.g. Banerji and Ghanem 1997; Milner and Kubota 2005; Giavazzi and Tabellini 2005; Eichengreen and Leblang 2008; Giuliano et al. 2010).[6] However, the causality of these relationships have been difficult to show because of data problems and the existence of potential feedback effect (Giavazzi and Tabellini 2005; Milner and Mukherjee 2009).

Part of this literature also compares different types of democratic systems, such as presidential regimes with dispersed political power and parlia-

---

[6] Some studies have argued that this effect depends on the country's resource endowment. O'Rourke and Taylor (2007) find that although democratization generally reduces trade protection, it does so only in countries where workers stand to gain from free trade. Kono (2006) shows that democracy, which increases the median voter's influence, leads to liberalization of trade in wealthier countries but to increased protection in poorer ones. However, politicians' support for free trade may depend on their time horizon. Conconi et al. (2011) show that in the US congressional system, six-year senators support more free trade policies than do two-year House members, except in the final two years before a senator is up for re-election.

mentary regimes with more concentrated political power. In general, these theories predict that compared with majoritarian and presidential systems, proportional electoral systems and parliamentary regimes will be associated with broad forms of redistribution, such as welfare programs, as well as with higher levels of government spending and redistribution (Persson et al. 1997, 2000; Persson and Tabellini 2000). A few studies have tried to test for these effects in agricultural policy. Olper and Raimondi (2010) find that agriculture is more protected/less taxed under a proportional electoral rule than under a majoritarian one. Olper and Raimondi (2013) find that presidential democracies support agriculture more (or tax it less) than parliamentary systems.

3.4.2   *Democratization and Agricultural Policies*

The very factors that make it difficult for farmers to organize politically for lobbying (such as their large number and their large geographic dispersion—see further in Sect. 3.6) render them potentially very powerful in democratic settings (Bates and Block 2010; Varshney 1995). However, early econometric studies on the effect of political institutions on agricultural policy find mixed and often weak evidence of the effect of democracy on agricultural protection (Lindert 1991; Beghin and Kherallah 1994; Swinnen et al. 2000; Olper 2001). There are both conceptual and empirical reasons for these weak results.

While it is intuitively obvious that when decision-makers are more insulated from repercussions, they can follow their preferences to a greater extent, this argument, by itself, has little predictive power because there are no good data on autocrats' preferences. One implication of this result, however, is that if dictatorial leaders are less constrained in setting policies, all else constant, there should be more variation in observed policy choices under dictatorial regimes than under democracy. Olper (2007) tests this hypothesis and does indeed find more variation in policy choices under dictatorial regimes than under democracy. That is, governments' responses to pressure from interest groups are stronger in democracies.

Early empirical studies typically used cross-sectional data and were subject to problems of reverse causality and omitted-variables bias.[7] More recent studies use long-run historical data and new methods such as a synthetic

---

[7]One should be careful in interpreting measured correlations as causal effects, since policies may also influence governance structures (reverse causality), or because unobserved factors may influence both the dependent and the explanatory variables (omitted variables). Cross-sectional data are particularly prone to such empirical problems.

control method (SCM) to address causality problems. Olper et al. (2014) analyzed the impact of democratic reforms over the past 50 years in developing and emerging countries and find that democratization on average tends to reduce agricultural taxation and/or increase agricultural subsidization. Masters and Garcia (2010) also find that governments with "more checks and balances" induce less price distortions. Swinnen et al. (2001) using long-term data show that changes in electoral rules that have disproportionately benefited agriculture (e.g. by extending voting rights to small farmers and tenants in the early twentieth century) have induced an increase in protectionism. In contrast, other electoral changes did not affect agricultural protection because they increased the voting rights of both those in favor of and those against protection. Overall, these results support the notion that political institutions do affect agricultural policies, but the average effect seems to be limited and complex.

One illustration of this complex interaction is the fact that as their economies further develop, agricultural policies of Communist autocracies often shift from taxing to subsidizing agriculture, as is also true in democracies (Swinnen and Rozelle 2006; Rozelle and Swinnen 2010). This suggests that there may be a complex interaction between political regimes, ideology, and economic development (see Chaps. 6 and 7).

Finally, a few studies have analyzed the impact of democratization on food consumers' welfare. However, since food security data are insufficient to measure the impacts, studies have used key health indicators (such as child mortality) as indicators of both food security and health policies. Many argue that democracy is good for health because (a) it gives the poor a stronger voice in political decision-making, leading to better public health policies, and/or (b) because it stimulates economic growth and thus income and health (Ruger2005; Sen 1999).

However, as with the impact on agricultural policies, empirical evidence is neither strong nor robust because of the difficulty of establishing causality (Besley and Kudamatsu 2006; Ross 2006). Pieters et al. (2016) analyze the impact of democratic reforms on health (child mortality) using the synthetic control method (SCM) to assess the impacts of 33 democratic reforms between 1960 and 2010. They find that democratic reforms reduced child mortality, especially in countries with high levels of child mortality. This finding is consistent with median voter model predictions.

3.4.3 Bureaucracies and Institutions

Political institutions determine the role played by the government administration and bureaucracy. Bureaucracies can have an impact both on the policy decision because of their agenda-setting powers and because of their role in policy implementation.

The important impact of the bureaucracy in policy implementation was emphasized in the reform processes in Asia and Europe in the 1980s and 1990s (Swinnen and Rozelle 2006—see also Chaps. 7 and 12). The support of officials for reforms in China was sustained by their personal interests as farm village leaders (Oi 1989) and later by reforms of the bureaucracy (Qian and Weingast 1997). A mandatory retirement program effectively removing the old guard which was opposed to reforms and replaced them by younger and more pro-reform people (Lee 1991). In the 1980s, it allowed bureaucrats to quit government positions and join business, which stimulated bureaucrat interest in economic growth and enterprise development (Li 1998). These changes stimulated interest of bureaucrats in local economic growth.

In Eastern Europe in the 1990s old-system bureaucrats were often an obstacle to the reform processes. Reformist governments tried to prevent bureaucrats from obstructing the reform processes by excluding them from the implementing institutions (Swinnen 1996).

The influence of the agenda-setting bureaucracy (the European Commission) and how their influence depends on political institutions was also emphasized by Pokrivcak et al. (2006) and Pirzio-Biroli (2008) in the 2000s reforms of the EU's agricultural policies and in recent failures to reforms. In the 2000s there was a shift from unanimity voting to qualified majority voting on agricultural policy issues in the EU Council of Agricultural Ministers (where agricultural ministers from all EU states are represented and have voting rights). This change removed national ministers' veto power. While the new rules still caused a "status quo bias" (Pokrivcak et al. 2006), they allowed the European Commission (the agenda-setting bureaucracy) to propose important reforms with a chance of success in the policy-making process. Swinnen (2008) argues that the change in voting rules played a crucial role in major reforms of the EU's Common Agricultural Policy in the 2000s (see also Chaps. 6 and 7).

The EU changed its decision-making procedures again in recent years, giving "co-decision power" to the European Parliament. This political reform caused a new shift of political power from the European Commission (the agenda-setting bureaucracy) to the European Parliament (consisting of elected representatives) (Crombez et al. 2012). The impact on agricultural policies was one of the enhanced impacts of farm lobbies (which had more influence in the agricultural committee of the European Parliament) and less support for reform (as the European Commission lost power) (Swinnen 2015).

3.5 IDEOLOGY[8]

As previously noted, greater insulation of decision-makers implies that they can follow their private preferences to a greater extent in selecting policies. This makes the preference of rulers—their ideology or other types of preferences—a key variable. For example, Bates and Block (2010) document that the regional backgrounds of leaders in Africa significantly affected their policy preferences, given the autocratic political systems' influence on agricultural policies. Leaders who drew their political support from cities and semi-arid regions (as in Tanzania and Ghana) seized a major portion of revenues generated by the export of cash crops (coffee and cocoa). In contrast, in countries where leaders came from and were supported by regions where cash crops were important sources of income (such as in Kenya and Ivory Coast), leaders employed the power of the state to defend the fortunes of their (wealthy) regions and imposed little if any taxation on coffee and cocoa exports. In their econometric analysis, Bates and Block's results are consistent with these case study arguments that the regional (political) associations of political leaders have significantly affected food policies in Africa.

Dutt and Mitra (2005) analyze the interaction between political institutions and preferences of rulers and find that a more left-wing government (i.e. one that assigns greater weight to the welfare of workers and labor) is more protectionist in the case of capital-abundant countries but less protectionist in the case of capital-scarce countries. They interpret their results as conveying that dictators who have consolidated their power may not face any electoral threats and may have fewer incentives to formulate trade policies according to their ideological affinities. However, if they do decide to favor their core constituent groups, they face fewer constraints in implementing redistributive trade policies.

---

[8] See Rausser et al. (2011, Chap. 7) for a formal treatment of the role of ideology and organization in public policy decision-making.

An extension of this model to agricultural policy is complex, since increasing food costs through agricultural protection hurts both urban workers and industrial capitalists. Hence, rulers who support either labor or capital should oppose agricultural protection—as they did historically in Europe (Kindleberger 1975; Schonhardt-Bailey 1998; Findlay and O'Rourke 2007). Empirically, Olper (2007) found that in OECD countries, on average, right-wing governments are more protectionist in the case of agriculture than are left-wing governments. This difference is consistent with studies such as those by Bates (1983), who argues that socialist rulers in Africa taxed farmers (by imposing low commodity prices), and by Tracy (1989), who found that right-wing governments in Europe (such as those dominated by Catholic parties and conservative parties, including the Nazi party in Germany) tended to support farm interests and protectionism.

Empirical observations also suggest that ideology and economic development may not be independent effects. As an illustration, consider the agricultural policies of extreme left-wing regimes in the twentieth century. Communist dictators such as Stalin in Russia, Mao in China, and Hoxha in Albania heavily taxed agriculture. In each of these cases average incomes in society were low. However, farmers were subsidized under Brezhnev in the Soviet Union and in most East European Communist countries in the 1970s and 1980s and recently in China—where incomes were considerably higher (Rozelle and Swinnen 2010 and Chaps. 6 and 7).

The ideology effect also appears to be conditional on inequality. Although, on average, left-wing governments support agriculture less, they tend to support farmers more in unequal societies (Olper 2007). For example, for more than a century in France, large farmers and landowners have been organized in different unions and associated with different political parties than small farmers, tenants, and farm workers: large farms are associated with right-wing political parties and small farms with left-wing parties. This empirical observation may hold more generally: right-wing dictators are more inclined to support agriculture if this sector is dominated by large-scale farms and estates, whose owners typically support right-wing rules. Similarly, right-wing dictators tend not to support agriculture if it is dominated by small farms and peasants, who constitute a potential revolutionary group. Conversely, left-wing regimes do the opposite.

3.6 POLITICAL ORGANIZATION

Regardless of ideology, in order to effectively influence political choices, interest-group members must coordinate their actions and use their collective bargaining power. Moreover, in order for their collective action to yield meaningful results, they must form an organization that can mobilize resources and direct individual action. But not all members of an interest group need to participate actively in the political organization. Admittedly, it is reasonable to expect that the greater the number of politically active members in an organization and the more resources at its disposal, the greater will be its political power base.

However, as Olson (1965) explained in his influential book *The Logic of Collective Action*, individuals of a group often prefer to free ride. If individuals cannot be excluded from the policy gains obtained through collective action, individuals who are solely concerned with their personal costs and benefits will often prefer to free ride as their marginal costs will often exceed their marginal utility of efforts spent on collective action. Olson explains that collective action by relatively large groups can come about only if free riding is controlled by means of "selective incentives." That is, the group must provide private goods desired by individual members on favorable terms only to those who decide to join the politically active organization. Examples of the selective incentives often provided by interest-group organizations to their members include insurance and information important to the members. In contrast, within relatively small groups, collective action may be induced by intragroup direct interactions even without the use of selective incentives.

Factors contributing to lower organizational set-up and maintenance costs enhance the group's political power. Geographic concentration of group members, a strong commitment to a broadly shared ideology, and closely knit inter-member communication networks (which often result from members' organized activities, such as trade and professional associations) contribute to cohesiveness within the interest group and decrease the organizational set-up and maintenance costs. Such forces strengthen the group's political power.

This collective-action theory predicts that in poor countries, food consumers will wield more political power than farmers. Consumers are often concentrated in cities with lower political action–coordination and enforcement costs relative to farmers, who are dispersed in rural areas. However, as the economy develops, and especially, as the share of agriculture in employment declines and rural infrastructure improves, the cost of political organization for farmers decreases. This cost reduction is likely to increase the effectiveness of farmers' representation of their interests and, as a consequence, of their lobbying activities.

The nature of agricultural structures also may determine the effectiveness of collective political action. Traditional arguments predict that a sector with mainly large-holding farmers can more easily overcome collective action problems because its members are typically fewer and its collective-action costs lower compared to the political rents they receive. However La Ferrara (2002) argues that inequality among farmers may make it harder for collective action to succeed because small and large farmers have conflicting incentives and because free riding is likely to be more common in a heterogeneous group setting. Historical evidence from Europe also supports this result (Schonhardt-Bailey 2006; Swinnen 2009). Significant inequality among farmers in England, Germany, and France at the end of the nineteenth century weakened the pro-tariff demands of major grain farmers because they were opposed by small farmers, many of whom were livestock producers.

There is debate in the literature whether changes in relative collective-action costs can explain major changes in agricultural policies. Although rural infrastructure and information have improved significantly as countries have developed, even in developed countries, there remain a very large number of farmers. The persistence of such large numbers of farmers, whose interests are not necessarily aligned, might imply that collective action obstacles remain important.

However, improvements in rural infrastructure and lower information costs (see Sect. 3.7) reduced the costs of farmer organizations. In addition, an important element here seems to have been the growth and concentration of agribusinesses and food-processing companies (Anderson 1995), which have often (though not always) aligned with farm interests in lobbying for agricultural policies. Since farm lobbies and agribusiness interests have often coalesced and are increasingly well capitalized and concentrated, they have been an important force in orchestrating public policies that benefit their interests. In Europe, the growth of agricultural protection was associated with the growth of cooperative agribusiness and food-processing companies (Swinnen 2009). Econometric studies by Gawande and Hoekman (2006) and López (2008) show empirically the influence of agribusiness and food companies' political contributions on US policies. Related arguments have been advanced by Francois et al. (2008), who explicitly integrate vertical relationships in the agri-food system. By integrating factor-market rivalry and input-output linkages in a Grossman-Helpman model, Cadot et al. (2004) show that protection escalates with the degree of processing. This finding helps explain why rich countries protect agriculture more than industry whereas poor countries do the reverse.

3.7 INFORMATION

3.7.1 The Rationally Ignorant Voter

Information plays a crucial role in political markets and policy design. In his path-breaking book *An Economic Theory of Democracy*, Anthony Downs (1957) explains the concept of the *rationally ignorant voter*. According to Downs, it is rational for voters to be ignorant about certain policy issues, if the costs of information are higher than the (potential) benefit from being informed. This argument implies that policies will be introduced that create concentrated benefits and dispersed costs, since the information costs are relatively large for those who carry the burden of financing transfers and relatively small for those who receive the benefits. Given the changing nature of agricultural and food consumers with economic development, this information mechanism has major implications for agricultural policies and contributes to the taxation of farmers in poor countries and the provision of rents to concentrated industries.

Factors that change information costs may therefore cause changes in public policies. One example is enhanced rural infrastructure, including communication infrastructure, that occurs either through public investments (as in many high-income countries earlier in the twentieth century) or through technological innovations and commercial distributions (as in the recent dramatic increase in mobile-phone use in developing countries). Another influencing factor is the spread of commercial mass media.

3.7.2 Mass Media

The literature on the economics of mass media is growing rapidly and has generated important new insights (Mullainathan and Shleifer 2005). An important segment of this literature investigates the role of mass media in political markets and its effect on public—policy-making. Mass media

FACTORS INFLUENCING POLICY CHOICES 51

affects policy-making through several mechanisms (McCluskey and Swinnen 2010), three of which are particularly relevant here.[9]

First, access to mass media empowers people politically, and a more informed and politically active electorate increases the incentives for a government to be responsive (Besley and Burgess 2001; Strömberg 2004a). This influence has been found for various types of government programs in various countries, such as unemployment programs and disaster relief (Eisensee and Strömberg 2007; Strömberg 2004b; Francken et al. 2012), better governance and less corruption in public food provision (Besley and Burgess 2002), and rural educational spending (Reinikka and Svensson 2005; Francken et al. 2009).

Second, mass media tends to target large audiences because of scale economies. In essence, mass media can play an important role in agricultural policy by altering the political economy mechanisms through which small special-interest groups influence policy. As explained above, the literature on the political economy of agricultural policy suggests that group size (e.g. the number of farmers versus the number of food consumers in the economy) helps determine lobbying effectiveness. Group size is thought to play an important role because it affects collective-action costs as well as per capita costs and benefits of agricultural policy (Peltzman 1976; Rausser and Foster 1990). In turn, these costs and benefits influence political outcomes in the presence of voter information costs as well as investments in political activities.

Recent papers in the media-economic literature claim that mass media can play an important role in public policy precisely by altering political economy mechanisms (Strömberg 2001, 2004a; Kuzyk and McCluskey

---

[9] Mass media can also affect policy-making by creating a bias in the provision of information (Baron 2006; Gentzkow and Shapiro 2006; Groseclose and Milyo 2005; Sutter 2001). Media bias can take various forms, and there is no generally accepted definition. Media bias can result from preferences of owners, editors, or journalists. It can also result from falsehoods or from information hidden or distorted by sources or journalists eager for a scoop or under pressure to attract attention, or it can result from consumer preferences. For example, the media's incentives to appeal to a larger audience and to attract advertisers may induce editors to moderate their political messages (Gabszewicz et al. 2008; Petrova 2008). Biased information will affect agents' behavior in economic and political markets. These studies have been found to be material to agricultural and food policy (Marks et al. 2003; McCluskey and Swinnen 2010; Swinnen and Francken, 2006).

2006). Oberholzer-Gee and Waldfogel (2005) argue that the link between group size and political mobilization depends on the structure of media markets. In a series of influential papers, Strömberg (2001, 2004a) shows that competition leads mass media outlets to provide more news and information to large groups such as taxpayers and dispersed consumer interests, thus potentially altering the landscape of political competition. Strömberg refers to this outcome as "mass-media competition-induced political bias."

Olper and Swinnen (2013) analyze empirically whether there is evidence that mass media affects global agricultural and food policies. While it is difficult to establish causality with available data, they find that mass media is associated with substantive changes in food policy. In developing countries, agricultural taxation is reduced when mass media grow in importance, while in rich countries, agricultural support is reduced. Their findings are consistent with the argument that by increasing government accountability, competition in the mass media market reduces distortions to agricultural and food prices.

3.7.3   The Bad News Hypothesis

Another factor is that commercial mass media has a tendency to publish negative aspects of issues, including economic news. This "Bad News Hypothesis" was first presented by McCluskey and Swinnen (2004) and formalized by McCluskey et al. (2015). This tendency of the media is driven by the demand side of the news market. As people are loss averse of have stronger marginal utility effects from avoiding income declines than from income gains, there is a demand for bad news. Commercial media responds to this demand by disproportionately publishing negative news items. For example, Heinz and Swinnen (2015) find that (on a per job basis) mass media are 20 times more likely to report employment declines than employment growth.

This tendency, combined with the fact that both voters and politicians receive a very large share of their information from commercial media will reinforce the "relative income effect" (explained in Sect. 3.1). With mass media covering income declines disproportionately, there is an extra mechanism that induces politicians to react. This media factor also played an important role in policy responses to the recent food price spikes (see Chap. 9).

3.7.4   *Information and Policy Instrument Choice*

The influence of information costs on how much a certain group lobbies, or is aware of policies and their effects, will not just affect the level of the policy intervention but also affect the choice of policy instruments. If voters are differently informed about the effects of different policies, politicians have an incentive to select policy instruments that are less transparent (Tullock 1983; Olson 1982). This "obfuscation" argument implies that governments use policies that obfuscate the costs of the policies to those hurt by the policies or use policies that obfuscate the transfer itself (Magee et al. 1989; Hillman and Ursprung 1988; Ray 1981; Trebilcock et al. 1982).

Kono (2006) argues that electoral competition reinforces obfuscation effects because some policies are easier to explain to voters. Magee et al. (1989) push this argument further and argue that there is a *voter information paradox* because as voters become more sophisticated, parties must disguise their redistributive activities more effectively, leading to an increase in the equilibrium level of distortions.

3.8   Crises

Empirical evidence indicates both significant changes but also considerable stability in agricultural and food policies for many countries (Anderson 2009; Anderson et al. 2013). The empirical data reveal that minor adjustments occur frequently but that major reforms are evidently difficult to achieve. Major obstacles to substantial reforms are institutional factors.

Political institutions induce interest groups, including bureaucracies, to organize themselves in particular ways. This process may lead to "political institutional equilibria" that create political power for certain interest groups (Rausser et al. 2011). In such equilibria, policy inertia is often the stationary political economic equilibrium. Large external changes ("crises") are often needed in order to overcome the inherent status quo in such equilibria, or to break the power of interest groups that are entrenched in the institutions. In terms of trade policy, Blanchard and Willmann (2011) show with a dynamic political economy model that in a democracy there may be two steady states: one protectionist and one liberal. They also find that shifting from one steady state (the protectionist) to the other (the liberal) is politically feasible only with sufficiently radical policy change.

Dramatic changes in agricultural-policy distortions that have occurred in the past decades have often been triggered by significant external changes, suggesting the importance of institutional inertia in constraining policy reforms. For example, major budgetary problems played an important role in stimulating radical agricultural-policy liberalization in Sweden and New Zealand in the 1980s (Anderson 2009). Policy reforms were also triggered by global financial (institutional/political) crises, including the financial crises in Latin America in the 1980s and in Asia in the 1990s; the liberalization reforms after the political changes in the Soviet Union in the 1990s; and the structural-adjustment programs in Africa in the 1980s and 1990s (Bates 1989; Moyer and Josling 2002; Orden et al. 1999).

Significant policy reversals sometimes require the combination of changes in political regimes and an economic crisis. In Africa, important changes in agricultural policies in the 1980s and 1990s followed the combination of fiscal crises and democratization (Bates and Block 2010). Similarly, in China in the mid-1970s, the combination of widespread hunger in the countryside and leadership change after the death of Mao allowed major reforms to occur (Swinnen and Rozelle 2006; see also Chaps. 7 and 12). In Europe at the end of the nineteenth and early twentieth centuries, the combination of enhanced political rights for farmers and rural households, along with a dramatic fall in rural incomes when prices collapsed, caused major changes in agricultural policies, including land reforms (Swinnen 2002, 2009; see also Chap. 7). In the EU, the combination of the accession of new member states, WTO constraints, and changes in voting procedures all contributed to important agricultural policy reforms in the 1990s and 2000s. The interaction of large external changes ("crises") and political institutional reforms caused a "*Perfect Storm*" leading to the radical reform of the EU's Common Agricultural Policy in 2003 (Swinnen 2008). Another crisis of a different nature (several food safety crises) in the 1990s induced a complete overhaul of food safety regulations and food standards in the EU in the 2000s (see Chap. 10).

3.9   International Institutions

In addition to domestic political institutions, other governance structures influence food policies. International governance can be a very important factor for agricultural and food policies. It can take such forms as bilateral, plurilateral, or multilateral trade integration, as well as broader regional, economic, and even political integration.

Changes in international governance structures have, on occasion, had dramatic effects on agricultural and food policies. One example is that of the dramatic transformation of policies in Central and Eastern Europe which moved from being fully integrated in the Soviet Union up to the 1980s, where economic policy was set by Communist rule in Moscow, to complete independence in the early 1990s. Ten years after this transition occurred, many of those newly independent states decided to shift much decision-making power (again) to (other) international governance structures. Most notably, they acceded to the WTO and the European Union. These international governance changes had dramatic effects on many of their policies, including those related to agriculture and food. The governance changes induced reforms from a highly distortive price and trading regime in the 1980s to a much more liberal system in the 1990s, and then to a renewed use of subsidies, albeit in a very different form, in the 2000s.[10]

Another major international governance change is the gradual integration of (what is now) 27 European countries into the European Union (EU) over the past 50 years. This development provides an interesting case study of the impact of such international or multinational governance structures on agricultural and food policies. One can observe a complex set of effects on such policies (see also above). First, obviously, the integration of the countries—some of which had a highly interventionist food policy, while others had more liberal policies—into a single market with common policies significantly affected the food policies in the member countries (Josling 2009). Second, during the past decades, several reforms of the decision-making rules within the EU have occurred, such as the move from decision with unanimity by member states to one with a (qualified) majority, and the more recent move to introduce "co-decision"[11] with the European Parliament. Theoretical studies (e.g. Pokrivcak et al. 2006) predicted that these changes could significantly affect reforms of the EU's agricultural policy. Empirical analyses confirm that, in particular, the change in voting rules toward qualified majority voting allowed the 2003 Common Agricultural Policy (CAP) reform to be implemented

---

[10] The extent to which WTO accession restrained these countries' use of tariffs and subsidies depended strongly on whether they were members of the GATT prior to the WTO's formation in 1995.

[11] "Co-decision" refers to new institutional rules under which both the Council of European Ministers and the European Parliament must approve policies. (Previously, only the Council of European Ministers had to vote, and the effective role of the European Parliament was mostly advisory.)

(Swinnen 2008). Third, recent enlargements of the EU to include more countries whose WTO constraints were already in place have required reforms of the EU's agricultural policy in order to avoid conflicts with WTO governance rules.

Other international governance structures may have less dramatic impacts but may still have a significant influence on food policies. This influence is particularly evident in international trade agreements covering agricultural-policy distortions. This issue has received considerable attention over the past decade: examples include the effects of the GATT's Uruguay Round Agreement on Agriculture (URAA), the establishment of the WTO, and the creation of the North American Free Trade Agreement (NAFTA).

An extensive body of literature has studied the URAA and the WTO with authors predicting a significant reduction in agricultural production (e.g. Anania et al. 2004). The WTO's impact on agricultural policies differs considerably depending on whether or not countries were part of the GATT before 1995, the year in which the URAA was completed (Anderson and Swinnen 2010). The WTO conditions imposed on China and Russia during the WTO accession negotiations were much more stringent than has been the case for some of the older WTO members (Drabek and Bacchetta 2004; Evenett and Primo Braga 2006). Hence, the impact of the WTO on agricultural distortions depends not only on comparative advantage but also on countries' institutional stage of entry.

Accessions to the GATT and WTO have influenced not only the total level of policy interventions but also the nature of the interventions. Since a key purpose of the WTO is to reduce trade distortions, accession to the WTO has induced a shift toward less trade-distorting policies. Both case study and econometric evidence support this result (Eicher and Henn 2011). In the specific case of agriculture, Swinnen et al. (2016) find that the WTO has played a central part in shifting to more-decoupled farm support across a wide range of countries (see Chap. 5).

For the USA, Orden et al. (2010) argue that the impact of the WTO on American agricultural policy over the past two decades has been very limited and that agricultural lobbies have been quite successful in continuing to advance their domestic interests. However, it appears that the US administration has attempted to introduce policy reforms with an eye toward insuring that many US agricultural subsidies are classified as "green box" (i.e. non-trade-distorting) under the WTO agreement. In addition the WTO and its dispute settlement mechanism contributed to reduction in support to specific sectors which were subject to official complaints, such as the US cotton subsidy programs (de Gorter and Kropp 2014).

The URAA and later WTO Doha Round negotiations have also been important in causing changes in the agricultural-policy instrument choice in the EU over the past decades. This included the shift in the 1990s from price support to direct payments (Moehler 2008). Later, the interaction of the WTO constraints with EU enlargement triggered further agricultural-policy instrument changes at the end of the 1990s (under the Agenda 2000 reforms). In addition, the 2003 Reform of the Common Agricultural Policy (CAP) was influenced by the ongoing WTO discussions and, in particular, the anticipation that agreement to cut agricultural assistance further would develop once the Doha Round concluded (Pirzio-Biroli 2008). These consecutive reforms not only helped reduce the total agricultural support in the EU but also strongly reduced the extent of trade distortion by encouraging a shift to more-decoupled policy instruments.

A final issue is the impact of international financial institutions (such as the World Bank and the International Monetary Fund [IMF]) and the policy conditions they have imposed on developing countries as part of their lending. The structural-adjustment programs in Africa and Latin America in the 1980s and the programs in the transition countries in Europe and Asia in the 1990s were very controversial. These programs required the borrowing governments in these countries to liberalize their policies and reduce distortions, with the stated intention of improving the chances of repaying the loans on schedule. Certainly, some policy reforms were reversed after the loans were in place (Masters 2009), but many appear to have stuck. Williamson and Haggard (1994) suggest that the most useful effect of these conditions came not in the form of hard conditionality ("leverage") but rather from shifting the domestic intellectual climate in these countries toward favoring freer markets.

3.10   Conclusion

This chapter reviewed a set of factors which influence policy choices and already referred to and discussed several cases of how they affected agricultural and food policies as an illustration. The rest of this book discusses some specific cases of agricultural and food policies, using insights from this chapter on political economy mechanisms.

REFERENCES

Acemoglu, D., and J.A. Robinson. 2001. A Theory of Political Transitions. *American Economic Review* 91 (4): 938–963.

———. 2006. *Economic Origins of Dictatorship and Democracy*. Cambridge/New York: Cambridge University Press.

Aghion, P., A. Alesina, and F. Trebbi. 2004. Endogenous Political Institutions. *Quarterly Journal of Economics* 119: 565–611.

Alesina, A., and D. Rodrik. 1994. Distributive Politics and Economic Growth. *Quarterly Journal of Economics* 109 (2): 465–490.

Anania, G., M.E. Bohman, C.A. Carter, and A.F. McCalla, eds. 2004. *Agricultural Policy Reform and the WTO: Where Are We Heading?* London: Edward Elgar.

Anderson, K. 1995. Lobbying Incentives and the Pattern of Protection in Rich and Poor Countries. *Economic Development and Cultural Change* 43 (2): 401–423.

Anderson, K. 2009. *Distortions to Agricultural Incentives: A Global Perspective,* 1955–2007. London/Washington, DC: Palgrave Macmillan/World Bank.

Anderson, K., and S. Nelgen. 2012. Trade Barrier Volatility and Agricultural Price Stabilization. *World Development* 40 (1): 36–48.

Anderson, K., and J.F.M. Swinnen. 2010. How Distorted Have Agricultural Incentives Become in Europe's Transition Economies? *Eastern European Economics* 48 (1): 79–109.

Anderson, K., Y. Hayami, and M. Honma. 1986. The Political Economy of Agricultural Protection: East Asia in International Perspective. In *The Growth of Agricultural Protection*, ed. K. Anderson and Y. Hayami, 17–30. Sydney: Allen and Unwin.

Anderson, K., G.C. Rausser, and J. Swinnen. 2013. Political Economy of Public Policies: Insights from Distortions to Agricultural and Food Markets. *Journal of Economic Literature* 51 (2): 423–477.

Baldwin, R., and F. Robert-Nicoud. 2007. Entry and Asymmetric Lobbying: Why Governments Pick Losers. *Journal of the European Economic Association* 5: 1064–1093.

Banerji, A., and H. Ghanem. 1997. Does the Type of Political Regime Matter for Trade and Labor Market Policies? *World Bank Economic Review* 11 (1): 171–194.

Baron, D.P. 2006. Persistent Media Bias. *Journal of Public Economics* 90 (1–2): 1–36.

Bates, R.H. 1983. Patterns of Market Intervention in Agrarian Africa. *Food Policy* 8 (4): 297–304.

———. 1989. *Beyond the Miracle of the Market: The Political Economy of Agrarian Development in Rural Kenya.* Cambridge/New York: Cambridge University Press.

Bates, R.H., and S. Block. 2010. Agricultural Trade Interventions in Africa. Chap. 12 in *The Political Economy of Agricultural Price Distortions,* ed. K. Anderson. Cambridge/New York: Cambridge University Press.

Becker, G.S. 1983. A Theory of Competition Among Pressure Groups for Political Influence. *Quarterly Journal of Economics* 98: 371–400.

Beghin, J.C., and M. Kherallah. 1994. Political Institutions and International Patterns of Agricultural Protection. *Review of Economics and Statistics* 76 (3): 482–489.

Besley, T., and R. Burgess. 2001. Political Agency, Government Responsiveness and the Role of the Media. *European Economic Review* 45 (4–6): 629–640.

———. 2002. The Political Economy of Government Responsiveness: Theory and Evidence from India. *The Quarterly Journal of Economics* 117 (4): 1415–1451.

Besley, T., and M. Kudamatsu. 2006. Health and Democracy. *American Economic Review* 96 (2): 313–318.

Besley, T., T. Persson, and D.M. Sturm. 2010. Political Competition, Policy, and Growth: Theory and Evidence from the U. S. *Review of Economic Studies* 77 (4): 1329–1352.

Blanchard, E., and G. Willmann. 2011. Escaping a Protectionist Rut: Policy Mechanisms for Trade Reform in a Democracy. *Journal of International Economics* 85 (1): 72–85.

Buchanan, J.M., and G. Tullock. 1962. *The Calculus of Consent*. Ann Arbor: University of Michigan Press.

Cadot, O., J. de Melo, and M. Olarreaga. 2004. Lobbying, Counter-lobbying, and the Structure of Tariff Protection in Poor and Rich Countries. *World Bank Economic Review* 18 (3): 345–366.

Coase, R.H. 1960. The Problem of Social Cost. *Journal of Law and Economics* 3: 1–44.

———. 1988. The Nature of the Firm: Origin. *Journal of Law, Economics, & Organization* 4 (1): 3–17.

Conconi, P., G. Facchini, and M. Zanardi. 2011. *Policymakers' Horizon and Trade Reforms*, CEPR Discussion Paper 8561. Centre for Economic Policy Research, London.

Corden, W.M. 1997. *Trade Policy and Economic Welfare*. 2nd ed. Oxford: Clarendon Press.

Crombez, C., L. Knops, and J. Swinnen. 2012. Reform of the Common Agricultural Policy Under the Co-decision Procedure. *Intereconomics* 47 (2012): 336–342.

Dixit, A.K. 1996. *The Making of Economic Policy: A Transaction Cost Politics Perspective*. Cambridge, MA: MIT Press.

Downs, A. 1957. *An Economic Theory of Democracy*. New York: Harper and Row.

Drabek, Z., and M. Bacchetta. 2004. Tracing the Effects of WTO Accession on Policy-Making in Sovereign States: Preliminary Lessons from the Recent Experience of Transition Countries. *The World Economy* 27 (7): 1083–1125.

Dutt, P., and D. Mitra. 2002. Endogenous Trade Policy Through Majority Voting: An Empirical Investigation. *Journal of International Economics* 58 (1): 107–133.

60   J. SWINNEN

———. 2005. Political Ideology and Endogenous Trade Policy: An Empirical Investigation. *The Review of Economics and Statistics* 87 (1): 59–72.

Eichengreen, B., and D. Leblang. 2008. Democracy and Globalization. *Economics and Politics* 20 (3): 289–334.

Eicher, T.S., and C. Henn. 2011. In Search of WTO Trade Effects: Preferential Trade Agreements Promote Trade Strongly, But Unevenly. *Journal of International Economics* 83 (2): 137–153.

Eisensee, T., and D. Strömberg. 2007. News Droughts, News Floods, and U.S. Disaster Relief. *Quarterly Journal of Economics* 122 (2): 693–728.

Evenett, S.J., and C. Primo Braga. 2006. WTO Accession: Moving the Goalposts? Chap. 19 in *Trade, Doha and Development: A Window into the Issues*, ed. R. Newfarmer, 227–41. Washington, DC: World Bank.

Findlay, R., and K.H. O'Rourke. 2007. Preface. In *Power and Plenty: Trade, War and the World Economy in the Second Millennium*, The Institute for International Integration Studies Discussion Paper Series IIIS.

Francken, N., B. Minten, and J.F. Swinnen. 2009. Media, Monitoring, and Capture of Public Funds: Evidence from Madagascar. *World Development* 37 (1): 242–255.

Francken, N., B. Minten, and J. Swinnen. 2012. The Political Economy of Relief Aid Allocation: Evidence from Madagascar. *World Development* 40 (3): 486–500.

Francois, J.F., D. Nelson, and A. Pelkmans-Balaoing. 2008. *Endogenous Protection in General Equilibrium: Estimating Political Weights in the EU*, CEPR Discussion Paper 6979. London, October.

Freund, C., and C. Özden. 2008. Trade Policy and Loss Aversion. *American Economic Review* 98 (4): 1675–1691.

Gabszewicz, J.J., D. Laussel, and N. Sonnac. 2008. *The TV News Scheduling Game When the Newscaster's Face Matters*, CORE Discussion Papers 2008/32. Université Catholique de Louvain, Center for Operations Research and Econometrics, Louvain-la-Neuve.

Gardner, B.L. 1983. Efficient Redistribution Through Commodity Markets. *American Journal of Agricultural Economics* 65: 225–234.

———. 1987. *The Economics of Agricultural Policies*. New York: Macmillan Publishing Company.

Gawande, K., and B. Hoekman. 2006. Lobbying and Agricultural Trade Policy in the United States. *International Organization* 60: 527–561.

———. 2010. Why Governments Tax or Subsidize Agricultural Trade. Chap. 10 in *The Political Economy of Agricultural Price Distortions*, ed. K. Anderson. Cambridge/New York: Cambridge University Press.

Gentzkow, M., and J. Shapiro. 2006. Media Bias and Reputation. *Journal of Political Economy* 114 (20): 280–316.

Giavazzi, F., and G. Tabellini. 2005. Economic and Political Liberalizations. *Journal of Monetary Economics* 52 (7): 1297–1330.

Giuliano, P., P. Mishra, and A. Spilinbergo. 2010. *Democracy and Reforms: Evidence from a New Dataset*, IMF Working Paper No. 10/173.

de Gorter, H., and J. Kropp. 2014. Is It Time to Put the Cotton Dispute to Rest? *Bridges Africa* 5 (3): 4.

de Gorter, H., and J. Swinnen. 2002. Political Economy of Agricultural Policies. In *The Handbook of Agricultural Economics*, ed. B. Gardner and G.C. Rausser, vol. 2, 2073–2123. Amsterdam: Elsevier Science.

de Gorter, H., and Y. Tsur. 1991. Explaining Price Policy Bias in Agriculture: The Calculus of Support-Maximizing Politicians. *American Journal of Agricultural Economics* 73: 1244–1254.

de Gorter, H., D.J. Nielson, and G.C. Rausser. 1992. Productive and Predatory Public Policies. *American Journal of Agricultural Economics* 74: 27–37.

Groseclose, T., and J. Milyo. 2005. A Measure of Media Bias. *The Quarterly Journal of Economics* 120 (4): 1191–1237.

Heinz, M., and J. Swinnen. 2015. Media Slant in Economic News: A Factor 20. *Economics Letters* 132: 18–20.

Hillman, A.L. 1982. Declining Industries and Political-Support Protectionist Motives. *American Economic Review* 72 (5): 118087.

Hillman, A.L., and H.W. Ursprung. 1988. Domestic Politics, Foreign Interests, and International Trade Policy. *The American Economic Review* 78: 729–745.

Ivanic, M., and W. Martin. 2014. Implications of Domestic Price Insulation for Global Food Price Behaviour. *Journal of International Money and Finance* 42: 272–288.

Josling, T. 2009. Looking Ahead to 2050: Evolution of Agricultural Trade Policies. In *The Evolving Structure of World Agricultural Trade: Implications for Trade Policy and Trade Agreements*, ed. Alexander Sarris and Jamie Morrison. Rome: FAO.

Kahneman, D., and A. Tversky. 1979. On the Interpretation of Intuitive Probability: A Reply to Jonathan Cohen. *Cognition* 7 (4): 409–411.

Kindleberger, C.P. 1975. The Rise of Free Trade in Western Europe, 1820–1875. *The Journal of Economic History* 35 (1): 20–55.

Kono, D.Y. 2006. Optimal Obfuscation: Democracy and Trade Policy Transparency. *American Political Science Review* 100 (3): 369–384.

Kuzyk, P., and J.J. McCluskey. 2006. The Political Economy of the Media: Coverage of the U.S.-Canadian Lumber Trade Dispute. *The World Economy* 29 (5): 637–654.

La Ferrara, E. 2002. Inequality and Group Participation: Theory and Evidence from Rural Tanzania. *Journal of Public Economics* 85 (2): 235–273.

Lee, H.Y. 1991. *From Revolutionary Cadres to Party Technocrats in Socialist China*. Berkeley: University of California Press.

Li, D.D. 1998. Changing Incentives of the Chinese Bureaucracy. *American Economic Review* 88: 393–397.

62   J. SWINNEN

Lindert, P.H. 1991. Historical Patterns of Agricultural Policy. In *Agriculture and the State: Growth, Employment, and Poverty*, ed. C. Timmer. Ithaca: Cornell University Press.

López, R.A. 2008. Does 'Protection for Sale' Apply to the US Food Industries? *Journal of Agricultural Economics* 9 (1): 25–40.

López, R.A., and X. Matschke. 2006. Food Protection for Sale. *Review of International Economics* 14 (3): 380–391.

Magee, S.P., W.A. Brock, and L. Young. 1989. *Black Hole Tariffs and Endogenous Policy Theory*. Cambridge/New York: Cambridge University Press.

Marks, L., N. Kalaitzandonakes, and L. Zakharova. 2003. Media Coverage of Agrobiotechnology: Did the Butterfly Have an Effect? *Journal of Agribusiness* 21 (1): 1–20.

Masters, W. 2009. Trends in Agricultural Protection: How Might Agricultural Protection Evolve in the Coming Decades? In *The Evolving Structure of World Agricultural Trade*, 79. Rome: FAO.

Masters, W.A., and A.F. Garcia. 2010. Agricultural Price Distortions and Stabilization. Chap. 9 in *The Political Economy of Agricultural Price Distortions*, ed. K. Anderson. Cambridge/New York: Cambridge University Press.

McCluskey, J.J., and J.F.M. Swinnen. 2004. Political Economy of the Media and Consumer Perceptions of Biotechnology. *American Journal of Agricultural Economics* 86: 1230–1237.

———. 2010. Media Economics and the Political Economy of Information. In *The Oxford Handbook of Government and Business*, ed. D. Coen, W. Grant, and G. Wilson. Oxford: Oxford University Press.

McCluskey, J.J., J. Swinnen, and T. Vandemoortele. 2015. You Get What You Want: A Note on the Economics of Bad News. *Information Economics and Policy* 30: 1–5.

McGuire, M.C., and M. Olson Jr. 1996. The Economics of Autocracy and Majority Rule: The Invisible Hand and the Use of Force. *Journal of Economic Literature* 34 (1): 72–96.

Milner, H.V., and K. Kubota. 2005. Why the Move to Free Trade? Democracy and Trade Policy in the Developing Countries. *International Organization* 59 (1): 107–143.

Milner, H.V., and B. Mukherjee. 2009. Democratization and Economic Globalization. *Annual Review of Political Science* 12: 163–181.

Moehler, R. 2008. The Internal and External Forces Driving CAP Reforms. In *The Perfect Storm: The Political Economy of the Fischler Reforms of the Common Agricultural Policy*, 76–82. Brussels: Center for European Policy Studies.

Moyer, W., and T. Josling. 2002. *Agricultural Policy Reform: Politics and Process in the EU and US in the 1990s*. London: Ashgate.

Mullainathan, S., and A. Shleifer. 2005. The Market for News. *American Economic Review* 95: 1031–1053.

Munk, K.J. 1989. Price Support to EC Agricultural Sector: An Optimal Policy? *Oxford Review of Economic Policy* 5 (2): 76–89.

———. 1994. Explaining Agricultural Policy: Agricultural Policy for the 21st Century. *European Economy, Reports and Studies* 4 (Annex): 93–119.

North, D.C. 1990. A Transaction Cost Theory of Politics. *Journal of Theoretical Politics* 2: 355–357.

North, D.C., J.J. Wallis, and B.R. Weingast. 2009. *Violence and Social Orders: A Conceptual Framework for Interpreting Recorded Human History*. Cambridge: Cambridge University Press.

O'Rourke, K., and A.M. Taylor. 2007. Democracy and Protection. In *The New Comparative Economic History: Essays in Honor of Jeffrey G. Williamson*, ed. T. Hatton, K.H. O'Rourke, and A.M. Taylor. Cambridge, MA: MIT Press.

Oberholzer-Gee, R., and J. Waldfogel. 2005. Strength in Numbers: Group Size and Political Mobilization. *Journal of Law and Economics* 48 (1): 73–91.

OECD. 2007. *Agricultural Policy Monitoring and Evaluation 2007*. Paris: OECD Publishing.

Oi, J.C. 1989. *State and Peasant in Contemporary China: The Political Economy of Village Government*. Vol. 30. Berkeley: University of California Press.

Olper, A. 2001. Determinants of Agricultural Protection: The Role of Democracy and Institutional Setting. *Journal of Agricultural Economics* 52 (2): 75–92.

———. 2007. Land Inequality, Government Ideology, and Agricultural Protection. *Food Policy* 32: 67–83.

Olper, A., and V. Raimondi. 2010. Constitutional Rules and Agricultural Policy Outcomes. Chap. 14 in *The Political Economy of Agricultural Price Distortions*, ed. K. Anderson. Cambridge/New York: Cambridge University Press.

Olper, A., and J. Swinnen. 2013. Mass Media and Public Policy: Global Evidence from Agricultural Policies. *The World Bank Economic Review* 27 (3): 413–436.

Olper, Alessandro, and Valentina Raimondi. 2013. Electoral Rules, Forms of Government and Redistributive Policy: Evidence from Agriculture and Food Policies. *Journal of Comparative Economics* 41 (1): 141–158.

Olper, A., J. Fałkowski, and J. Swinnen. 2013. Political Reforms and Public Policy: Evidence from Agricultural and Food Policies. *The World Bank Economic Review* 28 (1): 21–47.

———. 2014. Political Reforms and Public Policy: Evidence from Agricultural and Food Policies. *The World Bank Economic Review* 28 (1): 21–47.

Olson, M., Jr. 1965. *The Logic of Collective Action: Public Goods and the Theory of Groups*. Cambridge, MA: Harvard University Press.

———. 1982. *The Rise and Decline of Nations: Economic Growth, Stagflation, and Social Rigidities*. New Haven: Yale University Press.

Orden, D., R. Paarlberg, and T. Roe. 1999. *Policy Reform in American Agriculture: Analysis and Prognosis*. Chicago: University of Chicago Press.

Orden, D., D. Blandford, and T. Josling. 2010. Determinants of United States Farm Policies. Chap. 7 in *The Political Economy of Agricultural Price Distortions*, ed. K. Anderson. Cambridge/New York: Cambridge University Press.

64   J. SWINNEN

Peltzman, S. 1976. Toward a More General Theory of Regulation. *Journal of Law and Economics* 19: 211–240.

Persson, T., and G. Tabellini. 1994. Is Inequality Harmful for Growth? *American Economic Review* 84 (3): 600–621.

———. 2000. *Political Economics: Explaining Economic Policy*. Cambridge, MA: MIT Press.

———. 2003. *The Economic Effects of Constitutions*. Cambridge, MA: MIT Press.

Persson, T., G. Roland, and G. Tabellini. 1997. Separation of Powers and Political Accountability. *Quarterly Journal of Economics* 112 (4): 310–327.

———. 2000. Comparative Politics and Public Finance. *Journal of Political Economy* 108: 1121–1161.

Petrova, Maria. 2008. Inequality and Media Capture. *Journal of Public Economics* 92 (1–2): 183–212.

Pieters, H., D. Curzi, A. Olper, and J. Swinnen. 2016. Effect of Democracy Reforms on Child Mortality: A Synthetic Control Analysis. *Lancet Global Health* 4: 627–632.

Pirzio-Biroli, J. 2008. An Inside Perspective on the Fischler Reforms. In *The Perfect Storm: The Political Economy of the Fischler Reforms of the Common Agricultural Policy*, ed. J. Swinnen. Brussels: Centre for European Policy Studies.

Pokrivcak, J., C. Crombez, and J.F.M. Swinnen. 2006. The Status Quo Bias and Reform of the Common Agricultural Policy: Impact of Voting Rules, the European Commission, and External Changes. *European Review of Agricultural Economics* 33 (4): 562–590.

Prendergast, C. 2007. The Motivation and Bias of Bureaucrats. *American Economic Review* 97: 180–196.

Qian, Y., and B.R. Weingast. 1997. Federalism as a Commitment to Preserving Market Incentives. *The Journal of Economic Perspectives* 11 (4): 83–92.

Rausser, G.C., and H. de Gorter. 1989. Endogenizing Policy in Models of Agricultural Markets. In *Agriculture and Gevernments in an Interdependent World*, ed. A. Maunder and A. Valdés, 259–274. Oxford: Oxford University Press.

Rausser, G.C., and W.E. Foster. 1990. Political Preference Functions and Public Policy Reforms. *American Journal of Agricultural Economics* 72 (3): 641–652.

Rausser, G., J. Swinnen, and P. Zusman. 2011. *Political Power and Economic Policy: Theory, Analysis, and Empirical Applications*. Cambridge: Cambridge University Press.

Ray, A.J. 1981. The Determinants of Tariff and Nontariff Trade Restrictions in the United States. *Journal of Political Economy* 89 (1): 107–121.

Reinikka, R., and J. Svensson. 2005. Fighting Corruption to Improve Schooling: Evidence from a Newspaper Campaign in Uganda. *Journal of the European Economic Association* 3 (2–3): 259–267.

Roelfsema, H. 2004. *Political Institutions and Trade Protection,* Discussion Paper Series 04–06. TC Koopmans Research Institute.

Rogowski, R., and M.A. Kayser. 2002. Majoritarian Electoral Systems and Consumer Power: Price-Level Evidence from the OECD Countries. *American Journal of Political Science* 46: 526–539.

Rørstad, P.K., A. Vatn, and V. Kvakkestad. 2007. Why Do Transaction Costs of Agricultural Policies Vary? *Agricultural Economics* 36 (1): 1–11.

Ross, M.L. 2006. Is Democracy Good for the Poor? *American Journal of Political Science* 50: 860–874.

Rozelle, S., and J.F. Swinnen. 2010. Why Did the Communist Party Reform in China, But Not in the Soviet Union? The Political Economy of Agricultural Transition. *China Economic Review* 20 (2): 275–287.

Ruger, J.P. 2005. Democracy and Health. *The Quarterly Journal of Medicine* 98 (4): 299–304.

Schonhardt-Bailey, C. 1998. Interests, Ideology and Politics: Agricultural Trade Policy in Nineteenth-Century Britain and Germany. In *Free Trade and Its Reception, 1815–1960: Freedom and Trade,* ed. A. Marrison, 63–79. London: Routledge.

———. 2006. *The Corn Laws to Free Trade: Interests, Ideas and Institutions in Historical Perspective.* Cambridge, MA: MIT Press.

Sen, A.K. 1999. *Development as Freedom.* New York: Knopf.

Strömberg, D. 2001. Mass Media and Public Policy. *European Economic Review* 45 (4–6): 652–663.

———. 2004a. Mass Media Competition, Political Competition, and Public Policy. *Review of Economic Studies* 71 (1): 265–284.

———. 2004b. Radio's Impact on Public Spending. *Quarterly Journal of Economics* 119: 189–221.

Sutter, D. 2001. Can the Media Be So Liberal? The Economics of Media Bias. *The Cato Journal* 20 (3): 431–451.

Swinnen, J. 1994. A Positive Theory of Agricultural Protection. *American Journal of Agricultural Economics* 76: 1–14.

Swinnen, J.F.M. 1996. Endogeneous Price and Trade Policy Developments in Central European Agriculture. *European Review of Agricultural Economics* 23 (2): 133–160.

Swinnen, J. 2002. Transition and Integration in Europe: Implications for Agricultural and Food Markets, Policy and Trade Agreements. *The World Economy* 25: 481–501.

———. 2008. *The Perfect Storm: The Political Economy of the Fischler Reforms of the Common Agricultural Policy.* Brussels: Center for European Policy Studies.

———. 2009. The Growth of Agricultural Protection in Europe in the 19th and 20th Centuries. *The World Economy* 32 (11): 1499–1537.

———. 2015. Changing Coalitions in Value Chains and the Political Economy of Agriculture and Food Policy. *Oxford Review of Economic Policy* 31 (1): 90–115.

Swinnen, J., and H. de Gorter. 1993. Why Small Groups and Low Income Sectors Obtain Subsidies: The 'Altruistic' Side of a 'Self-Interested' Government. *Economics and Politics* 5(3): 285–296.

Swinnen, J., and N. Francken. 2006. Trade Summits, Riots, and Media Attention: The Political Economy of Information on Trade and Globalisation. *The World Economy* 29 (5): 637–654.

Swinnen, J., and S. Rozelle. 2006. *From Marx and Mao to the Market: The Economics and Politics of Agricultural Transition*. Oxford: Oxford University Press.

Swinnen, J.F.M., H. de Gorter, G.C. Rausser, and A. Banerjee. 2000. The Political Economy of Public Research Investment and Commodity Policies in Agriculture: An Empirical Study. *Agricultural Economics* 22 (2): 111–122.

Swinnen, J., H. de Gorter, and A. Banerjee. 2001. Agricultural Protection and Economic Development: An Econometric Study of the Determinants of Agricultural Protection in Belgium Since the 19th Century. *Agricultural Economics* 26: 25–43.

Swinnen, J., A. Olper, and T. Vandemoortele. 2016. The Political Economy of Policy Instrument Choice: Theory and Evidence from Agricultural and Food Policies. *Theoretical Economics Letters* 6 (01): 106.

Tovar, P. 2009. The Effects of Loss Aversion on Trade Policy: Theory and Evidence. *Journal of International Economics* 78 (1): 154–167.

Tracy, M. 1989. *Government and Agriculture in Western Europe 1880–1988*. 3rd ed. New York: Harvester Wheatsheaf.

Trebilcock, M.J., L. Waverman, and J.R.S. Prichard. 1982. *The Choice of Governing Instrument*. Ottawa: Economic Council of Canada.

Tullock, G. 1983. *Economics of Income Redistribution*. Boston: Kluwer-Nijhoff.

Varshney, A. 1995. *Democracy, Development, and the Countryside: Urban-Rural Struggles in India*. Cambridge/New York: Cambridge University Press.

Vatn, A. 2002. Multifunctional Agriculture: Some Consequences for International Trade Regimes. *European Review of Agricultural Economics* 29 (3): 309–327.

Williamson, J., and S. Haggard. 1994. The Political Conditions for Economic Reform. Chap. 12 in *The Political Economy of Reform,* ed. J. Williamson, 527–596. Washington, DC: Institute for International Economics.

Wittman, D. 1989. Why Democracies Produce Efficient Results. *Journal of Political Economy* 97 (6): 1395–1424.

PART II

CHAPTER 4

The Development Paradox

In the conclusions of the famous World Bank study on the political economy of agricultural pricing policies in the early 1990s, Anne Krueger (1992, p. 2) wrote that: "One of the most puzzling stylized facts of economic policy is that developed countries subsidize their farmers, whereas developing countries tax them: the degree of discrimination against agriculture increases as farmers constitute a larger fraction of the population."

Figure 4.1 illustrates this "development paradox" as researchers observed it in the second half of the twentieth century. From the 1950s to the 1980s, the Nominal Rate of Assistance to agriculture (NRA)[1] was on average around −20% in poor countries, while on average around +30% in rich countries, a staggering difference of 50 percentage points. The NRA measures distortions caused by government policies that create a gap between actual prices and the prices that would exist under free markets. These differences in NRAs thus reflect major differences in agricultural and food policies between rich and poor countries, with negative NRAs implying that farmers were taxed and positive NRAs reflecting subsidization of farmers (and taxation of consumers).

This difference was not only huge, the positive relationship of the NRA with income was also counterintuitive. In countries where farmers were the majority of the population, and thus had most of the votes or, more

---

[1] See Anderson (2009, 2016) for details on the NRA methodology.

© The Author(s) 2018
J. Swinnen, *The Political Economy of Agricultural and Food Policies*,
Palgrave Studies in Agricultural Economics and Food Policy,
https://doi.org/10.1057/978-1-137-50102-8_4

69

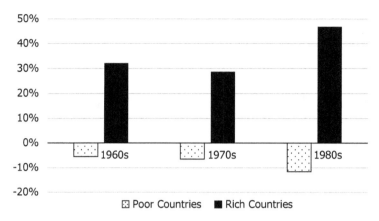

Fig. 4.1 Nominal rates of assistance to agriculture (NRAs), 1960s–1980s (%). (Source: Anderson 2009; Anderson and Nelgen 2012)

generally since many of these countries were not democracies, the political strength of numbers, they were losing out from agricultural policies which imposed a significant tax on them. In contrast, in countries where farmers were a minority, and often a small minority, farmers were subsidized, and often strongly so, despite the fact that their numbers in the political arena had declined. This observation was referred to as "*The Development Paradox*".

The differences in agricultural policies between rich and poor countries captured in the development paradox are due to differences in political economy equilibria caused by structural differences in economic forces, in information costs, in political organizations, and in changes in governance structures.[2] In the rest of this chapter I draw upon the mechanisms discussed in Chap. 3 to explain how these factors explain the development paradox. I also refer to Chap. 7 for an in-depth long-term analysis of dramatic changes in Chinese and European agricultural policies over the past century as an empirical illustration of the political economy forces explained here.

---

[2] This draws on studies explaining the relationship theoretically or empirically focusing on different time periods and different countries. See Anderson et al. (2013) and de Gorter and Swinnen (2002) for a more elaborate review and references to these studies.

4.1 Economic Growth, Restructuring, and Political Incentives

The most fundamental force in the development paradox is economic development itself. The structural changes that accompany economic development alter the economic and political costs and benefits of agricultural and food policies. Market structures affect the rents generated and the costs and benefits of policy distortions to various interest groups, and thus the incentives for political activities to be undertaken in order to influence governments. These costs and benefits, in turn, determine the government's political incentives and thus, adjust the political-economic equilibrium (Anderson 1995; Gardner 1987; Swinnen 1994).

Economic growth is associated with several important structural changes in the economy. First, economic growth typically coincides with a rise in urban-rural income disparities, as growth in industry and services outpaces growth in the agricultural sector, whose specific assets make it slow to adjust. As explained in Chap. 3, this income gap creates incentives for farmers and agricultural companies to demand—and politicians to supply—policies that redistribute income in order to reduce that income gap.

Second, economic structural factors other than income distribution also change with economic growth. The income-distributional effects of policy interventions that affect agricultural and food prices are vastly different in a poor agrarian economy than in a rich industrial economy. In a poor economy, most workers spend a large share of their income on food. In poor countries this is often more than 40% (see Table 4.1). They will

Table 4.1 The role of food and agriculture in economic development

Country	GDP per capita (current US$)	Employment in agriculture (% of total employment)	Agriculture, value added (% of GDP)	Share (%) of food consumption expenditure in total household consumption expenditure
USA	$56,207	1.6	1.1	13.9
EU	$32,048	4.5	1.6	12.4
Brazil	$8,757	10.3	5.0	19.8
China	$8,069	28.3	8.8	39.8
India	$1,346	51.1	18.9	49.5
Ethiopia	$571	71.4	41.9	50.8

Sources: World Bank, World Development Indicators and FAOstat

therefore strongly oppose an increase in food prices through government interventions, such as import tariffs on staple foods. Industrial capital will support worker opposition against food price increases because they are concerned about the inflationary effects on wages and their profits.

As Table 4.1 and Fig. 4.2 illustrate, the importance of agricultural raw materials in consumer expenditures declines strongly over time. In rich countries, workers generally spend a (much) smaller share of their income on food. The share is less than 20%, and only a relatively small part of this is the cost of raw materials (agricultural products). Most of the consumer food expenditures go to the processing, marketing, advertising, and retailing costs of food, not to the farmer's share. As a consequence, the impact of increased agricultural prices due to, for example, import tariffs on consumer welfare is much less. As a consequence, consumer opposition to agricultural protection declines with declining food shares in consumer expenditures. This effect is reinforced by declining opposition from industry as the inflationary pressure on wages from agricultural protection declines—through the same mechanism.

A related, but distinct, effect is how structural changes with economic development change the per capita impact of agricultural protection. Table 4.2 and Fig. 4.3 illustrate how the share of agriculture in employment

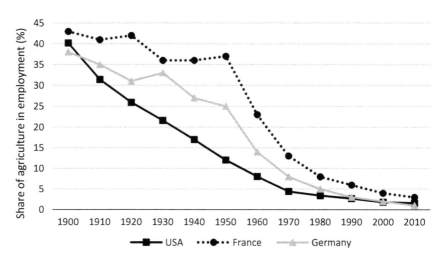

Fig. 4.2 Share of agriculture in employment in the USA, France, and Germany (%), 1900–2010. (Source: European Commission, Eurostat, NBER, ILO and Swinnen 2009, 2017)

THE DEVELOPMENT PARADOX   73

Table 4.2 History of taxation and subsidization of agriculture under communist political regimes in the Soviet Union and China

	GDP/capita	Country	Agricultural Policy	Ruler
1930	1450	Soviet Union	Tax (High)	Stalin
1940	2150	Soviet Union	Tax (High)	Stalin
1950	2850	Soviet Union	Tax (Low)	Kruzhnev
1960	3950	Soviet Union	Subsidy (Low)	Brezhnev
1970	5570	Soviet Union	Subsidy (High)	Brezhnev
1980	6420	Soviet Union	Subsidy (High)	Brezhnev
1970	780	China	Tax (High)	Mao
1980	1070	China	Tax (High)	Deng
1990	1860	China	Tax (Low)	Jiang
2000	3425	China	Tax (Low)	Jiang
2010	7100	China	Subsidy (Low)	Hu
2015	10,150	China	Subsidy (High)	Xi

Source: Updated from Rozelle and Swinnen (2009)

Note: GDP per capita in 1990 international Geary-Khamis dollars (for more details see http://unstats.un.org/unsd/methods/icp/ipc7_htm.htm) Maddison (2003)

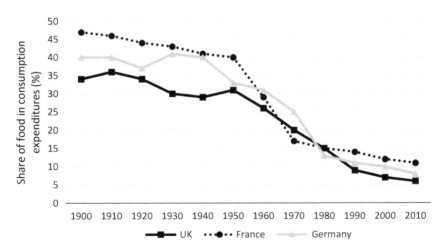

Fig. 4.3 Share of food in consumption expenditures (%) in the UK, France, and Germany, 1900–2010. (Source: European Commission, Eurostat, NBER, ILO and Swinnen 2009, 2017)

74   J. SWINNEN

declines with economic development. This share is typically 40% or more in poor countries and 10% or less in rich countries. This implies that, for a given per capita subsidy to farmers, it takes a much larger per capita tax on consumers (or workers in other sectors) when there are many farmers and fewer consumers (as in poor countries) than when there are few farmers and many consumers (workers in other sectors) as in rich countries. In other words, even though the share of farmers in the voting population declines, less opposition to protecting farmers arises when there are fewer of them. Swinnen (1994) shows that under plausible assumptions, the second of those two effects dominates.

In summary, as a result of these structural changes with economic development, government interventions that increase the price of farm products benefit farm households proportionately more than it harms non-farm households and industrialists in rich countries than in poor. As the economy becomes less agrarian the per-unit political cost of increasing farm incomes by policy interventions such as tariffs and price supports thus changes as opposition to agricultural protection declines. At the same time the demand for agricultural protection increases with the growing rural-urban income gap. The combination causes a shift in the political economy equilibrium from taxing farmers to subsidizing farmers with economic growth.[3]

4.1.1   Information Costs

Information plays a crucial role in political markets, organization, and policy design. As explained in Chap. 3, Downs' (1957) "rationally ignorant voter" principle means that it is rational for voters to be ignorant about certain policy issues if the costs of information are higher than the (potential) benefit of being informed.

McCluskey and Swinnen (2004) argue that rational ignorance, be it in the political arena ("voters") or in the economic arena ("consumers"), is still relevant today despite massive reductions of information costs and the emergence of mass media and social media. The reasons are that people's opportunity costs of processing information imposes limits of information

---

[3] Empirical studies that support these arguments include Anderson et al. (1986); de Gorter et al. (1992); Rausser and de Gorter (1989); Gardner (1987); and Swinnen et al. (2001); Gawande and Hoekman (2006, 2010); López and Matschke (2006); Masters and Garcia (2010); Olper and Raimondi (2010); and Olper et al. (2011).

consumption. Ideological divergences between the information (media) source and the reader and the price of some media sources may play a role as well.

The rationally ignorant voter argument implies that policies will be introduced that create concentrated benefits and dispersed costs, since the information costs are relatively large for those who carry the burden of financing transfers and relatively small for those who receive the benefits. As a result, forces that either change the distribution of the policies, or change information costs may cause changes in agricultural policies (Olper and Swinnen 2013).

The first factor is how economic development is associated with changes in the relative benefits of being informed. This is a direct implication from the structural changes explained above. In poor countries, for a given level of per capita subsidy to farmers, the per capita cost on consumers is large when there are many farmers and relatively fewer consumers; and the impact is further enhanced because of the large share of their budget spent on staple foods. That implies that consumers are likely relatively well aware of these costs since the benefits of learning about these impacts are higher than their information costs. With development, the per capita impact on consumers falls (as the relative numbers of farmers versus consumers declines) and their food expenditure share declines. This shift will change the costs and benefits of being informed. It makes it more likely that the costs of being informed about the policy becomes higher than the potential benefits for consumers. For farmers, the opposite happens: the more concentrated the benefits (as they become a smaller group with economic development), the more incentives they have of being well informed about the policy.

The second factor is how economic development is associated with changes in the cost of information. Typically with economic development, the cost of information declines, but also the relative cost of information in rural versus urban regions changes. A typical example is enhanced rural communication infrastructure, which occurs either through public investments (as in many high-income countries earlier in the twentieth century) or through technological innovations and commercial distributions (as in the recent dramatic increase in mobile-phone use in developing countries. This factor will typically reduce the relative costs of information in rural areas stronger compared to urban areas. As a consequence (a) farmers will be both better informed about policies and will thus more likely try to pressure politicians in shifting policies in their favor, and (b) they can better use this enhanced information infrastructure to organize themselves better, thus improving the effectiveness of their lobbying activities.

In summary, several information-related aspects of economic development (change in the relative benefits of information and changes in the relative costs of information) cause a shift in the political economy equilibrium from supporting consumers to supporting farmers in agricultural and food policies. We will come back to this issue in Chap. 6 to explain how recent changes in information markets and technology may have weakened the development paradox in recent years.

4.1.2 Political Organization

Not just information infrastructure but also other improvements in rural infrastructure with economic development also enhance agricultural interests' ability to organize for political action. In order to influence political choices effectively, farmers or consumers or other group members must act in unison. For their collective action to yield meaningful results, organizational structures must be established that can mobilize resources and direct individual action. As I explained in Chap. 3, Olson (1965) emphasized that collective action by relatively large groups is problematic because of free-riding incentives. In relatively small groups, collective action may be induced by intragroup direct interactions or by peer pressure.

This collective-action theory predicts that in poor countries, food consumers will wield more political power than farmers. Consumers are often concentrated in cities, where political action–coordination and enforcement costs are more favorable than in the rural areas where farmers reside. However, as the economy develops—and especially, as the share of agriculture in employment declines (see Table 4.2 and Fig. 4.3) and rural infrastructure improves—the cost of political organization for farmers decreases. This cost reduction is likely to increase the effectiveness of farmers' representation of their interests and, as a consequence, of their lobbying activities.

Researchers have debated whether changes in relative collective-action costs can explain major changes in agricultural policies (Rausser and Foster 1990; de Gorter and Swinnen 1996). Although rural infrastructure and information have improved significantly as countries have developed, even in developed countries, there remain a very large number of farmers. The persistence of such large numbers of farmers (whose interests are not necessarily aligned) implies that collective-action obstacles persist. Nonetheless, the growth and concentration of agribusinesses and food-processing companies, which are often aligned with farm interests in lobbying for agricultural policies, serve to strengthen pro-farm interests (Anderson 1995; Rausser et al. 2011). Since farm lobbies and agribusiness interests can coalesce and are increasingly well capitalized and concentrated, they have been an important force in orchestrating public policies that benefit their interests. In many countries the growth of agricultural protection has been associated with the growth of cooperative agribusiness and food-processing (and even transport and storage) companies.[4]

4.1.3   *Political Reforms*

There is a correlation between political regimes and economic development, with democratic regimes more prominent among richer countries than among poorer. From the arguments and review of the literature in Chap. 3, it is clear that the impact of differences in political regimes on agricultural policies is not obvious.

Theoretical models based on the median-voter theorem predict that democracies tend to redistribute from the rich to the poor. This is expected in democracies because the distribution of political power (measured by votes) is typically more equal than the distribution of income and wealth (Alesina and Rodrik 1994; McGuire and Olson 1996; Persson and Tabellini 1994). As farmers are typically among the poorer parts of the population, this suggests that farmers may benefit from democratization. Moreover, the very factors that make it difficult for farmers to organize politically in poor countries (such as their large number and geographic dispersion) render them potentially very powerful in electoral settings (Bates and Block 2010; Varshney 1995).

Yet it has been difficult to measure this empirically. Many early empirical studies relying on cross-sectional variation in the data are subject to problems of reverse causality (policies may also influence governance structures) and omitted-variables bias. Studies using long-run historical data allow more careful measurement of the impact of shifts from one set of political institutions to another. Swinnen et al. (2001) use detailed long-run data for Belgium and find that changes in electoral rules that have disproportionately benefited agriculture (e.g. extending voting rights to small farmers and tenants) have induced an increase in agricultural protectionism. In contrast, other electoral changes have not affected agricultural

---

[4] Econometric studies by Gawande and Hoekman (2006) and López (2008) also show the influence of agribusiness and food companies' political contributions on US policies.

protection because they increased the voting rights of both those in favor and those against protection. Olper et al. (2011) analyze the impact of democratic reforms since the 1960s covering most political reforms in developing and emerging countries. They do find that, on average, democratization tends to cause an increase in NRAs (that is, democratization tends to reduce agricultural taxation and/or increase agricultural subsidization).

However, there are also other observations which suggest that democratic reforms may only be a second-order effect compared to economic structural change. It is interesting to notice that the autocratic left-wing Communist regimes of the twentieth century in Asia and Europe also changed their agricultural policies with economic development and in line with the development paradox. As their economies evolved, agricultural policies of left-wing Communist autocracies shifted from taxing to subsidizing agriculture, as was the case in Western democracies (Rozelle and Swinnen 2010).

Communist dictators of poor countries (or when countries were poor) such as the Soviet Union under Stalin (1930s and 1940s), China under Mao, and Albania under Hoxha (1960s–1980s) all heavily taxed agriculture. However, as economic development occurred and overall incomes increased, agricultural policies changed and agriculture became (strongly) subsidized at higher incomes.

Table 4.2 illustrates the "development paradox" in the switch from agricultural taxation to agricultural subsidization in the Soviet Union and China, the dominant Communist countries. It presents data on the relationship between income and the shift from agricultural taxation to subsidization comparing the shift in the Soviet Union over the 1930–1980 period and the policy developments in China from 1970 to now. The switch from taxation to subsidizing agriculture came first in the Soviet Union, which had much higher incomes. While Stalin had been heavily taxing agriculture before World War II, agricultural subsidies increased strongly under the Brezhnev regime in the 1960s. Also in most East European Communist countries in the 1970s and 1980s, agriculture was strongly subsidized (Anderson and Swinnen 2008; Liefert and Swinnen 2002).[5]

---

[5] The main exception was Albania which was by far the poorest Communist country in Europe with roughly half its population still employed in agriculture in the 1980s. Remarkably this was the only country in Eastern Europe which was still taxing agriculture at the outset

A similar switch in agricultural policies occurred in China, but much later, when its income grew strongly (Huang et al. 2009). Whereas China's farmers were taxed heavily before 1980 under Mao's regime, in recent years they have begun to receive greater assistance from the state. China has clearly shifted from a country heavily taxing its farmers in the 1950s through the 1970s to gradually supporting agriculture as the nation's economy grew (see also Chap. 7). Interestingly, the income data in Table 4.2 suggest that the change in the Soviet Union occurred when GDP per capita was around $3500 (in real $1990), which, intriguingly, was roughly the income level of China when the switch occurred—around 2005.

If nothing else, these data suggest that the "development paradox" is a powerful force where economic structural changes may be stronger than ideology or political regimes in determining agricultural and food policies.

That said, more recently one has observed important changes in the relationship between economic growth and agricultural protection. More specifically, further economic growth in rich countries has not induced higher agricultural protection. These changes raise the question whether there are limits to the "development paradox". This is the main focus of the next chapter.

4.2   Development and Policy Combinations

Before focusing on recent changes in agricultural subsidies and taxes it is useful to consider that the tax and subsidy policies (which we discussed in Sect. 4.1) are only one part of a broader set of policies that governments have introduced in the course of economic development. The pressure on governments to intervene to support farmers and consumers at various times during economic history and development not only lead to changes in tax and subsidy regimes but also to the introduction of or changes in other policies (Barrett 1999; de Gorter and Zilberman 1990; Gardner 2002; Swinnen 2009).

In most countries during economic development, governments have at times attempted to stabilize markets and reduce price fluctuations or prevent shocks (see Chap. 8). They have introduced regulations and public standards to protect producers against fraud and consumers against products that may harm their health (see Chap. 10). The first major set of

---

of the liberalization process in the 1990s—having many features of China's agricultural economic structure (Cungu and Swinnen 1999; Macours and Swinnen 2002).

80   J. SWINNEN

public food standards were introduced between 1860 and 1910 in industrializing countries (Meloni and Swinnen 2015).

Governments have often supported the creation of farmer cooperatives to collectively purchase inputs (thus making quality inputs and better technology more easily and cheaply available), to sell products (thus enhancing bargaining power in commodity markets), and to stimulate rural credit through cooperative banks.

Governments have sometimes also introduced reforms to change land-ownership or land markets or policies to stimulate rural credit markets. In countries where poor tenants were suffering from low prices and tenure insecurity in the early twentieth century, land (tenure) reforms gave more security to tenants or made it easier for them to acquire land, often helped by public regulations to lower loan costs for small farmers buying land (Binswanger et al. 1995; Swinnen 2002) (see Chap. 12).

Other government policies include public investments in rural education to stimulate human capital development and in public research and development (R&D) programs to stimulate agricultural productivity growth (Alston and Pardey 1996; Pardey et al. 2016) (see Chap. 11). Public agricultural R&D and extension expenditures increased significantly over the course of the twentieth century in rich countries and in more recent years in emerging countries. Figures 4.4 and 4.5 illustrate for Belgium, a "rich" country, and China, a "poor/emerging" country (countries for which both data series were available over the period of economic growth), how public R&D investments and subsidies to agriculture (measured by the PSE or NRA indicators) have increased simultaneously with economic development. In Belgium (Fig. 4.4) this occurred over the course of the twentieth century and especially during the 1950–1980 period. In China (Fig. 4.5), the strong growth of agricultural R&D and subsidies occurred since 2000.

In countries with extensive public R&D investments, this has resulted in major productivity increases in agriculture (Alston 2018; Alston et al. 2009; Gardner 2002). This productivity growth benefited the economy as a whole. Whether consumers (through lower prices) or producers (through higher productivity) benefited most depended on the elasticity of supply and demand and the specific productivity effect of the R&D (see Chap. 11 for more analysis). As consumer incomes grew with economic development and demand became less elastic, benefits shifted increasingly to consumers. In this way, the pressure on farm incomes and the demand for agricultural subsidies to support farm incomes was partially caused by the effects of the government's R&D expenditures (de Gorter et al. 1992).

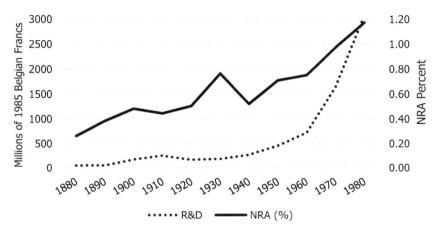

Fig. 4.4 Agricultural subsidies (NRA %) and public agricultural R&D expenditures in Belgium, 1880–1980. (Source: Data from Swinnen 1992, 2009, 2017)

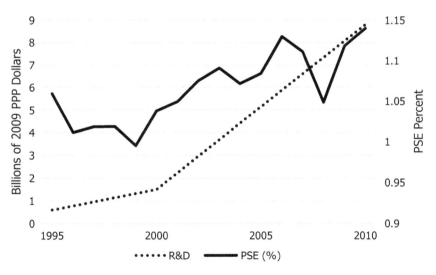

Fig. 4.5 Agricultural subsidies (PSE %) and public agricultural R&D expenditures in China, 1960–2010. (Source: Data from OECD 2017; Pardey, P.G., et al. 2016)

This is an example of an interaction effect between different public policies. These policies are often not independent from one another. Most policy interventions have both equity and efficiency effects, that is, they affect growth but also redistribute income among groups in society, thereby affecting political incentives. One can distinguish two forms of (potential) interactions between the policies: "*economic* interaction effects" and "*political* interaction effects" (Swinnen and de Gorter 2002). Economic interaction effects (EIEs) arise where one policy affects the economic effects of other policies. An example of such EIEs is when public R&D increased productivity and thereby the distortions caused by subsidy policies such as market interventions (Alston et al. 1993; Murphy et al. 1993)—see Chap. 13 for more on this.

Political interaction effects (PIEs) occur when the existence or introduction of one policy affects the political incentives of governments to introduce or change other policies. The example discussed above where the government's R&D expenditures caused productivity growth and price declines thereby put pressure on farm incomes, which in turn increased farmer's political demands for subsidies or price interventions (de Gorter et al. 1992; Swinnen and de Gorter 1998). These interaction effects are analyzed in more detail in Chap. 13.

References

Alesina, A., and D. Rodrik. 1994. Distributive Politics and Economic Growth. *Quarterly Journal of Economics* 109 (2): 465–490.

Alston, J.M. 2018. Reflections on Agricultural R&D, Productivity, and the Data Constraint: Unfinished Business, Unsettled Issues. *American Journal of Agricultural Economics* 100 (2): 392–413.

Alston, J.M., and P.G. Pardey. 1996. *Making Science Pay: The Economics of Agricultural R and D policy*. Washigton, DC: AEI Press.

Alston, J.M., M.A. Andersen, J.S. James, and P.G. Pardey. 2009. *Persistence Pays: US Agricultural Productivity Growth and the Benefits From Public R&D Spending*. Vol. 34. New York: Springer Science & Business Media.

Alston, Julian M., Colin A. Carter, and Vincent H. Smith. 1993. Rationalizing Agricultural Export Subsidies. *American Journal of Agricultural Economics* 75 (4): 1000.

Anderson, K. 1995. Lobbying Incentives and the Pattern of Protection in Rich and Poor Countries. *Economic Development and Cultural Change* 43 (2): 401–423.

———. 2009. *Distortions to Agricultural Incentives: A Global Perspective*, 1955–2007. London/Washington, DC: Palgrave Macmillan/World Bank.

———. 2016. *Agriculture Trade, Policy Reforms, and Global Food Security.* Palgrave Studies in Agriculture Economics and Food Policy book series (AEFP). New York: Palgrave Macmillan.

Anderson, K., and J. Swinnen. 2008. *Distortions to Agriculture Incentives in Europe's Transition Economies.* Washington, DC: World Bank Publications.

Anderson, Kym, and Signe Nelgen. 2012. Trade Barrier Volatility and Agricultural Price Stabilization. *World Development* 40 (1): 36–48.

Anderson, K., Y. Hayami, and M. Honma. 1986. The Political Economy of Agricultural Protection: East Asia in International Perspective. In *The Growth of Agricultural Protection*, ed. K. Anderson and Y. Hayami, 17–30. Allen/Unwin: Sydney.

Anderson, K., G.C. Rausser, and J. Swinnen. 2013. Political Economy of Public Policies: Insights from Distortions to Agricultural and Food Markets. *Journal of Economic Literature* 51 (2): 423–477.

Barrett, C.B. 1999. Stochastic Food Prices and Slash-and-Burn Agriculture. *Environment and Development Economics* 4 (2): 161–176.

Bates, R.H., and S. Block. 2010. Agricultural Trade Interventions in Africa. Chap. 12. In *The Political Economy of Agricultural Price Distortions*, ed. K. Anderson. Cambridge/New York: Cambridge University Press.

Binswanger, H.P., K. Deininger, and G. Feder. 1995. Power, Distortions, Revolt and Reform in Agricultural Land Relations. *Handbook of Development Economics* 3: 2659–2772.

Cungu, A., and J. Swinnen. 1999. Albania's Radical Agrarian Reform. *Economic Development and Cultural Change* 47 (3): 605–619.

de Gorter, H., and J. Swinnen. 1996. The Politics of Underinvestment in Agricultural Research. *American Journal of Agricultural Economics* 78 (5), ISSN 0002-9092.

de Gorter, H., and J. Swinnen. 2002. Political Economy of Agricultural Policies. In *The Handbook of Agricultural Economics, Volume 2*, ed. B. Gardner and G.C. Rausser, 2073–2123. North Holland/Amsterdam: Elsevier Science.

de Gorter, H., and D. Zilberman. 1990. On the Political Economy of Public Good Inputs in Agriculture. *American Journal of Agricultural Economics* 72: 131–137.

de Gorter, H., D.J. Nielson, and G.C. Rausser. 1992. Productive and Predatory Public Policies: Research Expenditures and Producer Subsidies in Agriculture. *American Journal of Agricultural Economics* 74 (1): 27–37.

Downs, A. 1957. An Economic Theory of Democracy.

Gardner, B.L. 1987. *The Economics of Agricultural Policies.* New York: Macmillan Publishing Company.

———. 2002. *American Agriculture in the Twentieth Century.* Cambridge, MA: Harvard University Press.

Gawande, K., and B. Hoekman. 2006. Lobbying and Agricultural Trade Policy in the United States. *International Organization* 60: 527–561.

———. 2010. Why Governments Tax or Subsidize Agricultural Trade. Chap. 10. In *The Political Economy of Agricultural Price Distortions*, ed. K. Anderson. Cambridge/New York: Cambridge University Press.

Huang, J., S. Rozelle, W. Martin, and Y. Liu. 2009. Distortions to Agricultural Incentives in China. Chap. 3. In *Distortions to Agricultural Incentives in Asia*, ed. K. Anderson and W. Martin, 117–161. Washington, DC: World Bank.

Johan F.M. Swinnen, Anurag N. Banerjee, Harry Gorter, (2001) Economic development, institutional change, and the political economy of agricultural protection An econometric study of Belgium since the 19th century. Agricultural Economics 26 (1):25–43

Swinnen, J.F.M., and H. de Gorter. 1998. Endogenous Commodity Policies and the Social Benefits from Public Research Expenditures. *American Journal of Agricultural Economics* 80 (1): 107–115.

Krueger, A.O. 1992. *A Synthesis of the Political Economy in Developing Countries*, Vol. 5 of The Political Economy of Agricultural Pricing Policy. Baltimore: Johns Hopkins University Press.

Liefert, W., and J. Swinnen. 2002. Changes in Agricultural Markets in Transition Economies. *USDA-ERS Agricultural Economic Report*, Vol. USDA-ERS 806, mimeo.

López, R.A. 2008. Does 'Protection for Sale' Apply to the US Food Industries? *Journal of Agricultural Economics* 9 (1): 25–40.

López, R.A., and X. Matschke. 2006. Food Protection for Sale. *Review of International Economics* 14 (3): 380–391.

Macours, K., and J. Swinnen. 2002. Patterns of Agrarian Transition. *Economic Development and Cultural Change* 50 (2): 365–395.

Maddison, A. 2003. *The World Economy: Historical Statistics*. Paris: OECD Development Centre.

Masters, W.A., and A.F. Garcia. 2010. Agricultural Price Distortions and Stabilization. Chap. 9. In *The Political Economy of Agricultural Price Distortions*, ed. K. Anderson. Cambridge/New York: Cambridge University Press.

McCluskey, J.J., and J.F.M. Swinnen. 2004. Political Economy of the Media and Consumer Perceptions of Biotechnology. *American Journal of Agricultural Economics* 86: 1230–1237.

McGuire, M.C., and M. Olson Jr. 1996. The Economics of Autocracy and Majority Rule: The Invisible Hand and the Use of Force. *Journal of Economic Literature* 34 (1): 72–96.

Meloni, G., and J. Swinnen. 2015. Chocolate Regulations. In *The Economics of Chocolate*, 268–303. Oxford: Oxford University Press.

Murphy, J.A., W.H. Furtan, and A. Schmitz. 1993. The Gains from Agricultural Research Under Distorted Trade. *Journal of Public Economics* 51: 161–172.

OECD. 2017. *Agricultural Policy Monitoring and Evaluation 2017*. Paris: OECD Publishing.

THE DEVELOPMENT PARADOX 85

Olper, A., and V. Raimondi. 2010. Constitutional Rules and Agricultural Policy Outcomes. Chap. 14. In *The Political Economy of Agricultural Price Distortions*, ed. K. Anderson. Cambridge/New York: Cambridge University Press.

Olper, A., and J. Swinnen. 2013. Mass Media and Public Policy: Global Evidence from Agricultural Policies. *The World Bank Economic Review* 27 (3): 413–436.

Olper, A., J. Falkowski, and J. Swinnen. 2011. *Political Reforms and Rent Distribution: Evidence from Agricultural Policies*, LICOS Discussion Paper. Leuven: Katholieke Universiteit Leuven.

Olson, M., Jr. 1965. *The Logic of Collective Action: Public Goods and the Theory of Groups*. Cambridge, MA: Harvard University Press.

Pardey, P.G., C. Chan-Kang, S.P. Dehmer, and J.M. Beddow. 2016. Agricultural R&D Is on the Move. *Nature* 537: 301–303.

Persson, T., and G. Tabellini. 1994. Is Inequality Harmful for Growth? *American Economic Review* 84 (3): 600–621.

Rausser, G.C., and H. de Gorter. 1989. Endogenizing Policy in Models of Agricultural Markets. In *Agriculture and Governments in an Interdependent World*, ed. A. Maunder and A. Valdés, 259–274. Oxford: Oxford University Press.

Rausser, G.C., and W.E. Foster. 1990. Political Preference Functions and Public Policy Reforms. *American Journal of Agricultural Economics* 72 (3): 641–652.

Rausser, G., J. Swinnen, and P. Zusman. 2011. *Political Power and Economic Policy: Theory, Analysis, and Empirical Applications*. Cambridge: Cambridge University Press.

Rozelle, S., and J.F. Swinnen. 2009. Why Did the Communist Party Reform in China, But Not in the Soviet Union? The Political Economy of Agricultural Transition. *China Economic Review* 20 (2): 275–287.

Rozelle, S., and J.F.M. Swinnen. 2010. Agricultural Distortions in the Transition Economies of Asia and Europe. Chap. 8. In *The Political Economy of Agricultural Price Distortions*, ed. K. Anderson. Cambridge/New York: Cambridge University Press.

Swinnen. 1992. Essays on the Political Economy of Agricultural Policies. PhD diss., Cornell University.

Swinnen, J. 1994. A Positive Theory of Agricultural Protection. *American Journal of Agricultural Economics* 76: 1–14.

———. 2002. Transition and Integration in Europe: Implications for Agricultural and Food Markets, Policy and Trade Agreements. *The World Economy* 25: 481–501.

Swinnen, J.F. 2009. The Growth of Agricultural Protection in Europe in the 19th and 20th Centuries. *The World Economy* 32 (11): 1499–1537.

Swinnen, J. 2017. *A Historical Database on European Agriculture, Food and Policies*, LICOS Discussion Papers No. 399.

Swinnen, J., and H. de Gorter. 2002. On Government Credibility, Compensation and Under-Investment in Public Research. *European Review of Agricultural Economics* 29 (4): 501–522.

Swinnen, Johan F.M., Anurag N. Banerjee, and Harry Gorter. 2001. Economic Development, Institutional Change, and the Political Economy of Agricultural Protection An Econometric Study of Belgium Since the 19th Century. *Agricultural Economics* 26 (1): 25–43.

Varshney, A. 1995. *Democracy, Development, and the Countryside: Urban-Rural Struggles in India*. Cambridge/New York: Cambridge University Press.

CHAPTER 5

Anti-Trade Bias and the Political Economy of Instrument Choice

5.1 Anti-Trade Bias

The development paradox is not the only stylized fact of agricultural and food policies. Another is the *anti-trade bias*. The anti-trade bias refers typically to the observation that import-competing sectors are protected by taxing imports and that exportable commodities have received much less support and, in particular, in poor countries, have been taxed severely. Both types of interventions hurt trade. Empirical analyses show that around 60% of all the variation in NRAs across countries and over time is explained by only two variables: per capita income (which captures *the development paradox*) and comparative advantage (which partially captures *the anti-trade bias*) (Anderson et al. 2013).

To document the anti-trade bias, one can separate the average NRA for all agricultural commodities presented in Fig. 4.1 into the average NRA for imported and exported commodities. Figure 5.1 illustrates the dramatic differences in agricultural policies for import-competing versus exportable commodities both in rich and in poor countries. In poor countries exportable commodities were heavily taxed with the NRA varying between −25% and −35%; while import-competing sectors were protected, with NRAs between 5% and 20%. In rich countries both groups of commodities have positive NRAs (reflecting protection), but the NRAs were much higher for import-competing (between 43% and 53%) than for exportable (between 10% and 17%) commodities. Hence in both rich and poor countries, the

© The Author(s) 2018

J. Swinnen, *The Political Economy of Agricultural and Food Policies*,
Palgrave Studies in Agricultural Economics and Food Policy,
https://doi.org/10.1057/978-1-137-50102-8_5

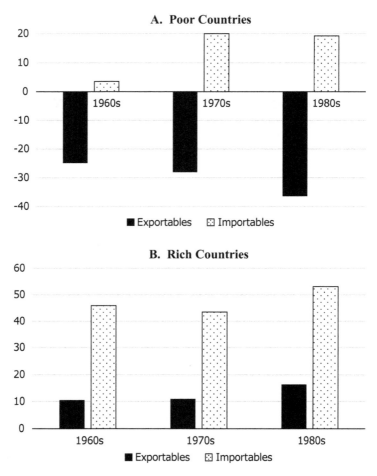

Fig. 5.1 NRAs to exportable and import-competing agricultural products, 1960s–1980s (%). (Source: Anderson 2009, 2016; Anderson and Nelgen 2012)

difference in NRA between the two groups of commodities was between 35 and 55 percentage points.

Throughout history, trade-policy instruments such as export and import taxes and subsidies or quantitative restrictions,[1] along with multiple exchange

---

[1] Since the inception of the WTO in 1995, most non-tariff barriers (NTBs) such as import quotas have been converted to tariffs. In many countries, however, those tariffs have been

rates, are the most important agricultural and food policies used globally to redistribute income between consumers and producers (Anderson et al. 2013). This was very clearly the case in earlier history when they were often the main (or even only) policies.[2] However, even today these trade-policy instruments account for more than 50% of agricultural NRAs globally (Anderson 2009, 2016). More recently, in particular, in the years 2007–2012, the anti-trade bias has taken on a particular version as many governments responded to rising food prices on world markets by restricting, sometimes outright banning, food exports, thereby exacerbating the global price spikes (Anderson et al. 2014; Pinstrup-Anderson 2015; Sedik and Sun 2012).

The anti-trade bias is related to the choice of instruments in agricultural policy. Trade policies are often part of a package of redistributive policy instruments. For example, when governments want to guarantee farmers high prices by intervening in the markets, they need to complement this with trade barriers to keep foreign producers and traders from benefiting from the market interventions. The same holds with price interventions to protect domestic consumers. Without export constraints domestic traders would export their products to world markets. This makes the analysis of the "anti-trade bias" part of a broader analysis of the political economy of policy instrument choice.

5.2   Political Economy of Instrument Choice

Many political economy studies of agricultural policy, as, for example, discussed in the previous chapter, have focused on explaining the *level* of policy intervention. However, at least as important is the explanation of the *instruments* used for intervention. From an economic welfare perspective, the key question should be why governments have introduced so many

---

legally bound at well above applied rates, so that such countries have been able to continue to vary border measures as international prices or domestic supplies have fluctuated from year to year.

[2] The analysis in Chap. 7 on Europe's long-run agricultural policies also documents that in the late nineteenth and early twentieth centuries, mainly import tariffs were used to protect farmers. In the 1930s quantitative measures such as milling rations and import quota were imposed in many European countries. These were combined with minimum prices, export subsidies, and marketing boards in some countries—typically referred to as "market organizations". Many of these instruments became part of the EU's Common Agricultural Policy in the 1960s. These policies caused major market and trade distortions in the 1970s and 1980s.

market distortions through agricultural policies.[3] The distortionary effects of government interventions are equally dependent on the choice of the instrument as on the level of the intervention. Therefore the choice of instrument is of equal concern as the intervention level.

Political economy explanations of the anti-trade bias, and instrument choice more generally, focus on several factors, some of which we identified in Chap. 3. The first is the relative income effect. Import-competing sectors have lower comparative advantage than exporting sectors. That means that the without-distributive-policy-incomes in import-competing sectors are lower than in exporting sectors. Hence the political economy mechanisms that lead policies that distribute from sectors with a comparative advantage (exports) to sectors with a comparative disadvantage (imports) are the same as the one we discussed earlier that lead to increased protection of agriculture as a whole with a growing rural-urban income gap (see Chaps. 3 and 4). Since benefits from market returns are lower in sectors with a comparative disadvantage, those sectors' incentives to seek income from government support are also relatively higher. In these (sub-) sectors, returns to investment in lobbying activities dominate returns from market activities and so indirectly support an anti-trade bias.

A second factor is the so-called "revenue motive" of public policy. Differential effects on government revenues also help explain why protection of sectors decreases as their trade surplus increases and why taxation is higher for industries that are net exporters. Obviously, tariff revenues and export taxes increase government revenues, while export and import subsidies require outlays. It is always less contentious for governments to tax than to subsidize trade: taxing raises government revenue and, in the case of larger economies, improves their terms of trade, whereas trade subsidies do the opposite.

Third, different instruments and comparative (dis)advantages imply different deadweight costs in redistribution. Demand and supply elasticities affect the distortions and costs of policies (Gardner 1983, 1987; de Gorter et al. 1992). The distortions (deadweight costs) and budgetary costs of policy intervention typically increase with higher supply elasticities. Because of the inherent changes in the distribution of costs and benefits of policies and the associated political incentives, sectors with higher supply elasticities (typically exports) will be subsidized less because it is more costly to do so and causes more distributions (Becker 1983; Gardner 1983).

---

[3] There is an extensive literature comparing the transfer efficiency and the distortions of various policy instruments in trade and agricultural policies (see, e.g. Alston and James 2002; Bullock et al. 1999; Gardner 1983).

Fourth, policy instruments differ not only in deadweight costs but also in implementation costs. The most obvious explanation for the broad use of trade taxes (either import tariffs or export taxes) is that they are easiest and least costly to implement (Dixit 1996; Rodrik 1995). In many developing countries, the system for administering and enforcing income taxes and/or subsidies may simply not exist (or be too costly to implement). Hence, in poor countries in which tax-collection institutions are weakly developed, trade taxes (either import tariffs or export taxes) are often an important—or the only substantive—source of tax revenue. If the tax infrastructure is less developed, governments have greater incentives to use tariffs instead of direct income support to assist farmers.

Fifth, policy instruments also differ in their "transparency", the information available concerning policies, and their incidence. Politicians have an incentive to select less-efficient policy instruments if the costs of more-efficient ones are more transparent (Tullock 1983; Olson 1982). Thus, governments use policies that mask the costs of the policies or use policies that obfuscate the transfer itself (Magee et al. 1989). This obfuscation perspective helps explain the persistence of trade policies and why non-budget methods of redistribution, such as tariffs, are politically preferable to production subsidies and direct income payments.

Sixth, governments may prefer distortionary policies, such as tariffs, when they have imperfect information on their target group. Foster and Rausser (1993) show that governments may prefer price supports or tariffs over lump-sum transfers because the more-distorting instruments allow discrimination among heterogeneous producers. The total transfers—even in the face of deadweight costs—may be lower than would be the case with lump-sum transfers when governments need to secure a minimum amount of political support. Mitchell and Moro (2006) advance a related argument: they maintain that compensation through distortive policies, such as tariffs, may be more attractive if the amount of transfer needed is unknown ex ante, resulting in inefficient targeting.[4]

In summary, these different political economy factors contribute to explain the choice of policy instruments. In terms of the anti-trade policy bias, we can conclude that this bias results from a combination of several political economy factors: (a) the relative income effect induces policy-makers

---

[4] These arguments are related to theories of inefficient redistribution based on contractual problems, such as those proposed by Acemoglu and Robinson (2001) and Acemoglu (2003). In these analyses, "inefficient" policies are chosen because they serve the interests of politicians or interest groups that hold political power and are reluctant to make commitments that bind their future actions.

to redistribute income from exporting sectors (with a comparative advantage) to importing sectors (with a comparative disadvantage); (b) the revenue motive and low implementation cost stimulate governments to use import tariffs and export taxes over other instruments, especially in countries where tax infrastructure is weakly developed; (c) subsidizing exports causes more distortions and is more costly than subsidizing imports because of higher supply elasticities and international spillovers; and (d) information costs, both for those affected by the policies (interest groups) and those introducing the policies (governments), stimulate the use of import tariffs and export taxes as they are less transparent than, for example, direct income payments and also allow selection among their political target group.

5.3 Instrument Choice, Trade, and International Institutions

The combination of these factors presents a powerful set of political economy forces leading to inefficient policy instruments and causing distortions in domestic and international markets. Most of the factors we have discussed are domestic in nature. However, through international trade (and in some cases international finance), domestic political equilibria can be influenced by foreign 'interests'—which can be affected by domestic policies.

The most obvious form of such foreign influence is when domestic policies affect trade and thereby affect trading partners. If these trading partners are dissatisfied with the policy choices they may try to influence the policy setting through negotiations or through retaliation. There are many examples of "trade wars" in history.

Negotiations may lead to trade agreements where governments voluntarily commit to constrain their policy choices (e.g. by agreeing to limits on import tariffs) in exchange for similar commitments from their trading partners. There are numerous examples of trading agreements, which can be bilateral (between two countries) or multilateral (between many countries).

The most encompassing institution regulating trade in the world is the World Trade Organization (WTO). The WTO does not restrict governments to support farmers or consumers but imposes restrictions on the instruments that can be used for this, in particular, on policy instruments that affect trade.

The trade-distorting effects of specific agricultural and food policy instruments are central to the WTO agreements (and negotiations regarding future agreements) (Tangermann 1999). The WTO explicitly classifies agricultural support from different policy instruments in "green", "blue", and "amber" boxes according to their distortionary impact. The green box includes subsidies that do 'not distort trade, or at most cause minimal distortions'. WTO agreements limit the use of distorting measures while non-distorting measures are not regulated (Josling and Tangermann 1999). This distinction between the *level* of support and policy *instrument* (related to the extent of market and trade distortions) is essential in the WTO and has contributed to some important agricultural policy reforms, such as those of the EU's Common Agricultural Policy (CAP) over the past two decades (see also Chaps. 6 and 7).

Not only trade agreements but also other forms of international institutions can influence domestic policy-making. One form that has been particularly influential in some developing countries in the 1990s and beyond is the impact of international financial institutions such as the IMF and the World Bank which have imposed policy conditionalities on developing countries as part of loan agreements. As will be explained in Chap. 6, these agreements required important policy reforms which have contributed to, among others, the reduction of agricultural export taxes and liberalization of exchange rates in, for example, African countries, thereby reducing taxation of African farmers and their anti-trade bias.

References

Acemoglu, D. 2003. Why Not a Political Coase Theorem? Social Conflict, Commitment, and Politics. *Journal of Comparative Economics* 31: 620–652.

Acemoglu, D., and J.A. Robinson. 2001. A Theory of Political Transitions. *American Economic Review* 91 (4): 938–963.

Alston, J.M., and J.S. James. 2002. The Incidence of Agricultural Policy. *Handbook of Agricultural Economics* 2: 1689–1749.

Anderson, K. 2009. *Distortions to Agricultural Incentives: A Global Perspective, 1955–2007*. London/Washington, DC: Palgrave Macmillan/World Bank.

———. 2016. *Agricultural Trade, Policy Reforms, and Global Food Security*. New York: Springer.

Anderson, K., G.C. Rausser, and J. Swinnen. 2013. Political Economy of Public Policies: Insights from Distortions to Agricultural and Food Markets. *Journal of Economic Literature* 51 (2): 423–477.

Anderson, Kym, and Signe Nelgen. 2012. Trade Barrier Volatility and Agricultural Price Stabilization. *World Development* 40 (1): 36–48.

Anderson, K., M. Ivanic, and W.J. Martin. 2014. Food Price Spikes, Price Insulation, and Poverty. In *The Economics of Food Price Volatility*, ed. J.P. Chavas, D. Hummels, and B.D. Wright, 311–339. Chicago: University of Chicago Press.

Becker, G.S. 1983. A Theory of Competition Among Pressure Groups for Political Influence. *Quarterly Journal of Economics* 98: 371–400.

Bullock, D.S., K. Salhofer, and J. Kola. 1999. The Normative Analysis of Agricultural Policy: A General Framework and Review. *Journal of Agricultural Economics* 50 (3): 512–535.

de Gorter, H., D.J. Nielson, and G.C. Rausser. 1992. Productive and Predatory Public Policies. *American Journal of Agricultural Economics* 74: 27–37.

Dixit, A.K. 1996. *The Making of Economic Policy: A Transaction Cost Politics Perspective*. Cambridge, MA: MIT Press.

Foster, W.E., and G.C. Rausser. 1993. Price-Distorting Compensation Serving the Consumer and Taxpayer Interest. *Public Choice* 77: 275–291.

Gardner, B.L. 1983. Efficient Redistribution Through Commodity Markets. *American Journal of Agricultural Economics* 65: 225–234.

———. 1987. *The Economics of Agricultural Policies*. New York: Macmillan Publishing Company.

Josling, T., and S. Tangermann. 1999. Implementation of the WTO Agreement on Agriculture and Developments for the Next Round of Negotiations. *European Review of Agricultural Economics* 26 (3): 371–388.

Magee, S.P., W.A. Brock, and L. Young. 1989. *Black Hole Tariffs and Endogenous Policy Theory*. Cambridge: Cambridge University Press.

Mitchell, M., and A. Moro. 2006. Persistent Distortionary Policies with Asymmetric Information. *American Economic Review* 96 (1): 387–393.

Olson, M., Jr. 1982. *The Rise and Decline of Nations: Economic Growth, Stagflation, and Social Rigidities*. New Haven: Yale University Press.

Pinstrup-Anderson, P. (ed.). 2015, Forthcoming. *Food Price Policy in an Era of Market Instability: A Political Economy Analysis*. Oxford: Oxford University Press.

Rodrik, D. 1995. The Political Economy of Trade Policy. In *Handbook of International Economics*, ed. G. Grossman and K. Rogoff, vol. 3. Amsterdam: North-Holland.

Sedik, T.S., and T. Sun. 2012. *Effects of Capital Flow Liberalization: What Is the Evidence from Recent Experiences of Emerging Market Economies?* (No. 12–275). International Monetary Fund.

Tangermann, S. 1999. Europe's Agricultural Policies and the Millennium Round. *The World Economy* 22 (9): 1155–1178.

Tullock, G. 1983. *Economics of Income Redistribution*. Boston: Kluwer-Nijhoff.

CHAPTER 6

Development Paradox and Anti-Trade Bias Revisited?

6.1   Introduction

In the 30-year period between 1955 and 1984, the Nominal Rate of Assistance to agriculture (NRA) was an average around—20% in developing countries, while on average around 30% in high-income countries, a difference of 50 percentage points—as explained in Chap. 4 (and see Fig. 4.1). However, as Fig. 6.1 illustrates, since then, there have been dramatic changes in the NRAs, both in rich and in poor countries. There has been significant growth in NRAs of developing countries. Average NRAs have increased from around—20% in the 1980s to around 10% in the 2000s. These are large changes, reflecting significant changes in agricultural and food policies in developing countries. The changes are arguably at last as significant in high-income countries. In rich countries the average NRA peaked in the late 1980s at around 60%. Since then the average NRA has fallen to around 20%—also a dramatic reversal. This means that—rather that the *divergence* observed in the 1950s to 1980s—there is significant *convergence* in NRAs, as is clearly illustrated in Fig. 6.1. What is more, the two groups' average rates of assistance to agriculture have converged toward zero (Anderson et al. 2013).

An obvious explanation of the rise of NRA in developing countries could be the that it is the result of income growth in these countries, which has been strong in many countries over the past 25 years. The positive impact of economic growth on agricultural protection as explained in Chap. 4

© The Author(s) 2018   95
J. Swinnen, *The Political Economy of Agricultural and Food Policies*,
Palgrave Studies in Agricultural Economics and Food Policy,
https://doi.org/10.1057/978-1-137-50102-8_6

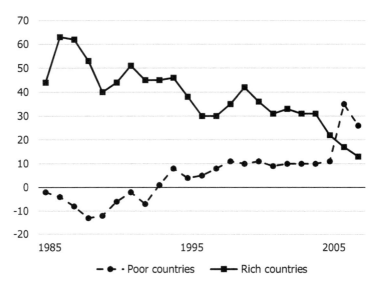

Fig. 6.1 Nominal rates of assistance to agriculture (NRAs), 1960s–2010s (%). (Source: Anderson 2009; Anderson and Nelgen 2012)

would indeed suggest the growth of NRAs. However, this obviously does not explain the reduction of agricultural protection in high-income countries since one would expect further increases in NRAs as also these countries' incomes have grown over the past three decades. One would therefore expect further increases in NRA, not a decline. Hence: is there a need to revisit the development paradox?

Another remarkable change is the significant reduction in the anti-trade bias, in particular, in developing countries, as is illustrated in Fig. 6.2. The tax on exportables has fallen from almost 40% in the 1980s to around zero in recent years. Hence: is there also a need to revisit the "anti-trade bias"?

6.2 Reform and Decline of Agricultural Taxation in Poor Countries 1980–2010

Many developing countries heavily taxed their agricultural sectors in the post-war decades up to the 1980s. However, since the 1980s there have been significant changes, including the phasing out of developing countries' multiple exchange rates as well as the phasing out of explicit taxation

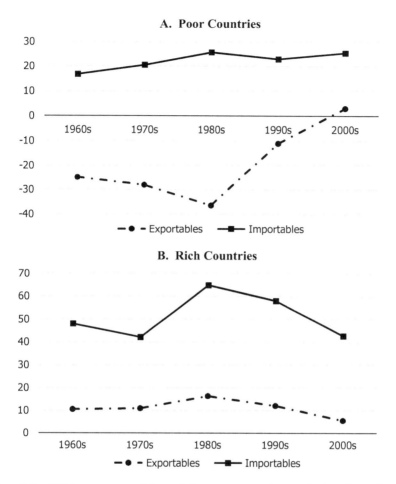

Fig. 6.2 NRAs to exportable and import-competing agricultural products, 1960s–2000s(%). (a) Poor Countries; (b) Rich Countries. (Source: Anderson 2009; Anderson and Nelgen 2012)

of agricultural exports (Anderson 2016). These changes can be explained by relating them to the adjustment of political economy equilibria because of changes in fundamental economic forces, including economic growth, structural adjustments, information costs, and changes in governance structures.

6.2.1 Economic Growth: The Development Paradox at Work

A key reason for the reduction in agricultural taxation in developing countries is economic growth (see Chap. 7 and Fig. 7.3 for the correlation between economic growth and the increase in NRAs for China) (Fig. 6.3).

As explained in Chap. 4, economic growth causes a shift in the political economy equilibrium of agricultural policies. Economic growth is associated with several important structural changes in the economy. With economic growth the share of agriculture in GDP and in employment declines. Figure 6.4 illustrates how in China and India agriculture's share in GDP has declined from around 40% in the 1970s to less than 10% (China) and less than 20% (India) today. This typically coincides with a rise in urban-rural income disparities, as growth in industry and services outpaces growth in the agricultural sectors. This income gap creates incentives for farmers and agricultural companies to demand—and politicians to supply—policies that redistribute income in order to reduce that income gap. The second is that consumers spend less of their income on food. This will reduce opposition to an increase in food prices through

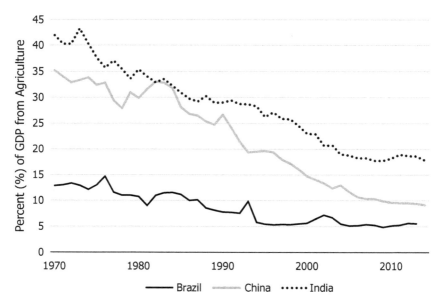

Fig. 6.3 Share of agriculture in GDP (%) in Brazil, China, and India (1970–2015). (Source: World Bank)

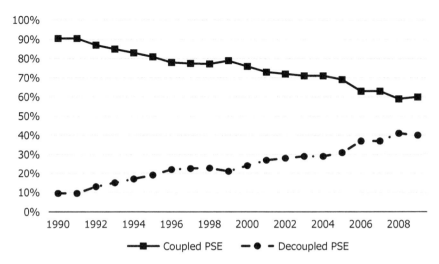

Fig. 6.4 Agricultural policy instruments in OECD countries (coupled and decoupled PSE as % of total), 1990–2009. (Source: Based on Swinnen et al. 2010 using data from OECD)

government interventions, such as import tariffs. Third, for a given per capita subsidy to farmers, it takes a lower per capita tax on consumers when there are fewer farmers. These structural changes with economic development reduce opposition to agricultural protection. At the same time the demand for agricultural protection increases with the growing rural-urban income gap. The combination causes a shift in the political economy equilibrium from taxing farmers to subsidizing farmers with economic growth. This political economy effect driven by economic structural changes is reinforced by improvements in infrastructure which lower information costs and collective-action costs (relatively more) for farmers, as we also explained in Chap. 3.

Two factors which were discussed earlier but seem to have played a more significant role in the reduction of taxation in developing countries (and/or for which there are now better data to measure their impact) are changes in information costs and political reforms.

100 J. SWINNEN

6.2.2 Political Reforms and Mass Media

Although China has formally remained a one-party political regime, many other developing and emerging economies have experienced democratization over the past three decades. Chapter 3 discussed theoretical empirical studies on how democratization will affect public policies. The impact on agricultural policies is not straightforward. The very factors that make it difficult for farmers to organize politically (such as their large geographic dispersion) render them potentially very powerful in electoral settings but that the impact also depends on the level of development and the preferences or ideology of autocratic governments.

Olper et al. (2014) exploit both the time-series and cross-sectional variation in NRA data to measure the impact of political reforms on agricultural policy changes in developing countries in the past 30 years. They find that, on average, democratization processes in developing countries have contributed to better policies for farmers (i.e. an increase in NRA) over the past decades.

Another major development has been the spread of mass media and improvements in rural communication infrastructure. Both reduce information costs which may cause changes in agricultural policies. Enhanced rural communication infrastructure can occur through public investments or through technological innovations and/or commercial distributions (as in the recent dramatic increase in mobile-phone use in developing countries)[1] and through the spread of mass media and social media (McCluskey and Swinnen 2010). In the past 30 years there has been rapid growth of commercial mass media in many (developing) countries. Several studies have shown that access to mass media can empower people politically, and a more informed and politically active electorate increases the incentives for a government to be responsive (Besley and Burgess 2001; Strömberg 2004).

The political economy literature (see Chap. 3) also argues that mass media can alter these political economy mechanisms between group size and political mobilization by providing more information to larger groups (Kuzyk and McCluskey 2006; Oberholzer-Gee and Waldfogel 2005). Strömberg (2001; 2004) refers to this outcome as "mass media competition-induced political bias". Olper and Swinnen (2013) argue that mass media will therefore increasingly weaken the political power of

---

[1] See Nakasone et al. (2014) for a review.

small groups (in rich countries, farmers; in poor countries, consumers) and reinforce that of large groups and groups attractive to advertisers (in rich countries, consumers and urban interests; in poor countries, farmers). The implication of this theory is that the spread of mass media will shift agricultural policies to the benefit of farmers for developing countries.

Using the NRA data, Olper and Swinnen find that the spread of mass media is indeed associated with a reduction in taxation of farmers and/or an increase in agricultural protection. Their empirical findings are thus consistent with the hypothesis that mass media benefits farmers in developing countries by empowering them politically.

6.2.3 Structural-Adjustment Programs and Policy Conditionality

Another key factor is the impact of international financial institutions (such as the World Bank and the International Monetary Fund) and the policy conditions they imposed on developing countries as part of their lending. The structural-adjustment programs in Africa and Latin America in the 1980s and the 1990s were very controversial. These programs often required the borrowing governments to liberalize their trade policies and reduce taxation of agriculture, with the justification that such changes would enable them to repay the loans on schedule. Some policy reforms were reversed after the loans were in place, but many appear to have stuck (Akiyama et al. 2001; Kherallah et al. 2002). Williamson and Haggard (1994) suggest that the most useful effect of these conditions came not in the form of hard conditionality ("leverage") but rather from shifting the domestic intellectual climate and public discourse in these countries toward favoring freer markets. In sub-Saharan Africa, the structural-adjustment programs have contributed to a significant reduction of taxes on farmers and thus an increase in the NRAs (Swinnen et al. 2010).

The anti-trade bias has declined in recent decades with declines in agricultural export taxation. Up to the 1980s it was quite common for developing country governments to intervene in the market for foreign exchange. Such interventions added to the anti-trade biases that were targeted at tradable sectors, including agriculture. However, these interventions largely disappeared by the mid-1990s, as initiatives took hold to reform overall macroeconomic policy and in developing countries (Anderson 2009). The political economy factors we identified here thus not only reduced taxation of farmers but also the anti-trade bias in developing countries.

6.2.4 Summary

Reduced taxation of agriculture in many developing countries that experienced income growth during recent decades is caused by a combination of political economy factors. The reduction of anti-agricultural and food policies in developing countries during the past decade has been caused by economic growth, by the shift in the political-economic equilibria induced by growth-induced structural change, and by changes in governance and media structures. As rural infrastructure improved and communications costs fell, farmers have become politically more effective. Moreover, as economies develop, the role of agribusiness and food companies expands and these more concentrated and better capitalized organizations often form powerful lobby coalitions with farmers' interest groups. The reduction of agricultural taxation has been reinforced by structural-adjustment programs imposed by international institutions and by changes in media structure and political institutions. In many cases, income growth has coincided with political reforms (democratization) and with the growth of commercial media. Democratic reforms have, on average, benefited farmers in developing countries, although in countries such as China there have been important policy reforms without political liberalization. The growth of commercial media may have contributed to less distortion, including the reduction of taxation of agriculture in developing countries.

6.3 REFORM OF AGRICULTURAL SUBSIDIES IN RICH COUNTRIES

Agricultural protection increased as rich countries' incomes have grown from the 1950s to the mid-1980s. Based on the development paradox arguments, one would expect further increases in NRAs as countries' incomes have grown. However, since then, there has been a change in the trend of agricultural protection for several of these high-income countries, as is illustrated in Fig. 6.1. Also here several factors have played a role in this recent reversal of the positive relationship between income and NRAs for higher-income countries.

The fall in agricultural protection was strong in Australia and New Zealand, where most support was abolished, and in both Western and Eastern Europe.

In Eastern Europe economic and political liberalizations removed much of the heavy subsidies to farms that existed under the Communist regimes in the 1970s and 1980s. The state-organized agricultural and food systems in the Soviet Union and Eastern Europe fixed prices, trade, and production levels and regulated farm organizations. This system fixed food (consumer) prices at low levels and farm (producer) prices at high levels, thereby distorting incentives along the food chain. The government-fixed prices that collective and state farms received for their agricultural production were well above the (world) market price levels. Although it was difficult to measure subsidy rates since also the exchange rates were fixed by the government, estimates of NRA-type indicators put the protection rates at between 50% and 100% (Liefert and Swinnen 2002). After the fall of the Berlin Wall in 1989, both the political and economic institutions collapsed in this part of the world. One result was that food prices increased and farm prices decreased to market price levels, and agricultural protection indicators fell to close to 0 (Anderson and Swinnen 2010). Since then agricultural protection has increased somewhat but is nowhere close to the Communist era levels.

Since 2004 many of the Eastern European countries have been integrated in the EU, and their agricultural and food policy has since been determined by the EU's Common Agricultural Policy (CAP). The CAP of the EU has itself been reformed significantly over the same period. Both the level of subsidies and the distortions caused by them have significantly reduced since 1990. The reasons, however, are very different than the political changes that caused dramatic changes in agricultural and food policies in Eastern Europe. In the EU, international trade negotiations played an important role in inducing policy reforms (see also Chap. 7).

6.3.1 *The WTO and Policy Reforms*

The change in the relationship between income and NRAs coincides with the integration of agricultural policies in the GATT/WTO as part of the Uruguay Round Agreement on Agriculture (URAA) in 1994. The relationship between the URAA and NRAs in high-income countries is complex: many of these countries were involved in the URAA negotiations, and from a political economy perspective, at least before an agreement is forged there is potential bi-causality between countries' NRA and the WTO negotiations.[2] However, once the agreement is reached, causal flow should largely go in one direction.

---

[2] For example, the inability of the EU's trading partners to constrain the EU's subsidization of exports induced these countries to insist on including agriculture in the GATT (Sumner and Tangerman 2002).

The impact of the URAA differs between countries that participated in the negotiations and those that joined later. That the URAA's effects were different for countries that joined afterwards or went through institutional changes that affected their WTO constraints is well illustrated by the transition countries. The WTO's impact on their agricultural policies differs considerably depending on whether or not they were part of the GATT before the end of 1994, the year in which the URAA was completed (Anderson and Swinnen 2010). Similarly, the WTO conditions imposed on China and Russia during their WTO accession processes have been much more stringent than was the case for some of the older WTO members (Drabek and Bacchetta 2004; Evenett and Primo Braga 2006). Hence, the impact of the WTO on agricultural distortions depends on countries' institutional stage of entry.

Studies suggest that the WTO/URAA has done less to reduce NRAs in the countries that were contracting parties to the GATT during the trade negotiations but has constrained the growth of agricultural protection afterward (Anania et al. 2004; Swinnen et al. 2012). For example, Orden et al. (2010) argue that the WTO's impact on agricultural policy in the USA has been limited and that agricultural lobbies have been quite successful in continuing to advance their domestic interests. However, in the EU there was a significant impact, partially because the EU itself changed in the following years because of the integration of East European countries.

Eastern expansion of the EU in 2004 and 2007 integrated mostly poorer countries. Some of these poorer countries (such as Poland and Romania) brought millions of new and predominantly poor farmers into the EU. This factor by itself reduced the pressure to increase NRAs (following the (inverse) economic growth effect explained earlier). In addition, several of these poorer countries were not initially part of the WTO/GATT, and their integration in the European Union caused WTO constraints for the EU as a whole in the 2000s. These constraints generated pressure to reduce total agricultural support and induced a change in policy instruments.

A reduction of trade-distorting policies in rich countries since the 1980s comes from a shift toward subsidies that are decoupled from production. This can be best illustrated by indicators on instrument choice from the OECD. Since 1986 the OECD calculates policy support given to agriculture. The total amount of support to agriculture is referred to as Producer

Support Estimate (*PSE*).[3] The OECD's calculation of agricultural policy support distinguishes between several instruments. The first group of instruments, "coupled PSE", includes all policy transfers (such as tariffs, price support, and subsidies) directly linked ("coupled") to agricultural production. These instruments are the most distortive markets and trade. The second group of instruments, "decoupled PSE", includes decoupled agricultural payments. These instruments distort markets and trade less (or not at all).

In the 1980s, by far the most important instruments in OECD agriculture were coupled policies—consistent with the strong anti-trade bias (see Fig. 6.4). Their share in total support was 82%, whereas decoupled support made up only 10%. However, in the 1990s and 2000s, the share of coupled support declined and that of decoupled support increased substantially in OECD countries. By the late 2000s the former had decreased to 60% and the latter increased to 40%.

A key purpose of the WTO was to reduce trade distortions and it has caused a shift toward less trade-distorting policies. Swinnen et al. (2013) do find that the implementation of the GATT and WTO have significantly influenced the *nature* of the policy instrument interventions (less trade interventions and thus a reduction of the anti-trade bias).

The decline of the overall subsidies in Australia and New Zealand and of the EU's trade-distorting subsidies played an important role in the overall decline of high-income countries (see also Chap. 7). The WTO appears to have had less impact on US agricultural policies. Nonetheless, the US administration has attempted to introduce policy reforms with an eye toward insuring that many US agricultural subsidies are classified as "green box" (i.e. non-trade-distorting) under the WTO agreement (Orden et al. 2010). In this sense, the motivation for its policy reforms appears to be similar to the EU's. WTO constraints also induced emerging countries (such as China) to choose less-distorting policy instruments as they attempt to support the incomes of agricultural households in recent years (see also Chap. 7).

---

[3]The PSE is a similar indicator as the NRA but the methodologies differ somewhat (Anderson 2009; OECD 2016). Initially the *PSE* calculations were only for OECD member states but more recently also some other countries, such as China and Brazil, are covered. The *PSE* data cover 28 countries, 12 of which are not OECD members, over the period 1986–2009. For countries not belonging to the OECD, the time coverage is not complete: the first-year observation is around 1990–1992 and the last is 2007.

REFERENCES

Akiyama, T., J. Baffes, D.F. Larson, and P. Varangis, eds. 2001. *Commodity Market Reforms: Lessons of Two Decades.* Washington, DC: World Bank.

Anania, G., M.E. Bohman, C.A. Carter, and A.F. McCalla, eds. 2004. *Agricultural Policy Reform and the WTO: Where Are We Heading?* London: Edward Elgar.

Anderson, K. 2009. *Distortions to Agricultural Incentives: A Global Perspective, 1955–2007.* London/Washington, DC: Palgrave Macmillan/World Bank.

———. 2016. Agriculture Trade, Policy Reforms, and Global Food Security. *Palgrave Studies in Agriculture Economics and Food Policy* Book Series (AEFP).

Anderson, K., and J. Swinnen. 2010. How Distorted Have Agricultural Incentives Become in Europe's Transition Economies? *Eastern European Economics* 48 (1): 79–109.

Anderson, Kym, and Signe Nelgen. 2012. Trade Barrier Volatility and Agricultural Price Stabilization. *World Development* 40 (1): 36–48

Anderson, K., G.C. Rausser, and J. Swinnen. 2013. Political Economy of Public Policies: Insights from Distortions to Agricultural and Food Markets. *Journal of Economic Literature* 51 (2): 423–477.

Besley, Timothy, and Robin Burgess. 2001. Political Agency, Government Responsiveness and the Role of the Media. *European Economic Review* 45 (4–6): 629–640.

Drabek, Z., and M. Bacchetta. 2004. Tracing the Effects of WTO Accession on Policy-Making in Sovereign States: Preliminary Lessons from the Recent Experience of Transition Countries. *The World Economy* 27 (7): 1083–1125.

Evenett, S.J., and C. Primo Braga. 2006. WTO Accession: Moving the Goalposts? Chap. 19. In *Trade, Doha and Development: A Window into the Issues*, ed. R. Newfarmer, 227–241. Washington, DC: World Bank.

Kherallah, M., C. Delgado, E. Gabre-Madhin, N. Minot, and M. Jonson. 2002. *Reforming Markets in Africa.* Baltimore/London: John Hopkins University Press.

Kuzyk, P., and J.J. McCluskey. 2006. The Political Economy of the Media: Coverage of the U.S.-Canadian Lumber Trade Dispute. *The World Economy* 29 (5): 637–654.

Liefert, W., and J. Swinnen. 2002. Changes in Agricultural Markets in Transition Economies. *USDA-ERS Agricultural Economic Report*, USDA-ERS 806, pp. 1–32: mimeo.

McCluskey, J.J., and J.F.M. Swinnen. 2010. Media Economics and the Political Economy of Information. In *The Oxford Handbook of Government and Business*, ed. D. Coen, W. Grant, and G. Wilson. Oxford: Oxford University Press.

Nakasone, E., M. Torero, and B. Minten. 2014. The Power of Information: The ICT Revolution in Agricultural Development. *Annual Review of Resource Economics* 6 (1): 533–550.

Oberholzer-Gee, R., and J. Waldfogel. 2005. Strength in Numbers: Group Size and Political Mobilization. *Journal of Law and Economics* 48 (1): 73–91.

OECD. 2016. *Agricultural Policy Monitoring and Evaluation 2016.* Paris: OECD Publishing.

Olper, A., and J. Swinnen. 2013. Mass Media and Public Policy: Global Evidence from Agricultural Policies. *The World Bank Economic Review* 27 (3): 413–436.

Olper, A., J. Falkowski, and J. Swinnen. 2014. Political Reforms and Public Policy: Evidence from Agricultural and Food Policies. *The World Bank Economic Review* 28 (1): 21–47.

Orden, D., D. Blandford, and T. Josling. 2010. Determinants of United States Farm Policies. Chap. 7. In *The Political Economy of Agricultural Price Distortions*, ed. K. Anderson. Cambridge/New York: Cambridge University Press.

Strömberg, D. 2001. Mass Media and Public Policy. *European Economic Review* 45 (4–6): 652–663.

———. 2004. Mass Media Competition, Political Competition, and Public Policy. *Review of Economic Studies* 71 (1): 265–284.

Sumner, D., and S. Tangerman. 2002. International Trade Policy and Negotiations. Chap. 38. In *Handbook of Agricultural Economics*, ed. B. Gardner and G.C. Rausser, vol. 2B. Amsterdam: Elsevier.

Swinnen, J., A. Vandeplas, and M. Maertens. 2010. Liberalization, Endogenous Institutions, and Growth. A Comparative Analysis of Agricultural Reforms in Africa, Asia, and Europe. *The World Bank Economic Review* 24 (3): 412–445.

Swinnen, J., A. Olper, and T. Vandemoortele. 2012. Impact of the WTO on Agricultural and Food Policies. *The World Economy* 35 (9): 1089–1101.

Swinnen, J., L. Knops, and K. Van Herck. 2013. Food Price Volatility and EU Policies. In *Food Price Policy in an Era of Market Instability: A Political Economy Analysis*, ed. P. Pinstrup-Andersen. Oxford: Oxford University Press.

Williamson, J., and S. Haggard. 1994. The Political Conditions for Economic Reform. Chap. 12. In *The Political Economy of Reform*, ed. J. Williamson, 527–596. Washington, DC: Institute for International Economics.

CHAPTER 7

Policy Reform in History: Europe, the USA, and China

7.1 INTRODUCTION

In the previous chapters (Chaps. 4, 5 and 6), we have documented major differences in agricultural and food policies among countries and how the policies have changed over time, by using average indicators among countries and focusing on "stylized facts" and explained these differences and changes by analyzing a variety of changes/differences in political and economic structures. In this chapter we will study some specific cases of policy reforms in greater detail. More specifically, we analyze the political economy of important changes in agricultural and food policies in Europe[1], the USA, and China.[2]

These countries provide fascinating cases to study the political economy of agricultural and food policies. China is currently spending around 200 billion US dollars per year on subsidies to farmers—much more than

---

[1] This chapter focuses mostly on Western Europe. See Chap. 12 for more on Eastern Europe.

[2] For historical political economy studies in other regions of the world, see Anderson (2009), Anderson and Hayami (1986), Gardner (1987), and Krueger et al. (1992). Well-documented cases of dramatic changes in agricultural policy include the radical liberalizations of extensive agricultural regulations in Sweden and in New Zealand and Australia in the 1980s (e.g. Anderson et al. 2007).

© The Author(s) 2018
J. Swinnen, *The Political Economy of Agricultural and Food Policies*,
Palgrave Studies in Agricultural Economics and Food Policy,
https://doi.org/10.1057/978-1-137-50102-8_7

any other country in the world.[3] This is a huge turnaround from the situation in the 1950s and 1960s when approximately 50 million people died of hunger and many farmers were among them. The policy system imposed by Chinese rulers caused huge inefficiencies and taxed farmers—literally—to death.

Europe has seen huge reforms in its agricultural and food policies as well. In 1848 the abolishment of the British Corn Laws was the start of a series of trade liberalizations resulting in free trade in agricultural and food products in the 1860s and 1870s. A century later, in the 1960s and 1970s, the EU introduced a "Common Agricultural Policy" which protected European farmers and heavily distorted European and global markets. Since then Europe has continued to spend tens of billions of euros every year annually—the EU alone more than fifty billion—on its farmers. However in the 1990s and 2000s the policy system has been completely reformed so that the impact on domestic and global markets is dramatically reduced. The USA also went from a "laissez-faire" attitude in the nineteenth century to heavy interventions in agricultural markets in the twentieth century, and fluctuating levels of support to its farmers in recent decades following a series of economic and political changes.

In this chapter we analyze the political economy behind these amazing policy changes focusing on key elements of the political economy of these reforms. While some of these factors are specific to the reforms, the key mechanisms described here are consistent with the larger and fundamental drivers in agricultural policy changes explained in earlier chapters.

7.2   Europe

Agricultural protection increased strongly in the twentieth century in Europe. The changes are reflected in the NRAs illustrated in Fig. 7.1. The average NRAs are close to zero in the 1870s and increase in the 1880s and 1890s. They fall again somewhat in the beginning of the twentieth century, and increase substantially in the 1930s, before declining rapidly in the 1940s. In the 1950s and 1960s the NRAs increase strongly, to a level

---

[3] "According to OECD calculations the Producer Support Estimate (PSE) to Chinese agriculture was 212 billion USD in 2016; and the Total Support Estimate (TSE) as 2.4% of Chinese GDP in 2014–16, thus about four times higher than the OECD average (OECD Agricultural monitoring report 2017)."

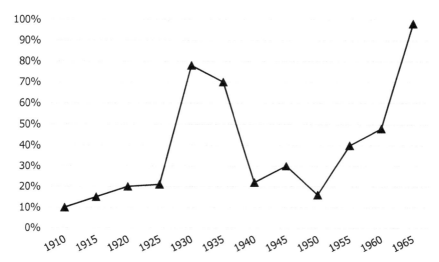

Fig. 7.1 Average NRA (%) for Belgium, the Netherlands, Germany, France, and the UK, 1910–1969. (Source: Swinnen 2009, 2017)

close to 100% in the second half of the 1960s and they stay high in the 1970s and 1980s.

These changes in agricultural policies are due to a combination of factors, in particular, the combination of changing incentives for farmers to demand protection, changed opposition to protection from the rest of society, and political institutional changes that influence how farmers and other interest groups impact the decision-making level.

There were three periods when European farmers intensely demanded protection and government support. This was at the end of the nineteenth century (1880–1895), in the 1930s, and in the post-1950 period. There were periods when either world market prices were depressed and imports increased strongly, putting pressure on domestic farms, or when the gap between incomes in farming and those in the rest of the economy grew significantly—consistent with Swinnen and de Gorter's (1993) "Relative Income Hypothesis". However, while farmers' demands for protection were intense during these three periods, there was a very different government response to farmers' demands, as I will explain.

7.2.1 Free Trade in Europe

Until the mid-nineteenth century there was substantial government intervention in agricultural markets in Europe. Probably the most well-known forms of protection were the Corn Laws in the UK. The Corn Laws were introduced centuries earlier to regulate grain prices and imposed import tariffs on grains (Kindleberger 1975). Other European countries also had import tariffs for agricultural commodities.

The Corn Laws were abolished in 1846 (Schonhardt-Bailey 1998, 2006), as were import tariffs on animals, meat, potatoes, and vegetables. A series of trade agreements contributed to the reduction of import tariffs and the spread of free trade throughout Europe. The first was the English-French trade agreement in 1860. Other trade agreements followed, including the 1862 French-German trade agreement. The German agricultural sector was strongly in favor of free trade. Large farms in Prussia benefited from grain exports and were opposed to tariffs (Tracy 1989).

While the move toward free trade is associated with the intellectual contributions of Adam Smith and his colleagues, it should be no surprise that liberalization of agricultural trade came in a period of relative prosperity for farmers. The 1840s through the 1870s was generally a period of relatively high incomes and productivity growth in agriculture. In England it is referred to as the period of "high farming". It was also a period of relatively high grain prices partly due to the Crimean War which reduced exports from Russia and the Black Sea region.

7.2.2 The Agricultural Crisis of the Late Nineteenth Century

However, the good times do not last. By 1875 cheap grain and meat start flooding Western Europe, especially from the USA where land was abundant and cheap. Technological innovations dramatically decreased transportation costs as the steam engine allowed much cheaper transport via trains and the steam boat and refrigeration made meat transport possible. Transportation costs declined by 60–70% between 1870 and 1900. Prices of imported grain fall by 40% over the same period (Fig. 7.2).

Farmers pressured governments to intervene. The reactions of European governments were mixed. Governments mostly resisted protectionist demands at the end of the nineteenth century, except in France and Germany. The French and German governments protected their farmers

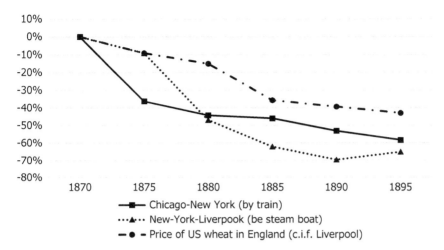

Fig. 7.2 Transport costs and wheat prices in England, 1870–1895 (index 1870=0). (Source: Own calculations based on Tracy 1989)

by increasing import restrictions. Countries such as the UK and Belgium, which were more industrialized, resisted the protectionist measures.

Opposition to import protection by the coalition of workers and industrial interests was so strong at the end of the nineteenth century, and for some basic food commodities still into the 1930s, that they were able to block substantive import tariffs for agriculture and in particular for (bread) grain. The opposition was strongest in the most industrialized countries, such as the UK, Belgium, and the Netherlands.[4] There, the share of employment in agriculture was lowest and both capital investment and employment in industry was largest. In France and Germany, the economic importance of agriculture was comparatively larger (and that of industry still smaller). In those countries grain tariffs were introduced in the late nineteenth century.

---

[4] In the UK, where the industrial revolution started, agricultural employment had fallen to 20% of total employment by 1880. On the continent, the shares were lowest in Belgium and Finland (less than 30%) and the Netherlands (35%). In contrast, farmers and farm workers still accounted for almost one-half of the population in France and Germany in 1880. By the late nineteenth century the share of agriculture in GDP had fallen to around 10% in Belgium and the UK while it was around a quarter of total output in France and around a third in Germany) (see also Figs. 4.2 and 4.3).

In addition, political coalitions within agriculture were complicated by heterogeneities among "farmers". In countries where livestock farming was well established (e.g. in the UK, livestock farms represented more than 60% of agricultural output by the 1880s, compared to less than 30% in France), livestock farms formed a powerful lobby against import tariffs for grains, rather than forming a coalition with grain farms.[5]

In addition, in feudal systems (as in the UK), farm workers opposed import tariffs on staple foods because they were to lose more as consumers (poverty was widespread and 80% of a farm worker's expenditure was on bread) than they would gain through increased wages (Burnett 1969). Moreover, in feudal systems small farms and tenants were more concerned with their tenure. They saw landlords as their main problem, not cheap imports. Their political struggle focused on improving land tenure conditions by opposing landlords, rather than forming a coalition with them to increase farm prices (see Chap. 12)—consistent with Olper's (2007) findings of a negative relationship between land inequality and agricultural protection.[6]

In countries which did not introduce high import tariffs (such as Belgium, the Netherlands and Finland) governments supported the restructuring of the agricultural sector from grains to livestock production. The governments of these countries considered that the restructuring of agriculture toward livestock production was the best development strategy in the face of cheap grain imports, which made competition in grains more difficult but also made feed costs cheaper for the livestock

---

[5] In the UK, the share of the livestock sector grew from 55% in 1860 to 70% of agricultural output in 1900.

[6] The agrarian crisis in the 1880s not only induced farmers to politically organize themselves to defend their interests against industrial capital and to demand protection but also to fight for changes in relationships within agriculture. In the UK, as farmers were forced off their land as they could no longer pay their rents with declining prices, the crisis induced social revolts by small farmers and tenants against the feudal relationships. In England tenants and small farmers organized themselves to defend their rights in the Farmers' Alliance (1879) and the Society of the Land for the People (1883). Their main objectives were to get a better deal from landlords, rather than import tariffs, as reflected in their demands for 'the Three F's': Fair land rents, Fixity of land tenure, and Free sale of commodities (Cannadine 1992). See Chap. 12 for a more extensive analysis.

sector.[7] More generally, European governments increased investment in public goods, such as agricultural research, extension and education, to increase agricultural productivity. Policies to reduce fraud and to improve rural transport were introduced. Ministries of agriculture and agricultural schools and universities were established throughout Western Europe in that period.

After 1900 the agricultural crisis subsided. Prices started increasing because production costs increased in grain exporting countries and because industrial growth increased demand for food, in particular for livestock and horticultural products.

The political economy changed completely with World War I in 1914. The war brought destruction and disruption in the food production and distribution systems and international trade. Food was scarce and expensive, and government regulation was introduced in order to secure sufficient food and limit price increases for consumers. Agricultural prices stay high in the beginning of the 1920s as reparation of war damages takes place.

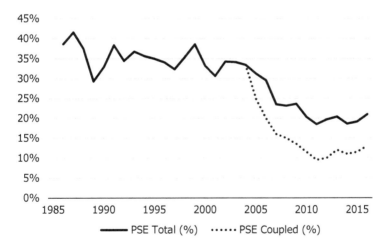

Fig. 7.3 Agricultural support in the EU (PSE-total and PSE-coupled), 1985–2015. (Source: OECD)

---

[7] Government initiatives to stimulate the shift to livestock production included: research and extension; the subsidization of activities that provided incentives for improved quality of livestock breeding; and compensation for farmers for the slaughter of infected animals.

7.2.3 The Growth of Agricultural Protection in the Mid-Twentieth Century[8]

The market turned in the late 1920s and 1930s. Supply increased by large farm investments in the 1920s, stimulated by high prices and profits. Demand fell after the 1929 stock market crash in Wall Street, the beginning of the economic depression. Agricultural prices and farm profits fell substantially in the 1930s resulting in strong pressure on the governments to intervene and support farmers (see Fig. 7.3).

However the political equilibrium is different compared to the 1880s. West European countries have become much more industrialized while at the same time the political organization of farmers is much stronger. While landlords and large farms were already powerful and politically well organized in the nineteenth century, new farm organizations, in particular representing small farmers, emerged during the crises, and a network of rural organizations linked to farming grew in importance in the first decades of the twentieth century. In addition, voting rights were extended to small farmers and farm workers in the beginning of the twentieth century. With voting rights being extended to small farmers, political parties saw rural households as an important source of votes. The political strategy of conservative (anti-socialist) parties was the social and political organization of the rural areas to create a strong power base and a reliable source of votes.[9] This new political strength gave farmers a much stronger influence on politics.

---

[8] See Swinnen (2009) for more details.

[9] The political organization of farmers coincided with the establishment of a broad social and educational network of rural schools, hospitals, and other rural organizations. Village priests often played a key role in the local organization. This strategy was very successful in several countries. For example, in Belgium the Catholic Party created a dominant political and social network in the rural areas in collaboration with the Catholic Church and the farmers' union. In France, conservative coalition of the Catholic Church and the (former) nobility was organized through the *Societé des Agriculteurs de France (SAF)*—and in reaction the Republican political movement established alternative farm organizations, focusing on small farmers. In Germany in the 1920s and 1930s, the National Socialist (Nazi) Party in Germany rose to power initially targeting urban areas. However, the Nazi Party soon realized the potential voting strength of a discontented peasantry and designed rural policies to address farmers' concerns. While their strategy focused strongly on the broad rural population, which dominantly voted for them in the 1930 elections, at the same time they joined forces with the large Prussian landlords with whom they shared preferences about the importance of protecting domestic food production and an autocratic political regime.

While governments faced strong pressure from industry and workers to keep basic food prices low in the midst of the economic depression, agricultural protection increased significantly in the 1930s, as illustrated by Fig. 7.1.

In the 1940s there was a temporary reversal of protectionism with World War II: average NRAs fell back to substantially lower levels (see Fig. 7.1). During World War II, food was scarce and policies that raised food prices were abolished. Maximum prices were imposed and harvests and stocks were claimed by the government. As in World War I, food prices were high on the black market.

After World War II, all factors in favor of more protection and more support to agriculture came together. First, farm incomes fell increasingly behind incomes in the rest of the economy. As economic growth took off in the 1950s, the income gap between farmers and people working in other sectors increased strongly. Farmers pressured European governments to intervene in the market to correct these growing income gaps and to support farm incomes. Second, opposition of industry and workers in the rest of the economy fell as the share of food in total consumer expenditures and its impact on wages declined and with this so did opposition to protection from workers and industry. Third, farm demands were now politically influential since political organizations of farms were well established and because of their still significant number of votes. Fourth, farm-related cooperatives and business organizations in the agri-food sector became important interest groups, with, for example, dairy and sugar processing companies joining farm unions in actively lobbying for government support and import protection for their sectors.

The combination of these factors caused an important and structural shift of the political equilibrium toward high levels of government intervention and support to agriculture. This led to a series of government interventions in European agriculture in the 1950s and 1960s. Minimum prices, target prices, import tariffs, quotas, and so on were introduced. As a result, agricultural protection increased strongly with the average NRA close to 100% by 1965.

7.2.4 The Common Agricultural Policy (CAP)

These national policy measures became the building blocks on which the EU's Common Agricultural Policy (CAP) was constructed and implemented in 1967. While these interventions provide strong support to farmers, they required significant taxpayer support and distorted markets heavily.

The introduction of high guaranteed prices and import tariffs at the EU level resulted in "wine lakes" and "butter mountains" emerged as surplus production needed to be stored, and in large trade distortions in the 1970s and 1980s. Tensions with the traditional agricultural exporting countries on the world markets increased (Josling 2009).

Pressure to reform came also from inside the EU, primarily from ministers of finance concerned about the cost of subsidies (Josling 2008; Moehler 2008). The first reforms came in the mid-1980s with the introduction of production quotas in the sugar and dairy sectors, limiting the size of surpluses. In the early 1990s price support and export subsidies were replaced by payments based on the area of land under cultivation, the so-called "direct payments" to further reduce the distortions on world markets.

7.2.5   A Perfect Storm

Despite the reforms, there were growing demands for further reforms, in particular, if a new WTO agreement was to be reached. Several factors came together in a "Perfect Storm" in the 2000s (Swinnen 2008). Pressures from other countries (trade partners) and EU ministers of finance were reinforced by food safety problems, by institutional reforms inside the EU, and by the opening of Eastern Europe.

The accession of Eastern European countries to the EU and their farms integration in the CAP was predicted to *"cause a flood of Eastern imports, bankrupt the EU and cause major WTO conflicts"* unless the CAP was reformed (Swinnen 2001). "Eastern enlargement" would add around 50% to the EU's farmland and more than doubled the number of farmers.

Major food safety and animal health crises in the late 1990s further contributed to a public perspective that despite the billions of euros in farm subsidies, European agriculture was running from one crisis to the next. In 2000, then-EU Commissioner Fischler argued that "the CAP had lost its legitimacy among the EU public". The CAP was seen as hurting EU trade interests with negative effects of agriculture on the environment and the climate.

Political institutional reforms also played a role. The governing political process had been fundamentally transformed by the 2001 Treaty of Nice, which introduced (qualified) majority voting in the decision-making on the CAP, effectively removing veto power of countries which opposed agricultural policy reforms.

This led to the 2003 reforms which "decoupled" farm payments through a "single farm payments" (SFP) system. From the mid-2000s onwards the vast majority of EU farm support remained at more than 50 billion euros per year, but most of this (35 billion euros) was given as decoupled direct payments. The result of these reforms, combined with increasing prices in the world market, is a significant decline in the NRA. Figure 8.1 illustrates how the average NRA gradually declined over the last decades and has fallen to much lower than the levels of the 1980s—and close to the levels of the early twentieth century—a century before. Moreover, the vast shares of these subsidies distort markets much less than they did in the 1960–1980 period.

7.3   USA

Agricultural and food policy discussions in the USA are largely concentrated and organized around the so-called Farm Bills. About every five years, a new Farm Bill is voted by the US House of Representatives and the Senate. The first Farm Bill was implemented in 1933. Before that, there was little intervention of the US government in agricultural markets.

US agriculture has traditionally been an export-oriented sector. It accounted for more than three-fourths of US exports in the eighteenth and early nineteenth centuries and still around 50% by 1900. With export success and domestic expansion, there was no government intervention (a "laissez-faire" approach) in agricultural markets. Instead the US government supported the expansion by investments in infrastructure (e.g. railroads, canals, and information) and education (the land-grant colleges), and by providing new settlers access to land through the Homestead Act (Gardner 2002).[10]

7.3.1   *The Emergence of the Farm Bills*

The policy debate changed in the first part of the twentieth century. While there were relatively high prices in the early years of the century, after World War I the agricultural economy became depressed as exports to

---

[10] Several key policies were introduced in the 1860s: the freeing of slaves, which radically altered southern agriculture; the Morrill Act and the start of land-grant colleges; and the Homestead Act that helped shape US farmland distribution.

Europe fell. With falling prices, many small and poor farmers were failing in the 1920s and pressure on the government to introduce support programs grew. The American Farm Bureau Federation (later known as the Farm Bureau) was formed during those days to organize lobby efforts (Orden et al. 1999).

However these pressures were not successful initially. As in Europe, farmers were not yet politically well-organized and faced strong opposition from industrial interests benefiting from low food prices and low inflationary pressure on wages and from industrial workers.

It took a further, and dramatic, decline in farm incomes to push the US government to introduce substantive support measures. The 1933 Farm Bill was introduced in response to economic hardships faced by farmers following the Great Depression (which started in 1929 and caused a reduction in demand and declining agricultural prices[11]) and the western Dust Bowl (which started in 1931 and caused yield declines and farm abandonment). The combined forces made per capita incomes in agriculture fall far below that of the rest of the population and triggered strong, sometimes even violent, political actions by desperate farmers.

A dramatic change in US policy came with the election of Franklin D. Roosevelt and commanding Democratic party majorities in the House and Senate. As part of his New Deal, the first Farm Bill in 1933 included measures to support farm incomes, with the explicit objective of achieving "parity of farm incomes", and stabilizing farm revenues. This was attempted by a combination of supporting farm prices (government "loan rates"), production controls, export subsidies, and direct payments to farmers, all targeted to "basic commodities". Soon afterward, import quotas and tariffs were added to protect other sectors (and to get the votes from the states where import-competing products such as sugar, dairy, wool, and fruits were important) (Gardner 2002).

The New Deal farm programs had a lasting impact on US agricultural policy (Orden et al. 1999, 2009). Later Farm Bills kept major parts of the 1933 legislations and have extended support to US agriculture, with important modifications being introduced later. As in Europe, the combination of a rapidly growing economy (causing an increasing urban-rural

---

[11] Orden et al. (1999) document how real agricultural prices fell by almost 50% from the late 1920s to the early 1930s—a decline which is very similar to that in European agriculture in the same period (Swinnen 2009), triggering similar political economy interactions (see also Sect. 7.2).

income gap, and thus pressure from farmers to reduce this), better political organization of farmers and their access to policy institutions (with Farm Bureau and National Farmers' Union membership rapidly increasing and farm organizations taking an active role in the institutions responsibly for local implementation of the Farm Bill), and reduced opposition from industry and workers shifted the political equilibrium toward agricultural interests.

With the Farm Bills, support to US agriculture increased and so did distortions in agricultural markets. The loan rate program allowed farmers to borrow against their crop, which had a huge impact on agricultural credit. However, with loan rates set above market prices, public stocks of grain grew rapidly, creating pressure for subsidized exports of US grain and the use of public grain stocks for food aid (see further).

Between 1955 and 1980 average NRA/PSEs in the USA fluctuated between 5% and 15%. However, average farm support remained below that in European countries and other OECD countries, such as Japan (compare Fig. 7.4 with Figs. 7.1 and 7.3). A key factor is that US agriculture was much more export-oriented than the agricultural sectors of the EU and Japan which were mostly protected by policies against imports (see also Chap. 5).

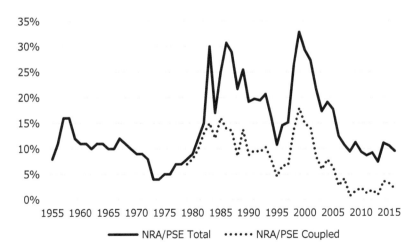

Fig. 7.4 Agricultural support in the USA (NRA/PSE-total and NRA/PSE-coupled), 1955–2016. (Source: 1955–1985: NRA from Anderson 2009 and Gardner 2009; 1986–2016: PSE from OECD)

122   J. SWINNEN

However, there are major differences among US commodities, in particular, among the import-competing and the export-oriented sectors—much in line with the "anti-trade bias" explained in Chap. 5. Support (as measured by NRA/PSEs) to import-competing sectors was around three times as much as support to exportable sectors. Some of the import-competing sectors, in particular the US dairy and sugar sectors, have received very high levels of assistance. Since 1980, NRA/PSEs for the dairy sector were most of the time above 60%, while NRA/PSEs for the sugar sector were often above 100% (Anderson and Nelgen 2012; Gardner 2009).

7.3.2 Political Coalitions in the Farm Bill

An intriguing characteristic of US Farm Bills is the interlinkage of agricultural policy (and the vested interests) with other policy areas, in particular environmental policy, food security policy, energy policy (biofuels), and (crop) insurance policy (and their vested interests)—which is much more explicit and elaborate in the USA than in most other countries. A typical Farm Bill has several "titles", that is, expenditure categories. The most important include commodity payments, conservation and other environmental payments, crop insurance, and nutritional assistance. All programs involve taxpayer costs. The nutritional assistance benefits primarily poor consumers. Most other programs benefit farms, but also other interest groups such as agribusiness and landowners.[12] Insurance companies benefit from crop insurance as the government heavily subsidizes administration costs. The environment benefits from conservation payments. Not surprising, this has influenced policy-making. In the words of Orden et al. (1999), these various interest groups (consumers, landowners, environmentalists, agribusiness, and crop insurance companies) have been "logrolling partners" to help defend farm programs at various times over the past century, and they argue that these coalitions have become increasingly important for farm organizations when the voting power of farmers declined over time.

From an international perspective, arguably the most intriguing coalition is between US consumers' and producers' interest in the Farm Bills. The Supplemental Nutrition Assistance Program (SNAP) was first known

---

[12] Farm subsidies, either linked to production or to land use, have spilled over into high land prices and rents in the USA (Goodwin et al. 2003; Roberts et al. 2003).

POLICY REFORM IN HISTORY: EUROPE, THE USA, AND CHINA   123

as the *food stamp* program. These programs are intended to support food security of low-income families and the program was originally designed to distribute surplus agricultural commodities to assist poor and needy families in the 1930s under the New Deal. It later became a part of President Kennedy's "War on Poverty". The food stamp program was initially allocated within the USDA and agricultural interest groups have lobbied strongly to keep it there, in order to create a coalition between supporters of domestic nutrition assistance and supporters of domestic farm subsidies in Farm Bill negotiations. Over time, SNAP has taken up a major share of expenditures. In the early 2010s, during the Great Recession, expenditures on nutrition assistance rose to over $100 billion, and it currently accounts for around 80% of the budgetary cost of the Farm Bill (Cueller et al. 2014; Wilde 2016).

7.3.3   Persistence and Policy Reforms

Despite the persistence of some farm programs, there have been significant changes and fluctuations in US farm support in the past 40 years. NRAs to US agriculture increased significantly in the 1980s, up to levels between 30% and 40%, and have fluctuated considerably since (see Fig. 7.4). The fluctuations are mostly in response to changing market situations—consistent with the relative income and loss aversion political economy theories (see above). In fact, an important element of the US farm policies is explicitly called "countercyclical payments". However, strategic coalitions of farm organizations with other lobby groups have also contributed to the persistence of US farm subsidies.

The decline in global commodity prices after the price boom in the mid-1970s triggered a rapid growth of the use of export subsidies, already used under the post-World War II treaties as food aid (mostly for wheat[13]), but now under the so-called Export Enhancement Program (EEP). The increase in support was continued in the 1980s. While the Reagan government (1980–1988) proposed several budget cuts for farm support, falling farm profits induced strong opposition from farm organizations. Macroeconomic reforms caused a rapid increase in interest rates and repayment problems for farms. In combination with falling agricultural prices, this caused declines in farm profitability and rising bankruptcies.

---

[13] In the 1950s and 1960s a large share of wheat exports was part of a heavily subsidized "food aid" program PL 480 (Barrett and Maxwell 2007; Gardner 2009).

124   J. SWINNEN

The resulting political reactions not only prevented budget cuts being approved in the US Congress but instead led to an increase in agricultural support in much of the 1980s.

Orden et al. (1999) argue that the coalition with environmental organizations also played a major role in raising farm subsidies in the 1980s, especially under the Conservation Reserve Program (CRP) for the protection of erodible land. Farmers can place their land in long-term CRP contracts in exchange for CRP payments. Environmental organizations had been an important lobby group in agricultural policy discussions going back to the Dust Bowl era of the 1930s; and their concerns took on new prominence in the 1985 and 1990 Farm Bill: the latter was entitled the "Food, Agriculture, Conservation and Trade Act."

A major reform came with the 1996 Farm Bill ("FAIR Act"), when Democratic President Clinton faced Republican controls of both the House and Senate, which further decoupled a significant share of farm subsidies—a policy decision which was considered "radical" at the time. With high market prices, decoupling subsidies from production decisions was attractive for both farmers and those interested in reducing market distortions. Orden et al. (1999) argue that the combination of a Republican political majority (favoring larger commercial farmers and agribusiness interests) and high prices (allowing for a windfall of fixed payments for farmers) was essential to make this reform politically feasible.

Decoupling farm subsidies had earlier been stimulated also by international trade negotiations. With the extensive use of export subsidies by the USA (under EEP), the EU, and other countries, such as Canada, world commodity prices continued to fall in the 1970s and 1980s. The turmoil in global agricultural markets eventually led agricultural trade policy to be discussed under the Uruguay Round of GATT negotiations and the introduction of reductions and limitations on export subsidies from the 1990s onward. This also stimulated the use of decoupled subsidies (see Fig. 7.4)

As agricultural prices fell in the late 1990s, US Congress introduced a "countercyclical" payment program that effectively re-introduced coupled payments with target prices. The (fixed) FAIR payments continued however, resulting in a rapid growth of farm subsidies. De Gorter (2008) refers to this as an example of commitment problems in agricultural policy reform.[14]

---

[14] See also Swinnen and de Gorter (2002) on credibility and commitment in agricultural policy.

POLICY REFORM IN HISTORY: EUROPE, THE USA, AND CHINA   125

In recent years (since 2002) there has been a significant decline in producer support, as measured by the NRA/PSE, primarily due to higher world commodity prices, which triggered a reduction in support policies that are linked to changes in prices (OECD 2016).

7.3.4   Recoupling Through Crop Insurance and Biofuels

While aggregate support (measured by the NRA/PSEs) has declined in recent years, two important US agricultural policy developments have been (a) the growing (economic and political) interaction with energy policy and (b) the recoupling of US farm subsidies through crop insurance programs (Coble and Barnett 2013; de Gorter et al. 2015; Orden and Zulauf 2015).

In the past decades, agricultural policy and energy policy became increasingly linked through biofuels (mostly corn-based ethanol).[15] Before 2006, using crops for alternative uses such as biofuels was seen as an opportunity to mitigate large crop surpluses and raise low agricultural prices; and to reduce dependency on foreign oil and mitigate climate change from fossil fuel gas emissions. The policy climate on biofuel changed after 2007 with (a) food price spikes on international markets (see Chap. 8) and (b) a re-assessment of the impact of biofuels on greenhouse gas emissions. The increased opposition to support to biofuels created new political coalitions with grain farmers, traders, and biofuel industries jointly lobbying for the continuation of biofuel mandates and subsidies against a coalition of livestock farmers, consumers, and other sectors hurt by rising feed and food costs (de Gorter et al. 2015).

Another policy which has grown in importance recently is crop insurance, and with it the role of the insurance industry in political negotiations on the Farm Bill. Since 1998, US agricultural policy has gradually increased subsidies to use private insurance to help combat risks (Glauber 2004). In the past decade, budget costs for crop insurance rose sharply, and in 2012, about 90% of US cropland was covered by the Federal Crop Insurance Program (FCIP). Crop insurance programs have become one of the larg-

---

[15] The growth in US biofuels was stimulated by tax exemptions and tariffs, and especially the introduction of mandates for the use of biofuels in transportation—the Renewable Fuel Standard (RFS) in 2005. After 2005, the US biofuel use grew rapidly: corn used for ethanol increased from about 1.2 billion bushels in 2004 to about five billion bushels (40% of US corn) in 2012 (de Gorter et al. 2015; Lobell et al. 2014).

126   J. SWINNEN

est expenditure items providing support to farmers in recent Farm Bills, with aggressive lobbying from farmers and the insurance industry to support these programs (Coble and Barnett 2013; Cuellar et al. 2014). This has contributed to a shift (back) from direct payments toward more coupled programs, such as crop insurance payments (de Gorter et al. 2015; Goodwin and Smith 2013).

7.4   CHINA

7.4.1   Political Changes, Grassroots Pressure, and Agricultural Reform

The situation in Chinese rural areas in the 1960s and 1970s was devastating. Households were forced to work together in communist-organized collective farms, and were forced to sell food they produced at very low prices to the state. As a result severe poverty and hunger were widespread. More than 30–40% of rural households lived below the one-dollar-per-day international poverty line (World Bank 1992) and faced famine in the recent past. It is likely that nearly 70% of households lived at less than the two-dollar-per-day international poverty line.

The administration of prices was a crucial element of the Chinese planning apparatus in the 1950s through the 1970s. Authorities used administrative prices to impose a heavy tax on agriculture by requiring farmers to deliver their output at artificially low prices (Lardy 1983; Sicular 1988; Green and Vokes 1997). Pro-urban policies used low procurement prices during the planning era to subsidize consumers (who also were workers on the front-line of East Asia's heavy industry-led development strategy). This led to artificially low farm gate prices.[16] Experts estimate that farms

---

[16] Input prices—especially that of fertilizer—were still controlled by the state's monopoly agricultural input supply corporations in China and Vietnam (Stone 1988; Pingali and Khiem 1995). Although in short supply, the governments in both countries controlled the price of fertilizer and other inputs (such as pesticides, diesel fuel, and electricity) as well as their distribution (Solinger 1987). Government-supplied, subsidized fertilizer was not sufficient to meet the needs of most farmers. Most farmers in China and Vietnam were not able to purchase fertilizer prices at subsidized rates. In fact, according to Huang and Chen (1999), during the 1980s the real price of China's fertilizer was above the national price. Vietnam was in a similar position early during its reforms (Pingali and Xuan 1992). Input prices were liberalized later (Rozelle 1996).

only received a small fraction of what they would if they could sell their products on the market (see Fig. 4.1).

The first price reforms came at the end of the 1970s. Between 1978 and 1983, in a number of separate actions, planners in China increased farm prices by around 50% (Sicular 1988). State-run procurement stations purchased grain from farmers as long as they had fulfilled their mandatory marketing delivery quota which was purchased at a lower price.[17]

These price reforms followed soon other reforms which gave land back from collective farms to households—the so-called household responsibility system (HRS). The HRS not only enhanced incentives in agriculture, stimulating productivity, but also allowed households to keep part of their production for which they received a higher price. The combined effect of these reforms gave a huge boost to Chinese agriculture. There was a confluence of interests of the leadership at the top and those at the grassroots, both farm households and local officials, in implementing these radical policies of decollectivization and market liberalizing (see also Chap. 12).

Credit for the reforms in China is often attributed to the new leadership that came to power after Mao died in 1976, and especially the new leader, Deng Xiaoping. However, a careful analysis of the reform discussions and decisions that took place at the top of the Communist Party and the changes that took place in the rural areas suggest a more nuanced picture. When decollectivization started in China's countryside in 1978, those that were in favor of reform at the top of the Communist Party were still in the midst of a power battle with conservative forces and not yet in charge. The power struggle continued throughout the 1978–1982 period (Yang 1996). It was not until 1983 that a central policy document formally adopted the HRS. By this time, more than 90% of China's villages had decollectivized.

Hence, grassroots pressure was a key element in the reforms. There had been pressure during the 1960s and 1970s. The pressure to decollectivize and reduce taxes on agriculture was most strong on the aftermath of the Great Leap Forward policy in the late 1950s and the famine that it created in the 1960s. The ideological pressure and the associated radical collectivization during those periods intensified the problems of the collective farming system and with that negatively affected the welfare of rural households.

In times of drought, the problems intensified. With such crises, the pressure to reform was strong at the grassroots levels. The reforms started

---

[17] For the case of rice, for example, the price was 50% below the above-quota price (Sicular 1995).

128   J. SWINNEN

where the pressure was strongest: in more drought-prone rural areas of China, before it was openly encouraged by reform-minded leaders in Beijing in the late 1970s. Yang (1996) documents how the willingness of rural households to risk punishment by the party traditionalists because of decollectivizing agricultural production is positively related to the intensity of famine that followed the Great Leap Forward. Household contracting started clandestinely in several regions that suffered heavily during the famine. Local cadres in these areas often tolerated the practices, and in many cases they were active collaborators because they witnessed firsthand the devastating effects of the famine and the benefits of the HRS.

The HRS reforms increased agricultural productivity and the agricultural pricing reforms contributed to higher farm incomes and food output. The performance of the agricultural sector strengthened the position of the new leaders by fueling China's first surge in economic growth and reducing the concerns about national food security. This provided legitimacy as leaders of a government that could raise the standard of living of its people.

The decentralized nature of China's economy affected the way that China reformed its markets. Regions were relatively self-sufficient. China's grain system was built around 30 separate provincial grain bureau systems that each ran its own network of county-level grain bureaus and township grain stations. A similar system existed for distributing fertilizer. In the mid-1980s, the government used reform experiments in some provinces to determine how the market could be allowed to play a more important role in the procurement of farm output (Sicular 1995).

China's leaders then slowly relaxed the restrictions on interregional trade of grain and fertilizer by partially commercializing the state-owned grain stations and fertilizer supply branches. Managers of these organizations were allowed to engage in trading as long as it did not interfere with their policy duties and keep part of their profits (such as continuing to collect the state-imposed delivery quota or deliver ration-priced fertilizer). Competition among quasi-commercialized trading companies further improved terms of trade for farmers (McMillan 1997).

7.4.2   The World's Largest Agricultural Subsidy Program

Since the late 1970s, Chinese agriculture grew at an average rate of 4.6% annually in the following three decades (NBSC 2015). Growth in agriculture and off-farm employment raised farmers' income and massively

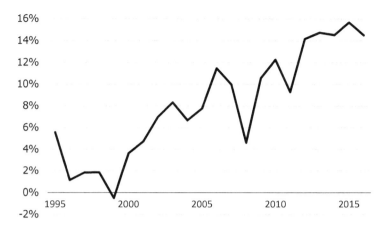

Fig. 7.5 Agricultural support in China (PSE), 2000–2016. (Source: OECD)

reduced rural poverty.[18] Over this period, the Chinese government had shifted from taxing farmers to heavily subsidizing agriculture, as is illustrated in Fig. 7.5.

Huang and Yang (2017) explain how in the past years (2004–2016), the Number One Document, the first and most important national policy document each year released by the Central Committee of the Communist Party of China, has emphasized the so-called *San Nong* issues (agriculture, rural areas, and farmers), signaling the Chinese leadership's strong commitment to supporting farmers and rural areas. By now China spends more on agricultural subsidies than any other country in the world (OECD 2017).

Not surprisingly, this dramatic policy shift has coincided with a similar dramatic increase in incomes in China—as the "development paradox" principles (see earlier chapters) would suggest.[19] Figure 7.6 illustrates how the growth of income and agricultural protection in China are positively correlated.

Economic growth in China, as in other countries, has coincided with an increase in the rural-urban income gap. Figure 7.7 illustrates how the ini-

---

[18] China was the first developing country to meet the Millennium Development Goals on reducing poverty population by half ahead of the 2015 deadline.

[19] Lopez et al. (2017) confirm that structural changes in the Chinese economy, such as the declining share of agriculture, are correlated with the growth in subsidies.

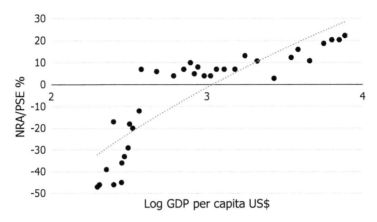

Fig. 7.6 Income and agricultural support in China (NRA/PSE %) 1980–2015. (Note: NRA % until 2005 and PSE % from 2006 onward; Source: OECD and Anderson and Nelgen 2012)

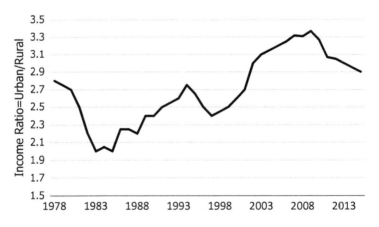

Fig. 7.7 Urban/rural income ratio in China, 1978–2015. (Source: Huang and Yang 2017; NBSC data)

tial economic reforms in the Chinese countryside (the HRS and price reforms) reduced the urban-rural income gap over the 1978–1984 period. However, as reforms in the rest of the economy stimulated growth outside agriculture, the urban-rural income gap has continuously widened over the 1985–2010 period. This growing inequality has induced the Chinese government to increase subsidies to agriculture and to support farm incomes. In recent years, growing subsidies to agriculture may have helped to reduce the rural-urban income gap.

The growth in subsidies has also coincided with a change in the nature of the subsidy instruments (Hejazi and Marchant 2017). Accession of China to the WTO in 2001 has played a role in this. Huang and Yang (2017) document the main policy changes since 2000 as follows: in 2004 remaining taxes on farmers were abolished and a direct subsidy program was launched. From 2006 onward several price and market interventions were introduced to raise farmer incomes, initially for rice and later extended to other grains, oilseeds, cotton, and sugar. As in the EU in the 1970s and 1980s these interventions created large market distortions in the past decade in China. These distortions, in combination with WTO constraints, induced a significant reform of Chinese agricultural subsidy programs from market interventions to direct subsidies. A significant share of these direct subsidies is no longer market distorting (Huang et al. 2011, 2013).

Hence albeit in different times and under quite different political regimes, both China, the USA, and the EU have dramatically increased agricultural subsidies during times of rapid economic growth (in the EU and the USA after 1930 and especially in the second half of the twentieth century and in China since 2000). The countries first installed distortionary policy systems, and later reformed their agricultural subsidy systems to less distortionary policy instruments and capping their subsidy levels, especially after accession to the WTO.

REFERENCES

Anderson, ed. 2009. *Distortions to Agricultural Incentives: A Global Perspective, 1955–2007.* London/Washington, DC: Palgrave Macmillan/World Bank.

Anderson, K., and Y. Hayami. 1986. *The Political Economy of Agricultural Protection: East Asia in International Perspective.* London/Boston: Allen and Unwin.

Anderson, Kym, and Signe Nelgen. 2012. Trade Barrier Volatility and Agricultural Price Stabilization. *World Development* 40 (1): 36–48.

Anderson, K., P. Lloyd, and D. MacLaren. 2007. Distortions to Agricultural Incentives in Australia Since World War II. *Economic Record* 83 (263): 461–482.

Barrett, C.B., and D. Maxwell. 2007. *Food Aid After Fifty Years: Recasting Its Role.* London/Routledge: Routledge.

Burnett, J. 1969. *A History of the Cost of Living.* Harmondsworth: Penguin Books.

Cannadine, D. 1992. *The Decline and Fall of the British Aristocracy.* New York: Anchor Books.

132   J. SWINNEN

Cuellar, M., D. Lazarus, W.P. Falcon, and R.L. Naylor. 2014. Institutions, Interests, and Incentives in American Food and Agriculture Policy. In *The Evolving Sphere of Food Security*, ed. R.L. Naylor, 87–121. Oxford: Oxford University Press.

Coble, K.H., and B.J. Barnett. 2013. Why Do We Subsidize Crop Insurance? *American Journal of Agricultural Economics* 95 (2): 498–504.

De Gorter, H. 2008. Explaining Inefficient Policy Instruments, World Bank Research Paper No. 48638. World Bank.

de Gorter, H., D. Drabik, and D.R. Just. 2015. *The Economics of Biofuel Policies.* Palgrave Studies on Agricultural Economics and Food Policies. Springer.

Gardner, B.L. 1987. Causes of U. S. Farm Commodity Programs. *Journal of Political Economy* 95 (2): 290–310.

———. 2002. *American Agriculture in the Twentieth Century.* Cambridge: Harvard University Press.

———. 2009. United States and Canada. In *Distortions to Agricultural Incentives: A Global Perspective, 2007*, ed. K. Anderson, 177–220. Washington, DC: The World Bank.

Goodwin, B.K., A.K. Mishra, and F.N. Ortalo-Magné. 2003. What's Wrong with Our Models of Agricultural Land Value? *American Journal of Agricultural Economics* 85: 744–752.

Goodwin, B.K., and V.H. Smith. 2013. What Harm Is Done By Subsidizing Crop Insurance? *American Journal of Agricultural Economics* 95 (2): 489–497.

Glauber, J.W. 2004. Crop Insurance Reconsidered. *American Journal of Agricultural Economics* 86 (5): 1179–1195.

Green, D.J., and R.W. Vokes. 1997. Agriculture and the Transition to the Market in Asia. *Journal of Comparative Economics* 25 (2): 256–280.

Hejazi, Mina, and Mary A. Marchant. 2017. China's Evolving Agricultural Support Policies, Choice, the 2nd Quarter 2017 32 (2): 1–7.

Huang, J., and C. Chen. 1999. Effect of Trade Liberalization on Agriculture in China: Institutional and Structural Aspects. CGPRT Work. Pap. Series N 42. Indonesia: United Nations, ESCAP Centre for Research and Development of Coarse Grains, Pulses, Roots and Tuber Crops.

Huang, J., and G. Yang. 2017. Understanding Recent Challenges and New Food Policy in China, Global Food Security. *Global Food Security* 12: 119–126.

Huang, J., X. Wang, H. Zhi, Z. Huang, and S. Rozelle. 2011. Subsidies and Distortions in China's Agriculture: Evidence from Producer- Level Data. *The Australian Journal of Agricultural and Resource Economics* 55: 53–71.

Huang, J., X. Wang, and S. Rozelle. 2013. The Subsidization of Farming Households in China's Agriculture. *Food Policy* 41: 124–132.

Josling, T. 2008. External Influences on CAP Reforms: an Historical Perspective. In *The Perfect Storm: The Political Economy of the Fischler Reforms of the Common Agricultural Policy*, ed. J. Swinnen. Brussels: Center for European Policy Studies.

———. 2009. Distortions to Agricultural Incentives in the European Union. In *Distortions to Agricultural Incentives: A Global Perspective, 1955–2007*, ed. K. Anderson. London/Washington, DC: Palgrave Macmillan/World Bank.

Kindleberger, C.P. 1975. The Rise of Free Trade in Western Europe, 1820–1875. *The Journal of Economic History* 35 (1): 20–55.

Krueger, A.O., M. Schiff, and A. Valdes. 1992. *The Political Economy of Agricultural Protection in Developing Countries. A World Bank Comparative Study*. Baltimore: Johns Hopkins University Press.

Lardy, N. 1983. *Agriculture in China's Modern Economic Development*. Cambridge: Cambridge University Press.

Lobell, D.B., R.L. Naylor, and C.B. Field. 2014. Food, Energy, and Climate Connections in a Global Economy. In *The Evolving Sphere of Food Security*, ed. R.L. Naylor, 238–268. Oxford: Oxford University Press.

Lopez, R.A., X. He, and E. De Falcis. 2017. What Drives China's New Agricultural Subsidies? *World Development* 93: 279–292.

McMillan, John. 1997. Markets in Transition. In *Advances in Economics and Econometrics: Theory and Applications*, ed. David Kreps and Kenneth Wallis, vol. ii. Cambridge: Cambridge University Press.

Moehler, R. 2008. The Internal and External Forces Driving CAP Reforms. In *The Perfect Storm: The Political Economy of the Fischler Reforms of the Common Agricultural Policy*, ed. J. Swinnen, 76–82. Brussels: Center for European Policy Studies.

NBSC, National Bureau of Statistics of China. 2015. China Statistical Yearbook.

OECD. 2016. *Agricultural Policy Monitoring and Evaluation 2016*. Paris: OECD Publishing.

———. 2017. *Agricultural Policy Monitoring and Evaluation 2017*. Paris: OECD Publishing.

Olper, A. 2007. Land Inequality, Government Ideology and Agricultural Protection. *Food Policy* 32 (1): 67–83.

Orden, D., and C. Zulauf. 2015. Political Economy of the 2014 Farm Bill. *American Journal of Agricultural Economics* 97 (5): 1298–1311.

Orden, D., R.L. Paarlberg, and T. Roe. 1999. *Policy Reform in American Agriculture: Analysis and Prognosis*. Chicago: University of Chicago Press.

Orden, D., D. Blandford, and T. Josling. 2009. *Determinants of Farm Policies in the United States, 1996–2008*. Washington, DC: The World Bank.

Pingali, P.L., and N.T. Khiem. 1995. Rice Market Liberalization and Poverty in Vietnam. Working paper, Int. Food Policy Research Institute, Washington DC.

Pingali, P.L., and V. Xuan. 1992. Vietnam: Decollectivization and Rice Productivity Growth. *Economic Development and Cultural Change* 40 (4): 697–718.

Roberts, M.J., B. Kirwan, and J. Hopkins. 2003. The Incidence of Government Program Payments on Land Rents: The Challenges of Identification. *American Journal of Agricultural Economics* 85: 762–769.

Rozelle, S. 1996. Gradual Reform and Institutional Development: The Keys to Success of China's Rural Reforms. In *Reforming Asian Socialism: The Growth of Market Institutions*, ed. J. McMillan and B. Naughton, 197–220. Ann Arbor: The University of Michigan Press.

Schonhardt-Bailey, C. 1998. Interests, Ideology and Politics: Agricultural Trade Policy in Nineteenth-Century Britain and Germany. In *Free Trade and Its Reception, 1815–1960: Freedom and Trade*, ed. A. Marrison, 63–79. London: Routledge.

———. 2006. *The Corn Laws to Free Trade: Interests, Ideas and Institutions in Historical Perspective*. Cambridge, MA: MIT Press.

Sicular, T. 1988. Plan and Market in China's Agricultural Commerce. *Journal of Political Economy* 96 (2): 283–307.

———. 1995. Redefining State, Plan, and Market: China's Reforms in Agricultural Commerce. *China Quarterly* 144: 1020–1046.

Solinger, D.J. 1987. *Chinese Business Under Socialism: The Politics of Domestic Commerce, 1949–1980*. Berkeley: University of California Press.

Stone, B. 1988. Developments in Agricultural Technology. *The China Quarterly* 116: 767–822.

Swinnen, J. 2001. Will Enlargement Cause a Flood of Eastern Food Imports, Bankrupt the EU Budget, and Create WTO Conflicts? *EuroChoices* 1: 48–53.

———., ed. 2008. *The Perfect Storm: The Political Economy of the Fischler Reforms of the Common Agricultural Policy*. Brussels: Center for European Policy Studies.

———. 2009. The Growth of Agricultural Protection in Europe in the 19th and 20th Centuries. *The World Economy* 32 (11): 1499–1537.

———. 2017. A Historical Database On European Agriculture, Food And Policies, LICOS Discussion Papers No. 399.

Swinnen, J., and H. de Gorter. 1993. Why Small Groups and Low Income Sectors Obtain Subsidies: The "Altruistic" Side of a "Self-Interested" Government. *Economics and Politics* 5 (3): 285–296.

———. 2002. On Government Credibility, Compensation, and Under-Investment in Public Research. *European Review of Agricultural Economics* 29 (4): 501–522.

Tracy, M. 1989. *Government and Agriculture in Western Europe 1880–1988*. 3rd ed. New York: Harvester Wheatsheaf.

Wilde, P. 2016. The Nutrition Title's Long, Sometimes Strained, but Not Yet Broken, Marriage with the Farm Bill. *Choices*. Quarter 4, 31: 1–5.

World Bank. 1992. *China: Strategies for Reducing Poverty in the 1990s*. Washington, DC: The World Bank.

Yang, D. 1996. *Calamity and Reform in China: State, Rural Society, and Institutional Change Since the Great Leap Famine*. Stanford: Stanford University Press.

PART III

CHAPTER 8

Food Price Volatility

8.1 Introduction

With a brief exception in the early 1970s when prices moved up following the first oil crisis, global agricultural markets were characterized by relatively stable and low prices for the past 50 years. Most of the global agricultural and food policy discussions focused on the reduction of taxes on farmers in developing countries and the removal of policies which subsidized farmers in rich countries, thereby hurting farmers in other countries (see Chaps. 4, 5 and 6).

All this changed in 2007 and 2008. Prices suddenly spiked in global markets (see Fig. 8.1). There was much discussion on what caused the dramatic price increase. Several causes were proposed, including increasing energy prices, US biofuels policies, low global food stocks, and weather conditions. Heady and Fan (2010) referred to it as a "perfect storm".[1]

Whatever the cause, the impacts and reactions were quite dramatic (Barrett 2013; Pinstrup-Andersen 2015). Urban consumers across the world protested and governments reacted rapidly to the price spikes. Many governments, in particular, in developing and emerging countries,

---

[1] The most vigorous debate centered on the role of biofuel policies with some identifying it as the main culprit (e.g. Mitchell (2008) and de Gorter et al.), while others minimizing its role, or arguing that other factors were more important—such as the historically low levels of food stocks (e.g. Wright).

© The Author(s) 2018   137
J. Swinnen, *The Political Economy of Agricultural and Food Policies*,
Palgrave Studies in Agricultural Economics and Food Policy,
https://doi.org/10.1057/978-1-137-50102-8_8

Fig. 8.1 Global food price index, 1990–2017. (*2002–2004=100 index Source: FAO)

intervened to reduce the effect of the global food price spikes. Demeke and his coauthors (2009) showed that in 68 out of the 81 countries they investigated governments used price and trade policies to counter global price movements and to insulate the domestic market from the international price spikes.

The typical reaction of exporters of food was to impose restrictions, and sometimes outright bans, on food exports. For example, India suspended rice exports and Russia and Kazakhstan banned wheat exports (Sedik 2011). Countries with significant food stocks refused to release these in global markets and to hoard them for domestic purposes. This was the case in China and Japan in rice markets (Timmer). At the same time food importing countries removed policies that would increase domestic prices. Many introduced price regulations and other interventions to restrict price increases (see various chapters in Barrett 2013; Naylor 2014; Pinstrup-Andersen 2015).

Government interventions were often ad hoc using policies which were relatively easy to implement or which governments (sometimes erroneously) assumed would have immediate effect—resembling what Swinnen (1996) called "fire brigade policy-making" when governments are confronted with unfamiliar shocks in the external environment.

The market and price developments and government reactions triggered several debates. One relates to the impact of the price increases on global food security and its implications for development policy. We will address this in Chap. 9. Another relates to food price volatility and the optimality of public interventions in agricultural markets to counter the price fluctuations. The issue of price volatility became increasingly relevant as the 2007–2008 price spike turned out to be the beginning of a period of serious price volatility, with large price declines in 2009 and a new price spike in 2010–2011 (see Fig. 8.1).

The issue was a challenge for both economists and political scientists. There was no agreement among economists on how best to deal with price volatility. However, not only economists struggled with the implications of price volatility but political economists also. The political economy literature had largely ignored price volatility and focused mostly on explaining structural trends in government policies (as explained in previous chapters). This chapter first briefly discusses the costs and benefits of price stabilization through government policy and then discusses political economy considerations.

8.2 Benefits and Costs of Price Stabilization

The key argument in favor of policy interventions is that price volatility is undesirable as it causes inefficiencies and potentially reduces economic growth. Several economists and advisors pointed at the importance of reducing price volatility based on efficiency gains (FAO 2011; FAO and OECD 2011; Prakash 2011; World Bank 2012). This is because unexpected price changes make it difficult for consumers and producers to make optimal decisions and it reduces their confidence in the market and investment levels. A typical example is the problem of farmers to plan their output if prices are volatile and uncertain. Government interventions that reduce price instability could thus be efficiency enhancing in environments with important market imperfection (e.g. in insurance and other factor markets). (After all that is why one uses various insurance-type instruments in private markets.)

The critique on government policies that stabilize prices and insulate their domestic markets from global price fluctuations is that these policies (a) are ineffective, (b) cause distortions in the economy, and (c) reinforce price fluctuations (e.g. Anderson et al. 2013; Ivanic and Martin 2014).

The distortions and welfare costs of a policy that stabilizes prices are illustrated in Fig. 8.2. The graph shows a simple downward sloping demand curve D, with prices P and Quantity Q. P_H represents the high

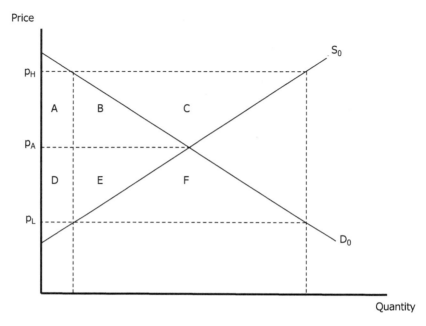

Fig. 8.2 Distortions from price stabilization

price, P_L the low price and $P_M = (P_H + P_L)/2$ the mean price. Area $A + B$ represents the loss in consumer surplus from price increases and $D + E + F$ the gain in consumer surplus from price declines. It is clear from the graph that consumers will have a higher combined surplus if prices increase to P_H and then fall to P_L than when they stay at P_M. The difference is Area F. In other words, with a downward sloping demand curve, the consumer will lose from a policy of price stabilization (Waugh 1944). The same conclusion holds when analyzing producer surplus with upward sloping supply curves (Oi 1961). Producers gain $A + B + C$ from high prices and lose $D + E$ from low prices, so their loss from stabilization is area C. The total distortions and welfare losses thus equal areas $C + F$.

Will Martin and Kym Anderson (2012) further argued that the result was even higher price volatility in the world market as food exporters reduced supply and food importers increased demand. They calculated how these policy changes exacerbated the crisis and compared the global effect with *everybody standing up in a stadium* so that the effect on individual visitors (countries) was annihilated by the combined effects. They therefore suggested that, just like in the case of import tariffs, export barriers should be included under WTO agreements to prevent such outcomes.

A fundamental critique on this is that if governments want to help farmers cope with price fluctuations they should do that by solving the imperfections in insurance and related markets, not by distortive trade and price interventions. The key argument in favor of policy interventions to stabilize prices is that price volatility is undesirable as it causes inefficiencies and potentially reduces economic growth. Several economists and advisors pointed at the importance of reducing price volatility based on efficiency gains (FAO 2011; FAO and OECD 2011; Prakash 2011; World Bank 2012). This is because unexpected price changes make it difficult for consumers and producers to make optimal decisions and it reduces their confidence in the market and investment levels. A typical example is the problem of farmers to plan their output if prices are volatile and uncertain. Government interventions that reduce price instability could thus be efficiency enhancing in environments with important market imperfection (e.g. in insurance and other factor markets). (After all that is why one uses various insurance-type instruments in private markets).[2]

However, these arguments ignore the fact that price changes are not always predictable and uncertainty affects consumer and producer decisions and welfare. To access, one also needs to take into account that people are heterogeneous in their risk preferences and how important the product is for their consumption. Combining these factors, Newbery and Stiglitz (1981) and Turnovsky et al. (1980) have shown that food price volatility fluctuations around the mean may benefit consumers if their budget spent on food is rather small and/or if they are risk loving. They argued that poor people in developing countries who spend a large amount of their budget on food and who are risk averse will likely benefit from stable prices. However, some economists argued that the impact of price volatility on poor consumers was less important than the high prices for the poor. Since consumers can switch between products relatively easily, the poor are more likely to suffer from high food prices than from volatile

---

[2] Some argue that because of (transaction) costs and capacity of governments to implement certain policy instruments, market and trade interventions may be the most effective (e.g. Munk 1989, 1994). The latter argument seems to be more relevant in the short run as it is difficult for governments to introduce policies to solve structural problems, but less so in the long run when governments should have the time and opportunity to do so—at least in theory.

prices. This argument was most forcefully presented in Chris Barrett and Marc Bellemare (2011)'s article *Why Food Price Volatility Doesn't Matter*. Producers use less inputs and have less profits if the prices of the agricultural products are volatile and uncertain (Sandmo 1971). In developing countries, many consumers in rural areas are at the same time also producing food. For these households, the impact of price stability on their welfare depends on their marketable surplus, risk aversion, and income and price elasticities. If the household is a net-seller of agricultural products and is risk averse, the household is more likely to benefit from price stabilization (Barrett 1996; Myers 2006; Gouel et al. 2014).

8.2.1 Balancing Volatility and Distortions

Without volatility concerns a social welfare maximizing (SWM) government will set the domestic price where it minimizes distortions. However with volatility concerns there is a trade-off for the government. The social optimum will then be to partially offset the price changes. The extent of the stabilization will depend on the marginal increase in production and consumption distortions caused by deviations of the price from the world market price (depending on the elasticities of supply and demand) and consumer and producer preferences for stability. Pieters and Swinnen (2016) derive the government's optimal distortions-volatility (DV) trade-off and the optimal combinations of the domestic volatility and distortions for different cases (levels of marginal distortions and preferences for stability) for a given price shock. With higher marginal distortions and less preference for stability, the government's choice will be closer to international prices, and vice versa.

This result is illustrated in Fig. 8.3. It shows that for a given fluctuation of world market prices how a social welfare maximizing government and a political government would introduce policies to influence domestic prices.

8.3 TRADING-OFF VOLATILITY AND DISTORTIONS? EMPIRICAL OBSERVATIONS

Figure 8.4 illustrates the evolution of rice prices in global markets and in China. The graph illustrates two important observations. First, rice prices in China have been much less volatile than in global markets. The sharp global price fluctuations in 2008–2010 have not occurred in China. This

FOOD PRICE VOLATILITY 143

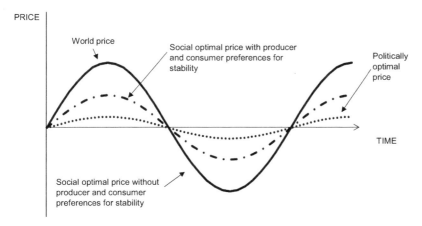

Fig. 8.3 Socially and politically optimal prices with global price volatility

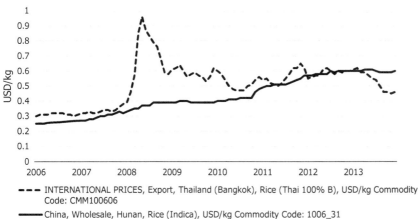

Fig. 8.4 Rice prices in China and on world markets (2006–2013). (Source: Pieters and Swinnen (2016), based on FAO data)

was due to important policy interventions by the Chinese government, including trade policy measures and the strategic use of rice stocks (Yang et al. 2008). The second observation is that, despite stabilizing prices, the Chinese government allowed rice prices to increase over the 2006–2013 period, thus passing on (apparently) structural changes in global rice markets (and food markets more general) to Chinese consumers and producers. Rice prices in China were very close to international prices both at the start and at the end of the 2006–2013 period. In fact, prices were close to the international prices throughout 2006 and 2007 and again since 2011. Hence they diverged only during the years of largest volatility on international markets: 2008–2010.

Figure 8.5 illustrates wheat prices in Pakistan and in global markets. The story here is similar. Domestic wheat markets have been less volatile than wheat prices in international markets, due to extensive interventions of the Pakistan government in wheat markets and trade (Dorosh and Salam 2008; Briones Alonso and Swinnen 2016). Yet at the same time, the government has allowed structural price changes to be transmitted to its domestic producers and consumers. Also here the domestic prices in

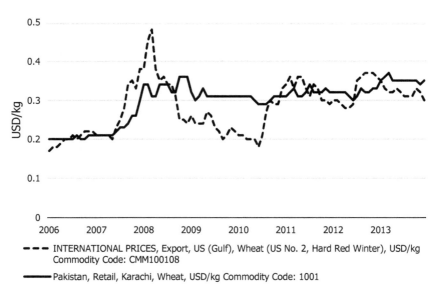

Fig. 8.5 Wheat prices in Pakistan and on world markets (2006–2013). (Source: Pieters and Swinnen (2016), based on FAO data)

Pakistan were very close to international prices both at the beginning and at the end of the 2006–2013 period, and more precisely until mid-2007 and again since 2011. As with rice, in China, wheat prices in Pakistan diverged strongly from international prices only during the most volatile price period: from mid-2007 till end of 2010.

In summary, in their interventions in their most important staple food markets, both the Chinese and Pakistani governments appear to have allowed (long run) structural changes in the global food markets to be transmitted to their producers and consumers—avoiding long-run distortions—while stabilizing the markets in the presence of large (short run) global price volatility, thus (possibly) avoiding short-run inefficiencies due to volatility and uncertainty.

Are these two cases exceptional cases or do they represent a larger pattern of government interventions? Pieters and Swinnen (2016) calculate "efficiency indicators" from many developing and emerging countries using quantitative indicators of price distortions and volatility. They find that China's rice policy and Pakistan's wheat policy are actually exceptional in a global context and that even when explicitly taking into account the DV trade-off (and the benefits of reducing volatility) that many countries (governments) are far removed from the optimal distortion-volatility (DV) combination.

China's policy intervention in the rice market is closest to the (theoretically) best outcome. Most countries are far away. Compared to the best outcome many countries are confronted with large deviations from the international food prices for similar volatility levels. A similar conclusion holds for the wheat policies. Pakistan performed much better in this framework than many other countries which had much higher inefficiencies in the D-V framework.

8.4 FOOD POLITICS WITH PRICE VOLATILITY

From a political economy perspective there is nothing surprising that governments have reacted to changes in world market prices. One of the basic stylized facts in agricultural and food price policies is the countercyclical nature of government policies. There is much evidence on this for other periods and regions (e.g. Gardner 1987; Swinnen 2009), as is explained in earlier chapters.

Chapter 3 explained that there are several mechanisms presented in the political economy literature which may explain these countercyclical policies.

One is the "relative income hypothesis" of de Gorter and Swinnen (1993) and Swinnen (1994) which is driven by changes in marginal utility which in turn determines political incentives for governments to respond to interest groups. Another is the "loss aversion" argument of, for example, Tovar where political action is driven by interest groups who want to avoid losses coming from changing market conditions.[3]

With fluctuations in world market prices, these political mechanisms will induce domestic price stabilization, irrespective of whether there are economic benefits from price stabilization. Note that in the model of de Gorter and Swinnen (1993) where political support is driven by the change in utility caused by the policy, price stabilization is never complete. International price fluctuations in either direction will be dampened in domestic markets, but not fully offset.

Hence, even without taking into account social welfare considerations coming from benefits for consumers or producers from price stability, political mechanisms will induce governments to respond to international price increases by policy interventions that reduce prices for the domestic markets (and vice versa when prices fall in the international markets). Hence this political motivation will result in less price volatility in domestic markets than in international markets in any case.

Efficiency effects of price stabilization as explained above reinforce these political considerations.[4] Hence, as illustrated by Fig. 8.1, price stabilization by politicians will typically be more extensive than the social optimum.

In summary, governments responded strongly to price volatility by introducing countercyclical policies to limit price volatility transmission. There is a trade-off between volatility and distortions in situations with limited policy options, both for welfare maximizing and politically optimizing governments. Political considerations will induce more price stabilization than is socially efficient, even when taking into account consumer

---

[3] Note that the basic Grossman-Helpman (1994) political economy model which is widely used in trade policy analysis does not yield such countercyclical policies.

[4] If one wants to fully explain empirical observations on government policy choices during periods of volatile price spikes, one also needs to take into account other factors that will influence government decision-making (Pieters and Swinnen 2017). These include the strength of the consumer and producer lobbies, the international trade status of the country (export versus import tariffs), affecting taxation or additional revenues for the government. These factors add to differences in relative preferences for stability of different interest groups, and so on.

and producer preferences for stability. Empirical observations are also influenced by traditional political economy factors, such as those identified in Chaps. 3, 4 and 5. This explains why some countries have performed well in the D-V trade-off framework, but many countries, even when explicitly taking into account this trade-off (and the benefits of reducing volatility) government policies, appear far removed from the optimal distortion-volatility (DV) combination.

REFERENCES

Anderson, K., M. Ivanic, and W. Martin. 2013. Food Price Spikes, Price Insulation, and Poverty. Chapter, In: *The Economics of Food Price Volatility*. National Bureau of Economic Research, Inc.

Barrett, C.B. 1996. On Price Risk and the Inverse Farm Size-Productivity Relationship. *Journal of Development Economics* 51 (2): 193–215.

———. 2013. *Food Security and Sociopolitical Stability*. Oxford: Oxford University Press.

Barrett, C., and M. Bellemare. 2011. Why Food Price Volatility Doesn't Matter. *Foreign Affairs*, July 12.

Briones Alonso, E., and J. Swinnen. 2016. Who Are the Producers and Consumers? Value Chains and Food Policy Effects in the Wheat Sector in Pakistan. *Food Policy* 61: 40–58.

Demeke, M., G. Pangrazio, and M. Maetz. 2009. Country Responses to the Food Security Crisis: Nature and Preliminary Implications of the Policies Pursued. FAO Initiative on Soaring Food Prices.

Dorosh, P., and A. Salam. 2008. Wheat Markets and Price Stabilization in Pakistan: An Analysis of Policy Options. *The Pakistan Development Review* 47 (1): 71–87.

FAO. 2011. The State of Food Insecurity in the World. How Does International Price Volatility Affect Domestic Economies and Food Security? Rome.

FAO and OECD (eds.). 2011. *Price Volatility in Food and Agricultural Markets: Policy Responses*. OECD.

Gardner, B.L. 1987. Causes of U.S. Farm Commodity Programs. *Journal of Political Economy* 95 (2): 290–310.

Gouel, C., M. Gautam, and W.J. Martin. 2014. Managing Food Price Volatility in a Large Open Country. The Case of Wheat in India, mimeo.

Grossman, G.M., and E. Helpman. 1994. Protection for sale. *American Economic Review* 84 (4): 833–850.

Heady, D., and S. Fan. 2010. Reflections on the Global Food Crisis: How It Happened? How It Hurt? And, How We Can Prevent the Next One?. *Research Monograph, 165.*

Ivanic, M., and W. Martin. 2014. Implications of Domestic Price Insulation for Global Food Price Behaviour. *Journal of International Money and Finance* 42: 272–288.

Martin, W., and K. Anderson. 2012. Export Restrictions and Price Insulation During Commodity Price Booms. *American Journal of Agricultural Economics* 94 (2): 422–427.

Mitchell, D. 2008. *A Note on Rising Food Prices*. Vol. 4682. Washington, DC: World Bank.

Munk, K.J. 1989. Price Support to EC Agricultural Sector: An Optimal Policy? *Oxford Review of Economic Policy* 5 (2): 76–89.

———. 1994. Explaining Agricultural Policy: Agricultural Policy for the 21st Century. *European Economy, Reports and Studies* 4 (Annex): 93–119.

Myers, R.J. 2006. On the Cost of Food Price Fluctuations in Low-Income Countries. *Food Policy* 31 (4): 288–301.

Naylor, R.L., ed. 2014. *The Evolving Sphere of Food Security*. New York: Oxford University Press.

Newbery, D., and J.E. Stiglitz. 1981. *The Theory of Commodity Price Stabilization. A Study in the Economics of Risk*. Oxford: Clarendon Press.

Oi, Walter Y. 1961. The Desirability of Price Instability Under Perfect Competition. *Econometrica* 29 (1): 58.

Pieters, H., and J. Swinnen. 2016. Trading-off Volatility and Distortions? Food Policy During Price Spikes. *Food Policy* 61: 27–39.

———. 2017. *Economics and Politics of Price Volatility and Stabilization*. LICOS Discussion Paper.

Pinstrup-Andersen, P., ed. 2015. *Food Price Policy in an Era of Market Instability: A Political Economy Analysis*. Oxford: Oxford University Press. forthcoming.

Prakash, A. 2011. Why Volatility Matters. In *Safeguarding Food Security in Volatile Global Markets*, ed. A. Prakash. Rome: Food and Agriculture Organization of the United Nations.

Sandmo, A. 1971. On the Theory of the Competitive Firm Under Price Uncertainty. *The American Economic Review* 61 (1): 65–73.

Sedik, D. 2011. Food Security and Trade in the ECA Region. *Presentation at the "Course on Food and Agricultural Trade for ECA"*, February, pp. 7–10.

Swinnen, J. 1994. A Positive Theory of Agricultural Protection. *American Journal of Agricultural Economics* 76 (1): 1–14.

———. 1996. Endogenous Price and Trade Policy Developments in Central European Agriculture. *European Review of Agricultural Economics* 23 (2): 133–160.

———. 2009. The Growth of Agricultural Protection in Europe in the 19th and 20th centuries? *The World Economy* 32 (11): 1499–1537.

Swinnen, J., and H. De Gorter. 1993. Why Small Groups and Low Income Sectors Obtain Subsidies: The 'Altruistic' Side of a 'Self-Interested' Government. *Economics and Politics* 5 (3): 285–296.

Turnovsky, S.J., H. Shalit, and A. Schmitz. 1980. Consumer's Surplus, Price Instability, and Consumer Welfare. *Econometrica* 48 (1): 135–152.

Waugh, F.V. 1944. Does the Consumer Benefit from Price Instability? *The Quarterly Journal of Economics* 58 (4): 602–614.

World Bank. 2012. Responding to Higher and More Volatile World Food Prices. Washington, DC.

Yang, J., H. Qiu, J. Huang, and S. Rozelle. 2008. Fighting Global Food Price Rises in the Developing World: The Response of China and Its Effects on Domestic and World Markets. *Agricultural Economics* 39: 453–464.

CHAPTER 9

Crises, Media, and Agricultural Development Policy

9.1 Introduction

As explained and illustrated in the previous chapter, the "food crisis" of the early twenty-first century is associated with the dramatic increase in food prices in the second half of the 2000s (see Fig. 8.1). The price spikes had major effects on agricultural and food policy decisions, as explained in Chap. 8. It also induced extensive policy discussions on the impact of food prices on poverty and hunger, and had a major impact on global investments in agriculture.

This chapter first discusses the impact of agricultural and food prices on poverty and hunger, and how the food crisis caused dramatic changes in the communication of these principles. It then explains some of the factors driving these policy communication strategies and how the interaction of mass media and food price shocks have pushed food security and agricultural development problems to the top of the agenda of governments, international agencies, and donors. It ends by reflecting on how negative shocks to consumers' food security has resulted in major increases in funding for agricultural development, benefiting both consumers and farmers in developing countries.

© The Author(s) 2018
J. Swinnen, *The Political Economy of Agricultural and Food Policies*,
Palgrave Studies in Agricultural Economics and Food Policy,
https://doi.org/10.1057/978-1-137-50102-8_9

151

9.2 The Right Price of Food

In his book *Getting Prices Right*, Peter Timmer (1986, p. 13) posed the question "What is the 'right' price for an agricultural commodity?". There is a long literature on the role of agriculture in economic development and the impact of high versus low agricultural prices, including the work by famous economists such as T.W. Schultz, John Mellor, Irma Adelman, Hans Binswanger, and others. The issue is well captured in the "food price dilemma" as explained by Peter Timmer et al. (1983, p. 11): "The incomes of the poor depend on their employment opportunities, many of which are created by a healthy and dynamic rural sector. Incentive prices for farmers are in the long run important in generating such dynamism and the jobs ... But poor people ... must eat in the short run or the prospect of a long-run job creation will be a useless promise...."

Agricultural prices thus affect the poor in two (opposing ways): they influence the price of food which is a major expenditure for the poor (as documented in Table 4.1) and they influence the incomes of most of the world's poor people. The vast majority (more than 70%) of poor people are still depending on agriculture for their incomes: around 50% are small farmers and around 20% don't have land but their main income source is a wage from working on a farm (UNDP 2005).

9.2.1 Some Basic Principles

To interpret the analyses and policy statements that have been made over the past decade, it is useful to go back for a moment to some basic principles on the effects of food price changes.[1] Consider first a simple model of an open economy with two groups, producers and consumers of food, where prices are determined at the world market with local production or consumption having no impact on global prices (i.e. the so-called small country assumption in international trade theory). In this situation, a change in world market prices (caused by some external factor which is exogenous to the country) affects producers and consumers, but in opposing directions: consumers gain and producers lose from a decline in prices, and vice versa when prices increase.

---

[1] For more elaborated and sophisticated models, see, for example, the textbooks on agricultural, food, and development policy analysis of Gardner (1987) and Sadoulet and de Janvry (1995).

To make this model more realistic one can consider several extensions. First, in reality the distinction between producers and consumers may not be so simple. Many rural households in developing countries are both producers and consumers of food and are thus affected in different ways by price changes. The net household effect depends on their net consumption status. Second, the change in world market prices may differ from the change in the local prices and the latter may even differ for local producers and local consumers, as these changes are affected by various policies (trade policy, taxes, …), by infrastructure and institutions, and by the industrial organization of the food chain. Third, local production and consumption may also affect local prices, in addition to exogenous external shocks. Fourth, the "exogenous" shocks may be caused by nature (e.g. the weather) or by men (e.g. changes in trade policies or consumption or production in other countries). Fifth, short-run effects may differ from long-run effects, as pass-through may take some time.[2]

What is important for our further discussion is that, first, all these extensions do not fundamentally change the basic result of the simple model: when prices go up consumers lose and producers gain, and vice versa. Hence, when rich countries increase (reduce) export subsidies which leads to a decline (increase) in world markets, this will benefit (hurt) urban consumers and net consuming rural households in poor countries and hurt (benefit) net producing rural households in poor countries. The size of the benefits/losses though will depend on various factors, such as local policies, institutions, the food chain organization, time, and so on.[3]

Second, the net benefits of price increases and decreases for a country should be roughly symmetric. Countries that benefit most from price decreases (e.g. if they consume lots of food but produce little) will lose most from price increases. The same holds at the household level within a country. Households which only consume food and do not produce food will be affected stronger when prices change than households which both produce and consume food. Another implication is that households which

---

[2] There are more factors that would need to be taken into account in a truly complete model. For example, not only "exogenous" shocks will affect producers and consumers, but also "endogenous" price changes, with the latter caused, for example, by faster productivity growth in agriculture. In addition, one would have to consider general equilibrium effects (considering not just food market effects but also effects through/on markets for labor, capital, services, other inputs and outputs). For example, as other prices (e.g. energy, fertilizer, etc.) changed together with food prices, this may need to be taken into account as well.

[3] In extreme cases the size of the effects could actually be reduced to zero.

154   J. SWINNEN

are directly affected by world market prices will gain or lose more than those living in areas largely isolated from market transactions when world prices change. A straightforward implication of these basic principles is that low food prices on the world market in most of the pre-2005 period benefited consumers and hurt farmers in developing countries, and vice versa in the 2006–2008 period. Another implication is that households which suffered strongly in 2007 from high food prices (e.g. they lived in urban market centers and produced little food themselves) would have benefited significantly from low food prices prior to 2005. Inversely, some rural households may not have benefited (much) from the high prices in 2007 (e.g. because they live in remote places with poor pass-through of prices from the world market or because they consume all their food production themselves). These rural households would also have experienced limited negative welfare effects from the low food prices prior to 2005.

9.3   COMMUNICATIONS ON PRICE EFFECTS ON POVERTY AND FOOD SECURITY

While these basic principles are well known, the food policy debate over the past decades was based on very partial interpretations and communications of these effects. Before the price spikes, the emphasis of policy communications and reports was that *low* food prices were a curse to developing countries and the poor. A typical statement on world markets and their implications for developing countries, representing a common perspective was: "The long-term downward trend in agricultural commodity prices threatens the food security of hundreds of millions of people in some of the world's poorest developing countries" (FAO 2005). However, after the dramatic increase of food prices in 2006–2008 and in 2010–2011, the vast majority of reports emphasized that *high* food prices were detrimental for poverty and food security of developing countries and the world's poor. Typical examples are: "rapidly rising food prices began to further threaten the food security of poor people around the world. ... The current food-price crisis can have long-term, detrimental effects on peoples' health and livelihoods, and can contribute to the further impoverishment of many of the world's poorest people" (IFPRI 2008), and "High global food prices risk hunger for millions of people" (Oxfam 2011). This reversal of emphasis was widespread (see Swinnen (2011) for details).

CRISES, MEDIA, AND AGRICULTURAL DEVELOPMENT POLICY   155

The shift from producer concerns to consumer concerns with increasing prices is not surprising—it is merely an illustration of the relative income driver of agricultural policies, as explained in several previous chapters. What is more surprising was that was hardly any mentioning of the benefits of low food prices for urban consumers and net consuming rural households during the pre-2006 low price era, and there was very little emphasis on the benefits for producers in poor countries from high food prices after the price spikes.[4]

These communication strategies raise several questions, such as why did they do it, what were the implications, and so on. Communications by these organizations are likely to influence policy thinking, government strategies, development priorities, and aid flows. Communication biases may draw in larger revenues through fundraising but may have negative welfare effects if it induces suboptimal behavior by other agents who use this advice for their decision-making.

9.4   THE MARKET FOR COMMUNICATION, MASS MEDIA, AND DONOR FUNDING

9.4.1   Communication Incentives

To answer these questions and to analyze potential bias in "policy communication", Swinnen et al. (2011) develop a model of the interaction between "policy organizations" (POs) and "donors".[5] POs engage in

---

[4] Only a few studies initially pointed at the mixed effects of the high food prices on poverty and food security (e.g. Aksoy and Hoekman 2010; Heady 2013; Jacoby 2013; Verpoorten et al. 2013). Recently there has been a growing consensus on the nuanced and mixed effects, as summarized in the review by Heady and Martin (2016). The observed heterogeneity among households and countries is consistent with economic predictions: net sellers and exporters of food benefit and net buyers and importers lose; the transmissions of price shocks to local markets have been mitigated by policy interventions and by institutional and infrastructure deficiencies; negative price effects on poverty and malnutrition have been offset by economic growth over the same period; and accounting for positive wage effects for the rural poor enhances poverty reduction.

[5] Their model builds on the work of Mullainathan and Shleifer (2005) on bias in mass media; of Andreoni and Payne (2003) on fundraising by charity organizations and the literature on bias in communication in mass media; on international organizations' lending and project implementation activities (Aldenhoff 2007; Dreher et al. 2009; Vaubel et al. 2007); the impact of fundraising on NGO strategies (e.g. Chau and Huysentruyt 2006; Andreoni and Payne 2003; Aldashev and Verdier 2010).

156   J. SWINNEN

both analysis and communication. The purposes of the POs' analysis are multiple: their analysis serves to support internal decision-making on funding and project implementation. Analysis also provides the basis for communication. The POs' communication strategy has two objectives. The first objective is policy advice, that is, to influence others (e.g. governments) to implement or reform certain policies. The second objective is fundraising, that is, to influence donors to contribute funds to the POs.[6]

POs will slant their communication depending on several factors, such as the relative importance of, respectively, fundraising and policy impact in the policy organizations' objective function, and the donors' sensitivity to slanting as well as their sensitivity and to reading reports that are inconsistent with their beliefs. When donors prefer donating to policy organizations that (claim to) address more severe problems, policy organizations have an incentive to depict situations as being more negative (severe) than they actually are. Swinnen (2013) show that there is a complex interaction between donors' perspectives and POs communication. Donors' beliefs are affected by POs' reports. This may create perverse dynamic effects. Even if donors' initial beliefs were correct they may become biased over time with slanted PO reports.

9.4.2   Mass Media and Social Media

However, these communications do not occur in a vacuum. They are influenced by other information sources, in particular, mass media and social media. This will also influence POs' communications. There are two mechanisms in the interaction between POs' communications and the mass media.

The first mechanism is the impact of stories that appear in the mass media on the communications of the organizations. Several characteristics of mass media are relevant to explain this mechanism (McCluskey and Swinnen 2010). Mass media may play an important role in influencing donors'

---

[6]All international organizations use funds from donors to operate and implement their projects—or subgroups within these organizations have to compete internally for funding. While their funding sources may differ, in a world where financial means are limited and where there is continuous pressure to demonstrate relevance and importance of budget spending on particular items, projects, or divisions within large organizations, all these organizations face a demand to demonstrate the importance of their work. Focusing their reports and analyses on those hurt by price changes may fit in such strategy to show relevance and importance—and may thus help in securing and raising funds.

beliefs, in particular initial beliefs, and thus POs' communication. Media attention is typically concentrated around 'events' or 'shocks'.[7] This agenda-setting effect of the media in international and aid policy, has sometimes been referred to as the "CNN factor" (Hawkins 2002). It refers to the process by which the media influences policy by invoking responses in their audiences through concentrated and emotionally based coverage, which in turn applies pressure to governments to react. Similarly, the absence of media coverage reduces priority in agenda-setting (Jakobson 2000).[8]

The second mechanism is the desire of the organizations to appear in mass media in order to achieve their objectives (Cottle and Nolan 2007). With mass media reports focusing on those hurt by changing food prices—in particular consumers post-2006—the donor community, the organizations' shareholders, and the public at large may expect (or even demand) that these organizations focus their attention on those who are suffering from price changes. If they would not publicly react ('communicate') on these problems, it would hurt their legitimacy as development organizations. This could undermine overall support for their existence. Hence, sudden changes with dramatic effects, such as the 2008 food crisis, not only present important challenges to the international organizations in addressing these, but also important opportunities for development organizations to capture media attention and signal their relevance and importance to their donors and the public.

A related factor is that the public at large is more interested in media reports concentrating on negative (development) effects. This follows from the so-called Bad News Hypothesis (McCluskey and Swinnen 2004). Media consumers in general tend to be more interested in negative news items than in positive news items, ceteris paribus. This demand effect of the media market drives mass media to pay more attention to "bad news" (McCluskey et al. 2015).[9]

In combination, these factors create a set of incentives for development organizations to emphasize the negative welfare implications in their anal-

---

[7]For example, Swinnen and Francken (2006) find that virtually all the attention to globalization, trade, and development issues in mass media is concentrated around "international summits".

[8]Van Belle et al. (2004) and Kim (2005) find that a higher level of media attention to developing countries problems leads to more aid. Eisensee and Strömberg (2007) argue that disaster relief and aid allocations are influenced by media coverage of disasters.

[9]For example, Heinz and Swinnen (2015) find that job market losses are reported 20 times more likely than job market gains in the media (on a per job basis).

ysis and policy communications, and to put less emphasis on the positive effects. In doing so, they are more likely to attract media coverage on their work and, in turn, more likely to reach a wide audience and to influence policy-makers. Such a media strategy could have a direct effect in influencing public and private donations and policies of governments in the short run and an indirect effect in encouraging appreciation and legitimacy for their work and the organizations themselves—which could lead to support in the long run.

How important are these media effects? To analyze the link between food prices and mass media coverage, Guariso et al. (2014) constructed a news coverage index on agriculture, food prices, and poverty, relying on a large archive of news sources for the 2000–2012 period. The correlation coefficient between the food price indicator and the media coverage indicators is a staggering 83% (Fig. 9.1). News coverage of food and agriculture related issues was low as long as food prices remained low. As food prices started to increase in 2007, news coverage quickly followed. As prices decreased, in the second half of 2008, news coverage dropped: the news effect was over. And as food prices increased again, in 2011 and 2012, the news coverage index peaked again as well, even if less impressively than in 2008. Hence, the increase in food prices significantly shifted media attention toward these topics (Fig. 9.2).

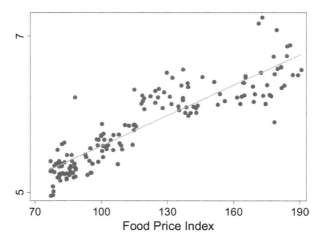

Fig. 9.1 Food prices and mass media coverage of agriculture and food security, 2000–2012. (Source: Guariso et al. (2014))

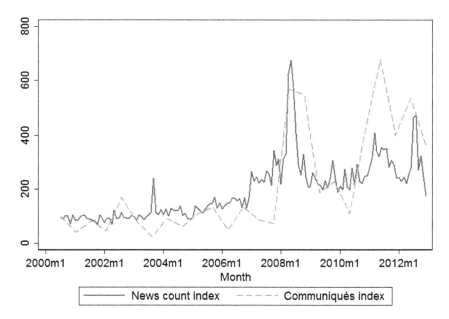

Fig. 9.2 Mass media coverage and development policy priorities* on agricultural development and food security 2000–2012. (*Indices of media coverage and WB-IMF development committee coverage of agriculture and food security* Source: Guariso et al. (2014))

Moreover, the shift is disproportionate as mass media coverage is strongly event-driven (Hawkins 2002; Swinnen and Francken 2006). Whenever there are significant and sudden changes, the number of articles jumps up more than proportionally. For the 2008 peak, for instance, while the price index increased by around 200% compared to the reference level, news coverage increased by more than 500%.

9.5 Food Prices and Development Policy Priorities and Funding

The food crisis also pulled food security and agricultural development from the bottom of the international development agenda and pushed it toward the top of policy-makers' priority list. While hunger and malnutrition have obviously been a major development problem in the past

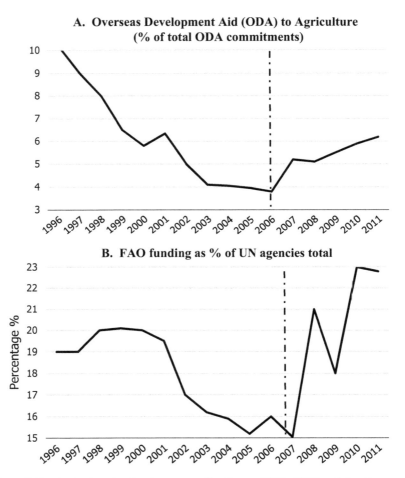

Fig. 9.3 Agricultural development funding, 1996–2012. (a) Overseas Development Aid (ODA) to Agriculture (% of total ODA commitments); (b) FAO funding as % of UN agencies total. (Source: Guariso et al. (2014) based on data from OECD and the Global Policy Forum)

decades, food security issues attracted relatively little public attention and were often low on policy-makers' priority list as is illustrated in Fig. 9.3. This figure, from a study by Guariso et al. (2014), shows that policy-makers' attention to food security and agricultural development was strongly correlated with food price changes and media attention.

The increase in food prices caused a significant increase in donor funding to agriculture and food security, reversing the downward trend that had characterized the previous years.

In the mid-2000s, almost 14% of the people in the world were undernourished (FAO 2012), and around 25% of the people were living below the $1.25/day poverty line (World Bank 2013), most of them farmers. Yet, poor farmers and food security did not figure prominently on the global development policy agenda and donor funding for developing country agriculture was declining significantly, despite economic growth in rich countries. As Fig. 9.3 illustrates, between 2000 and 2005, the share of global overseas development aid (ODA) going to agriculture fell from 5% to 3.8% (OECD 2013) and the budget share in the UN system going to agriculture (FAO) fell from 20.1% to 15.5% (Global Policy Forum 2013).

From 2007 onwards, global leaders moved food security and agricultural development to the top of their agendas. Between 2007 and 2011 the share going to agriculture (FAO) in the UN system increases from 15.2% to 22.2% and the share of global development aid going to agriculture jumps from 3.7% to 6.5% (Global Policy Forum 2013; OECD 2013). The World Bank doubled its lending for "agriculture and related sectors" and created a new Global Food Crisis Response Program. Oxfam and global agricultural research centers under the heading of the CGIAR also saw their funding increase strongly.

What made this impact particularly remarkable is that all this has occurred, while the shift from "low" to "high" food prices has induced a shift in (demographic or social) "location" of the hunger and poverty effects, but the total number of undernourished and poor people actually declined over the same period—and significantly so.

After the "food crisis" there are still a very large number of poor and undernourished people in the world, but the numbers are significantly better than before, as Fig. 9.4 illustrates. By 2010 around 12.5% of the people in the world were undernourished (FAO 2012) and more than 20% of the people were living below the poverty line (World Bank 2013). Studies estimate that the number of poor and food insecure people declined between 50 and 250 million people, depending on the source (Heady 2013; Ravallion 2013). The vast majority of these poor and food insecure people still depend mostly on agriculture for their incomes.

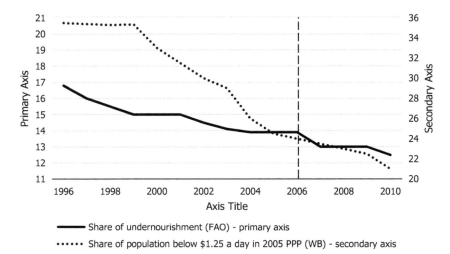

Fig. 9.4 Global poverty and hunger, 1996–2012. (Source: Guariso et al. (2014))

9.6 Bad News and Good Policies?

The food price hikes thus increased media coverage, policy priorities, and donor funding for agriculture and food security. However, as Figs. 9.1, 9.2, 9.3 and 9.4 illustrate, the observed increase in attention and donor funding is not correlated with actual increases in hunger and poverty. While the incidence of hunger has changed, the total number of food insecure households has not increased and poverty has declined since 2006. That is (a) because the transmission of global food prices to domestic markets has been imperfect, (b) because economic growth has enhanced incomes in developing countries, and (c) because food prices have mixed effects on food security (Heady 2013; Swinnen and Squicciarini 2012). In fact, the most recent estimates suggest that the high agricultural prices have reduced, not increased, hunger and malnutrition (Heady and Martin 2016).

That said, there obviously remain a very large number of poor and malnourished people and many of them are living in rural areas and the vast majority are depending on agriculture for their incomes, mostly as small farmers. The dire situation of developing countries' farmers has been caused at least partially by policies in the past which were said to be "urban biased", that is, favoring urban interests and at the detriment of rural farmers through (implicit) taxes—and a lack of (public and private) investment in agriculture (Lipton 1977; Krueger et al. 1992; Bezemer and Heady 2008).

There are a variety of explanations for the urban bias in developing countries as we have explained in Chap. 4. Urban consumers, when hit by a negative relative income shock, such as an increase in food prices, will react through demonstrations and other ways of pressuring government (Swinnen 1994).[10] Since they are concentrated in cities and are easier to mobilize (lower transportation and lower organization and communication costs) than dispersed farmers in distant rural areas, they may receive disproportionate attention and policy favors from policy-makers (Olson 1965).[11]

It appears that a similar urban bias effect played a role in drawing reactions and policy attention from international organizations and policy-makers. As we have documented, before 2006 there was little attention to the plight of poor farmers suffering from low prices and low productivity in policy-makers' priorities and agendas.

The high and volatile prices from 2007 to 2008 onward changed this. The spikes in food prices led to urban protests, and, in a number of cases, these demonstrations turned violent and created political instability (Cohen and Garret 2010). Hendrix and Brinkman (2013) document that following the increase in food prices, the number and the severity of conflicts experienced the largest year-to-year increase since the end of the Cold War. Probably the most documented case was the political unrest in the Middle East and Northern Africa. Maystadt et al. (2014) show that food price spikes were an important factor in triggering the unrest.

The price spikes also captured the attention of global policy-makers and donors. As soon as urban protests reached the streets, international organizations have reacted much like local politicians and paid a disproportionate amount of attention to the problems of urban consumers. While part of this shift in global policy attention may have been a direct result of information reaching policy-makers and donors through their own channels, or various reports, it appears that global mass media also have played

---

[10] This shift in policy attention reflects the relative income effect, which is widely observed to be a determinant of food and trade policy (see Chap. 2). When economic conditions change, government attention will typically shift from one social group (or economic sector) to another depending on how they are (relatively) affected, that is, who is benefiting and losing from the change.

[11] The organization cost argument was made first by Olson (1965) and has been applied to agricultural and food policy by, for example, Anderson and Hayami (1986) and Gardner (1987).

an important role in drawing reactions and policy attention from international organizations and global policy-makers.

The 2007–2008 price spikes, and the ensuing urban consumer unrests, created major "media events". Local media reports on urban protests were picked up by international mass media, paying a disproportionate amount of attention to the problems of urban consumers, compared to the long-run hunger and poverty problems among the rural population. Thus, while for many years experts pointed at the low level of investment in developing country agriculture as a source of poverty and food security, it was only after the "food crisis" that media attention increased and that policy-makers worldwide put rural poverty and underinvestment in agriculture on their priority list. Donor funding has followed.

While most international organizations changed their message on how food policies affect food security, their policy prescriptions of how to address food security and poverty problems have been relatively consistent. While there is a significant shift in the attention to food consumer concerns and in the emphasis of rural households as net food consumers, as well as on some specific policies (e.g. input vs. export subsidies, biofuels, etc.), there is much consensus on key structural policies, such as the need for public and private investments in agriculture to improve infrastructure, institutions, and rural factor markets—thereby reducing costs for farmers and lowering prices for consumers—empowering small farmers, enhancing value chains, and the importance of safety nets for consumers.[12]

In summary, there is a clear link between the movements of international food prices and changes in media attention, in the priorities on the global development agenda and in the targets of donor funding. The "food crisis" acted as a catalyst of attention on long-standing issues related to food security and agricultural production, which were made particularly salient by the fact that urban consumers—whose voice is typically heard the most by mass media and policy-makers—were hit the hardest by the spikes in food prices.

---

[12] In addition, the organizations have maintained their views on issues on which they differ in opinion. For example, organizations like the World Bank, OECD, FAO, and IFPRI have continued to emphasize the importance of trade liberalization and of concluding the Doha Round both before and after 2006, while NGOs, such as Oxfam and ActionAid, have continued to recommend the cut of rich country subsidies and the importance of government regulation and protection of poor countries' agri-food markets (Swinnen et al. 2011).

What is therefore remarkable in this story is that, despite the fact that rural malnutrition and poverty of farmers and low agricultural productivity in developing countries has been a major problem for a long time, it may have been an "urban (consumer) crisis" that helped to put poor farmers' situation on top of the agenda. Pressure from urban interests led to a surge in attention to food security issues and, somewhat paradoxically, to the problems of poor farmers.

Hence, food price spikes may have succeeded where others have failed in the past: to put the problems of poor and hungry farmers on the policy agenda and to induce development policies and donor strategies to help them.

References

Aksoy, M.A., and B. Hoekman. 2010. *Food Prices and Rural Poverty*. Washington, DC: World Bank.

Aldashev, G., and T. Verdier. 2010. Goodwill Bazaar: NGO Competition and Giving to Development. *Journal of Development Economics* 91: 48–63.

Aldenhoff, F.-O. 2007. Are Economic Forecasts of the International Monetary Fund Politically Biased? A Public Choice Analysis. *Review of International Organizations* 2: 239–260.

Anderson, K., and Y. Hayami. 1986. *The Political Economy of Agricultural Protection: East Asia in International Perspective*. London: Allen and Unwin.

Andreoni, J., and A.A. Payne. 2003. Do Government Grants to Private Charities Crowd Out Giving or Fund-Raising? *American Economic Review* 93: 792–812.

Bezemer, D., and D. Headey. 2008. Agriculture, Development, and Urban Bias. *World Development* 36 (8): 1342–1364.

Chau, N.H., and M. Huysentruyt. 2006. Nonprofits and Public Good Provision: A Contest Based on Compromises. *European Economic Review* 50: 1909–1935.

Cohen, M.J., and J.L. Garrett. 2010. The Food Price Crisis and Urban Food (In) Security. *Environment and Urbanization* 22: 467–482.

Cottle, S. and Nolan, D. (2007). Global humanitarianism and the changing aid-media field: 'Everyone was dying for footage'. Journalism Studies 8: 862–878.

Dreher, A., J.-E. Sturm, and J. Vreeland. 2009. Development Aid and International Politics: Does Membership on the UN Security Council Influence World Bank Decisions? *Journal of Development Economics* 88: 1–18.

T. Eisensee, D. Stromberg, (2007) News Droughts, News Floods, and U. S. Disaster Relief. The Quarterly Journal of Economics 122 (2):693–728

FAO. 2005. Agriculture Commodity Prices Continue Long-Term Decline, *FAO Newsroom*. http://www.fao.org/newsroom/EN/news/2005/89721/index. html.

166   J. SWINNEN

———. 2012. *The State of Food Insecurity in the World 2012.* Rome: FAO.

Gardner, B.L. 1987. Causes of U.S. Farm Commodity Programs. *Journal of Political Economy* 95 (2): 290–310.

Global Policy Forum. 2013. *Global Policy Forum – Financing of the UN Programmes, Funds and Specialized Agencies.* Available at http://www.global-policy.org/un-finance/tables-and-charts-on-un-finance/the-financing-of-the-un-programmes-funds-and-specialized-agencies.html

Guariso, A., M.P. Squicciarini, and J. Swinnen. 2014. Food Price Shocks and the Political Economy of Global Agricultural and Development Policy. *Applied Economic Perspectives and Policy* 36 (3): 387–415.

Hawkins, V. 2002. The Other Side of the CNN Factor: The Media and Conflict. *Journalism Studies* 3 (2): 225–240.

Headey, D. 2013. The Impact of the Global Food Crisis on Self-Assessed Food Security. *World Bank Economic Review* 27 (1): 1–27.

Headey, D.D., and W.J. Martin. 2016. The Impact of Food Prices on Poverty and Food Security. *Annual Review of Resource Economics* 8: 329–351.

Hendrix, C., and H. Brinkman. 2013. Food Insecurity and Conflict Dynamics: Causal Linkages and Complex Feedbacks. *Stability: International Journal of Security & Development* 2 (2): 1–18.

International Food Policy Research Institute (IFPRI). 2008. REPORT IFPRI Annual Report 2007–2008.

Jacoby, H.G. 2013. *Food Prices, Wages, and Welfare in Rural India*, Policy Research Working Paper 6412, World Bank, Washington, DC.

Jakobson, P. V. (2000). Focus on the CNN effect misses the point: the real media impact on conflict management is invisible and indirect. Journal of Peace Research 37: 131–143.

Jill J. McCluskey, Johan Swinnen, Thijs Vandemoortele, (2015) You get what you want: A note on the economics of bad news. Information Economics and Policy 30:1–5

Kim, J. S. (2005). Media Coverage and Foreign Assistance: The Effects of U.S. Media Coverage on the Distribution of U.S. Official Development Assistance (ODA) to Recipient Countries. Washington, DC: Georgetown Public Policy Institute.

Krueger, A.O., M. Schiff, and A. Valdes. 1992. The Political Economy of Agricultural Protection in Developing Countries. In *A World Bank comparative study*. Baltimore: Johns Hopkins University Press.

Lipton, M. 1977. *Why Poor People Stay Poor: A Study of Urban Bias in World Development.* London: Temple Smith.

Matthias Heinz, Johan Swinnen, (2015) Media slant in economic news: A factor 20. Economics Letters 132:18–20

Maystadt, J.F., J.F.T. Tanb, and C. Breisinger. 2014. Does Food Security Matter for Transition in Arab Countries? *Food Policy* 46: 106–115.

CRISES, MEDIA, AND AGRICULTURAL DEVELOPMENT POLICY 167

McCluskey, J. J. and Swinnen, J. F. M. (2004). Political economy of the media and consumer perceptions of biotechnology. American Journal of Agricultural Economics 86: 1230–1237.

McCluskey, J.J., and J.F.M. Swinnen. 2010. Media Economics and the Political Economy of Information. In *The Oxford Handbook of Government and Business*, ed. D. Coen, W. Grant, and G. Wilson. Oxford: Oxford University Press.

Mullainathan, S., and A. Shleifer. 2005. The Market for News. *American Economic Review* 95: 1031–1053.

OECD. 2013. *OECD Statistics – Creditor Reporting System*. Available at http://stats.oecd.org/Index.aspx?QueryId=33364. Accessed June 2014.

Olson, M. 1965. *The Logic of Collective Action*. New Haven: Yale University Press.

Oxfam UK. 2011. Food Prices at All Time High "Should Ring Alarm Bells", 4 February 2011. http://www.oxfam.org.uk/applications/blogs/pressoffice/2011/02/04/food-prices-at-all-time-high-%E2%80%9Cshould-ring-alarm-bells%E2%80%9D-oxfam/newsblog.

Ravallion, M. 2013. *How Long Will It Take to Lift One Billion People Out of Poverty?* Policy Research Working Paper 6325, World Bank, Washington, DC.

Sadoulet, E., and A. De Janvry. 1995. *Quantitative Development Policy Analysis (Vol. 5)*. Baltimore: Johns Hopkins University Press.

Swinnen, J. 1994. A Positive Theory of Agricultural Protection. *American Journal of Agricultural Economics* 76 (1): 1–14.

———. 2011. The Right Price of Food. *Development Policy Review* 29 (6): 667–688.

———. 2013. Factor Markets: Comparative Analysis of Factor Markets for Agriculture Across Member States. Some Findings & Implications (No. 152393). International Agricultural Trade Research Consortium.

Swinnen, J.F.M., and N. Francken. 2006. Summits, Riots and Media Attention: The Political Economy of Information on Trade and Globalization. *The World Economy* 29: 637–654.

Swinnen, J., and P. Squicciarini. 2012. Mixed Messages on Prices and Food Security. *Science* 335 (6067): 405–406.

Swinnen, J., P. Squicciarini, and T. Vandemoortele. 2011. The Food Crisis, Mass Media and the Political Economy of Policy Analysis and Communication. *European Review of Agricultural Economics* 38 (3): 409–426.

Timmer, C.P. 1986. *Getting Prices Right: The Scope and Limits of Agriculture Price Policy*. New York: Cornell University Press.

Timmer, C.P., W.P. Falcon, and S.R. Pearson. 1983. *Food Policy Analysis*. Baltimore: Johns Hopkins University Press.

UNDP. 2005. *Human Development Report 2005*. United Nations, New York.

Van Belle, D. A., Rioux, J. and Potter, D. M. (2004). Media, Bureaucracies, and Foreign Aid: A Comparative Analysis of the United States, the United Kingdom, Canada, France and Japan. New York: Palgrave Macmillan.

Vaubel, R., A. Dreher, and U. Soylu. 2007. Staff Growth in International Organizations: A Principal-Agent Problem? *Public Choice* 133: 275–295.

Verpoorten, M., A. Arora, N. Stoop, and J.F.M. Swinnen. 2013. Self-Reported Food Insecurity in Africa During the Food Price Crisis. *Food Policy* 39: 51–63.

World Bank. 2013. *World Development Indicators 2013*. Available at http://databank.worldbank.org/data/. Accessed June 2014.

CHAPTER 10

Food Standards

10.1 Introduction

Standards to prevent adulterations and frauds have existed as long as products have been exchanged and traded. The addition of water in wine or in milk to increase the volume has been documented throughout history and across the globe. However, in recent years, standards have increased rapidly, both geographically and in addressing new concerns. Production and trade are increasingly regulated through stringent public and private standards on quality, safety, nutritional, environmental, and ethical and social aspects. As an illustration of the growth of standards in agriculture and food markets, Fig. 10.1 shows the rapid growth of SPS notifications to the WTO since the mid-1990s. Food standards have spread through trade and foreign investments[1] and change the way trade and global value chains are organized (McCullough et al. 2008; Swinnen and Maertens 2007; Yueng et al. 2017).

The rise and spread of standards has triggered vigorous debates on the impacts on international trade and development. An important critique is

---

[1] The growth of foreign direct investment (FDI) has been triggered by several factors, including a wave of investment liberalizations in the past 20 years and strong economic growth in emerging and developing countries. A well-documented form of FDI is the so-called 'supermarket revolution' as large retail chains increasingly invested in emerging and developing countries (Dries et al. 2004; Reardon et al. 2003).

© The Author(s) 2018   169
J. Swinnen, *The Political Economy of Agricultural and Food Policies*,
Palgrave Studies in Agricultural Economics and Food Policy,
https://doi.org/10.1057/978-1-137-50102-8_10

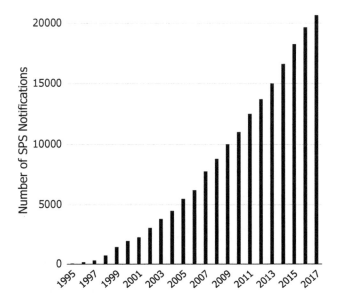

Fig. 10.1 The growth of food standards: SPS notifications to WTO (total number). (Source: Own calculations based on data from WTO)

that standards are (non-tariff) trade barriers.[2] As international trade agreements such as the WTO have contributed to a global reduction in tariffs, it is argued that countries have turned to new instruments to shield their domestic markets from foreign competition. However, others have disputed this. Convergence (or not) of standards is at the heart of recent trade negotiations such as CETA, TTIP, and so on.[3]

As other policies discussed in Chaps. 8, 9, 10, 11, 12 and 13, standards may enhance aggregate welfare, but they may also be set at suboptimal levels, causing welfare losses. The introduction of a standard may create winners and losers in society as its effects can differ for consumers and producers, and even within consumer and producer groups.

---

[2] For a discussion on the development and poverty effects, see Beghin et al. (2015), Maertens and Swinnen (2009) and Swinnen et al. (2015).

[3] Many studies argue that standards are non-tariff barriers to trade that protect domestic producers (Barrett 1994; Sykes 1995; Thilmany and Barrett 1997; Schleich 1999; Barrett and Yang 2001; Anderson et al. 2004; Fisher and Serra 2000; Sturm 2006; Sheldon 2012). Other authors have argued that standards are not necessarily protectionist (Tian 2003; Maertens and Swinnen 2007; Marette and Beghin 2010; Swinnen and Vandemoortele 2011).

These differential effects will determine preferences of different interest groups who will try to influence the government in the standard-setting process. While there is an extensive literature on the political economy of regulation and trade policy, only recently has some work been done on the political economy of public standards to explain why standards are set at certain levels, and how this affects trade (Anderson et al. 2004; Li and Beghin 2014; Li et al. 2017; Swinnen and Vandemoortele 2008, 2009, 2011).

A key finding in this literature is that lobbying of farmers, firms, and consumers may lead to standards being set "too low" or "too high" in the political equilibrium, depending, among other things, on relative costs of compliance and the benefits for consumers or companies (Swinnen and Vandemoortele 2008, 2011). Kerr (2009) also argues that "political precaution" may be an important factor in overregulation. Standards may both stimulate trade ("catalysts") or reduce trade ("barriers"). Hence the political economy analyses yield nuanced results on the protectionist impact of standards. Dynamic political economy effects may change the welfare effects of standards over time with potentially important persistence of suboptimal standards.

10.2 Efficiency and Equity Effects

To illustrate the equity and efficiency effect of standards, consider a case where standards[4] generate efficiency gains by solving (or reducing) externalities or asymmetric information problems, but they also involve

---

[4]The literature has adopted different modeling assumptions depending on which product or production process characteristic (safety, quality, social and environmental effects, etc.) is regulated by the standard. *Safety* standards, which guarantee safety characteristics, for example, by prohibiting dangerous substances in a product, are analyzed by incorporating risk in (expected) utility and/or profit functions (Cook and Fraser 2008; Swinnen and Vandemoortele 2009), based on the literature on product warranties (Cooper and Ross 1985; Emons 1988). *Quality* standards ensure characteristics concerning consumer preferences about aspects of nutritional value, taste, size, life span, performance, and so on. The literature on minimum quality standards (Ronnen 1991; Boom 1995; Crampes and Hollander 1995; Jeanneret and Verdier 1996; Valletti 2000) uses a vertical differentiation framework (Spence 1976; Mussa and Rosen 1978; Tirole 1988) in which consumers are heterogeneous in their willingness to pay for quality/standards. Standards that aim at regulating *social and environmental issues* such as the prohibition of child labor and the limitation of carbon dioxide emissions, are usually modeled as having an impact on externalities (Copeland and Taylor 1995; Anderson et al. 2004; Fisher and Serra 2000; Swinnen and Vandemoortele 2008, 2009).

172   J. SWINNEN

implementation costs.[5] Under these assumptions, standards can create welfare gains but also involve rent redistribution between different interest groups. The standard yields (positive) efficiency gains, that is, the value that consumers attach to the reduced informational asymmetries and an increase in the equilibrium price due to increased demand and the cost of implementing the standard. The impact on producer profits is a combination of a (positive) increase in revenue, due to increased consumption, and a second (negative) producer's *cost* of *implementing* the standard. The net impact depends on the relative size of the increase in revenue and the implementation cost.

The impact on aggregate welfare depends on the trade-off between the efficiency gain and increased cost due to the standard. The socially optimal level of the standard is where the marginal efficiency gain for consumers equals the marginal cost for producers. The magnitude of the rent distribution effect depends on how the standard affects demand and supply, and on elasticities and implementation costs. Moreover, when producers differ in terms of implementation costs, standards will also cause rent distribution among producers.

Figure 10.2 illustrates these effects. S_0 and D_0 represent the pre-standard supply and demand functions[6] and p_0 and x_0 the equilibrium price and consumption (which equals production in this closed economy). The introduction of a standard s shifts supply and demand functions to S_1 and D_1. The new equilibrium price and quantity are p_1 and x_1. The total price effect $(p_1 - p_0)$ is the result of rising prices due to the growth in demand $(p_D - p_0)$ and a cost increase $(p_S - p_0 = p_1 - p_D)$.

In the case illustrated by Fig. 10.1, the effect of the growth in demand (represented by the vertical shift in the demand curve) is stronger than the increasing cost effect (represented by the vertical shift in the supply curve).

---

[5] In general, a standard can be interpreted as a prohibition to use a cheaper technology (Swinnen and Vandemoortele 2011). Examples are the prohibition of an existing technology (e.g. child labor) or of a technology that has not yet been used but that could potentially lower costs (e.g. genetic modification (GM) technology). Most studies therefore assume that standards raise domestic production costs (Leland 1979; Ronnen 1991; Valletti 2000). In an open economy, the production costs of foreign producers (interested in) exporting to the standard-imposing country may also rise if the standard is also imposed and enforced on imported goods (Fisher and Serra 2000). The effect on prices depends on various factors such as demand and supply elasticities and trade.

[6] The figure can also be interpreted as from a lower to a higher standard.

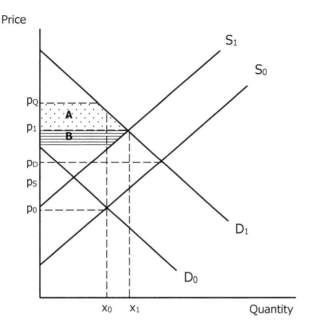

Fig. 10.2 Impact of standards in closed economy

As a consequence, consumption and production increase ($x_1 > x_0$) and both producers and consumers gain. Consumer surplus increases by area A_1 and producer surplus increases by area B_1. Total welfare increases by area A_1+B_1.

It is easy to illustrate that with different elasticities of supply and demand, the size of the effects would be different. With different shifts in (or rotations of) the supply and demand curves, the sign of the effects could be different—in particular if the cost effect is larger than the demand growth effect, the impact on welfare would be negative.

So far, I focused on two 'interest groups': domestic 'producers' and 'consumers'. Domestic producers gain (lose) if the price increase (due to higher demand with the standard) is higher than the cost increase. Consumers gain if the positive utility effect (from reduced uncertainty) is larger than the price effect from the standard, and vice versa. This simplified model may apply to various stages of the supply chain since the general terms 'producers' and 'consumers' may also point at different actors depending on which stage of the supply chain is under analysis. For example, at the processing stage, 'consumers' are retailers who source products from processors (the 'producers'). At the retail stage, the retailers are 'producers' who sell products to the final consumer.

However, other interest groups may be affected by the standard. For example, standards may require costly enforcement and monitoring by governments. Insofar that these costs are not born by producers and/or consumers, taxpayers may try to influence the government's standard-setting behavior.

Additionally, some interest groups may be foreign. Foreign supply chain participants may have an interest in influencing the standard-setting process, for instance, if they experience difficulties in meeting the importing country's standard. Moreover, if the standard-imposing country is a large economy that imports a significant share of that product's world market, its standard may have an impact on the world price and affect other countries' terms of trade (Baldwin 2000). Hence, foreign interest groups may have additional motives, be it as producers or consumers, to influence the standard-setting of a large country. These terms-of-trade effects could also influence the political economy in foreign countries, potentially through the World Trade Organization (WTO).[7]

Interest groups other than supply chain participants may also try to influence a country's standard-setting process. For example, for standards targeting externalities, NGOs may take an interest in the standard's implementation. Depending on the type of externality, that is, social versus environmental or local versus global, different domestic or international NGOs may be involved. An example of standards where many actors are involved in lobbying is GMO regulations. Multinational agribusiness companies and local and international NGOs have lobbied many governments on this issue.

---

[7] These issues are related to harmonization and mutual recognition of standards which—due to space limitations—we do not discuss in this review. We refer the reader to, among others, Baldwin (2000), Bagwell and Staiger (2001), Hensen and Wilson (2005), Costinot (2008), and Chen and Mattoo (2008) for analyses of these issues.

10.3 Government Decision-Making on Standards

Because of the distributional effects of standards, various groups in society have a vested interest in trying to influence governments' decision processes on standards. When interest groups have differing lobbying strengths, the political equilibrium will generally differ from the social optimum. In that case, the rent transfer affects the standard set by the government. Studies in this field have typically assumed that governments maximize a political objective function such as a political support function (e.g. Li et al. 2017) or a Grossman and Helpman (GH) (1994)-type protection-for-sale model which consists of a weighted sum of lobby contributions from interest groups and social welfare (e.g. Swinnen and Vandemoortele 2011).[8]

A key conclusion is that both 'over-standardization' or 'under-standardization' may result from the lobbying process. If producers are more influential than consumers over-standardization results when producers' profits increase with a higher standard and in under-standardization otherwise. In this case higher profits for producers are more likely when the standard's price effect is large and when the implementation cost is small. On the other hand, the resulting under-standardization reduces the negative effect of the standard on producers' profits, and producers benefit from under-standardization. (And vice versa when consumers are more influential than producers.)

Kerr (2009) and Yueng et al. (2017) explain that standards may be set too high because of additional political incentives where governments feel forced to respond to perceived risks of social groups, leading to an outcome they refer to as "political precaution". Paarlberg (2001) has also emphasized this factor in his book *The Politics of Precaution* when trying to explain differences in GM regulations.

Hence, the political equilibrium standard may be either too high or too low from a social welfare point of view. Influential lobby groups may push for both more stringent or less stringent standards depending on the relative magnitude of the price effect compared to the implementation cost (for producers) or the efficiency gain (for consumers).

---

[8] There are some differences in specific assumptions. For example, Swinnen and Vandemoortele (2011) assume that both consumers and producers are politically organized and that they lobby simultaneously. This assumption differs from Anderson et al. (2004) who assume that consumers are not organized—or do not effectively lobby. Foreign producers and consumers are typically assumed to be politically unorganized.

10.4 Development and Pro-Standard and Anti-Standard Coalitions

These results may explain the empirically observed positive relationship between standards and economic development. It is often argued that this relationship simply reflects consumer preferences. While our political economy analysis confirms that preferences (in the form of the efficiency gains) play a role, it also suggests other factors which affect the relationship between development and the political economy of public standards, causing different standards between developing ('poor') and developed ('rich') countries.

First, and most obvious, higher income levels are typically associated with higher consumer preferences for quality and safety standards as reflected in higher efficiency gains.[9] Second, the quality of institutions for enforcement of contracts and public regulations are positively correlated with development. Better institutions implies better enforcement and control of standards. While poor countries, with low wages and lower land rents, may have a cost advantage in the production of raw materials, better institutions of rich countries lower the marginal increase in production costs caused by standards. Third, a lower increase in production costs could also result from higher education and skills of producers, better public infrastructure, easier access to finance, and so on.

An additional factor may be the different organization and structure of the media in rich and poor countries. Mass media is the main source of information for many people. Commercial media is more likely to highlight potential food risks (McCluskey and Swinnen 2004, McCluskey et al. 2016). The cost of media information is higher and government control of the media is stronger in poor countries. Therefore, the media structure and information provision are likely to induce a more pro-standard attitude in rich countries than in poor, as increased access to media increases attention to risks and negative implications of low standards (Curtis et al. 2008).

---

[9] This is consistent with international survey evidence on consumer preferences for GM standards. Rich country consumers are generally more opposed to GM than poor country consumers. Consumers in rich countries have less to gain from biotech-induced farm productivity improvements compared to developing country consumers who have much to gain from cheaper food (McCluskey et al. 2016). This argument is also consistent with empirical observations that consumers from developed countries have generally higher preferences for other applications of biotechnology, such as medical applications (Costa-Font et al. 2008; Hossain et al. 2003) which have more (potential) benefits for richer consumers.

A related element is that poor countries have a larger rural/urban population ratio. Asymmetric information may be more important for urban consumers. For example, McCluskey et al. (2003) find that people associated with agriculture are more in favor of GM crops than urban consumers because they have a better idea of the amount of pesticides used on non-GM crops than urban consumers and hence of the benefits from GM (such as insect resistant crops).

In combination these factors are likely to induce a shift of the political equilibrium from low standards to high standards with development as the mechanisms identified here may result in a pro-standard coalition of consumers and producers in rich countries. Consumers may derive large efficiency gains from a standard, while producers incur only moderate increases in costs. In contrast, an anti-standard coalition may be present in poor countries if consumers are more concerned with low prices than with high quality (leading to small efficiency gains from a higher standard) while the implementation costs for producers (both in terms of production costs and transaction costs) may be large. Differences in asymmetric information may reinforce the positive relationship between standards and development.

10.5   STANDARDS AND TRADE

An important aspect of public standards which has attracted substantive attention is their potential use as 'protection in disguise' (Vogel 1995). The near explosion of standard-like NTMs in recent years brings the questions whether standards are non-tariff measures (NTMs) used for protectionist purposes, especially in the context of commitments to decrease or eliminate tariffs and expand imports under tariff-rate-quota schemes following multiple multilateral and preferential trade agreements (Bacchetta and Beverelli 2012). Much attention of trade economists focused on the potential or presumed protectionism of such standard-like NTMs. In fact, many studies on (the political economy of) standards in open economy models consider standards as protectionist instruments (Anderson et al. 2004; Fisher and Serra 2000; Sturm 2006).

Standards do affect trade. Only in very special circumstances would standards not affect trade: this is when the effect on domestic production exactly offsets the effect on consumption. However, the implicit comparison with tariffs in the trade debate is not entirely valid. In a small open economy, the socially optimal tariff level is zero. A positive tariff level constrains trade, is harmful to social welfare, and is by definition protectionist. However, the analogy to tariffs is not entirely valid. In a small open economy, the socially optimal tariff level is zero. A positive tariff level constrains trade, is harmful to social welfare, and is by definition protectionist. This is not necessarily the case for standards since this ignores the potential consumer or societal benefits induced by standards. The optimum standard in the presence of asymmetric information or externalities is more complex, and there is no simple relationship between the trade effects of a standard and the social optimum (Beghin 2013; Marette 2014; Marette and Beghin 2010; Sheldon 2012; Van Tongeren et al. 2009). This result however obviously does not imply that there are no political forces or protectionist elements in standards setting.

Standards may affect the comparative cost advantage between domestic and foreign producers, as standards may affect the production costs of foreign and domestic producers differently. Standards increase production cost advantages when they reinforce scale economies but not when they have a scale neutral impact or reinforce scale diseconomies. Differences in these effects induce different reactions to standards by domestic producers, but the effects are conditional. Producers oppose standards more (or support them less) if they have a comparative disadvantage and standards reinforce this, compared to when standards are scale neutral. The opposite holds when standards reduce the comparative disadvantage vis-à-vis foreign producers. Similarly, producers support standards more (or oppose less) if standards reinforce a comparative advantage—and vice versa.

These conceptual arguments imply that there is a need for empirical studies to identify whether standards are protectionist or not. However, for similar reasons, good empirical work in this area is difficult. The main reason is that it is very difficult to measure these effects if one wants to take into account the potential benefits of standards. Determining the socially optimum standard in the presence of asymmetric information or externalities is complex (see also Beghin (2013); Marette (2014), and Marette and Beghin (2010)). It depends, among others, on the relative ability of domestic and foreign industries to comply with the standard. Beghin et al. (2015) conclude that sorting out the protectionism of standard-like NTMs is complex once one moves beyond simple detection strategies. Policy prescriptions on standard-like NTMs depend on the particular context of the policies. In most situations, the trade impact of standard-like NTMs is not informative regarding their welfare impact, barring the absence of scientific basis for the policy (Baldwin 2000).[10]

In summary, political economy models which include both negative and positive aspects of standards yield nuanced/complex theoretical conclusions, and careful empirical analyses support such nuanced arguments and complex effects.

10.6 THE PERSISTENCE OF STANDARDS: DYNAMIC POLITICAL ECONOMICS

The arguments so far are based on static considerations. However, some of the most important political and economic aspects of standards related to their dynamic effects, have been much less studied. Dynamic economic and political aspects of standards can provide an explanation for different food standards and regulations in countries with similar levels of development, such as in the EU and the USA, and why such differences in standards may persist through history.[11]

In a dynamic framework, implementation costs depend on the current level of the standard and on previous standards because of past investments. Hence, differently from a static equilibrium, standards in the previous period will influence the optimal allocation of production and consumption, equilibrium price, and the optimal standard in the current period.

A key implication is that small or temporary variations in consumer preferences or implementation costs may determine long-term differences in standards. Once adopted, countries will tend to stick to the status quo in standards. Standards will persist because of changing producer or consumer interests. This hysteresis in regulation can be driven by protectionist

---

[10] Beghin et al. (2015) provide an overview of empirical studies and approaches to analyze the impact of standards on trade and welfare. An earlier review is by Maskus and Wilson (2001). Both reviews conclude that that stronger standards in developed countries may either diminish trade opportunities or expand market access for developing countries. Recent empirical studies also provide conflicting evidence. For example, Anders and Caswell (2009) find that US seafood safety standards had a negative impact on developing countries' exports to the USA, while Maertens and Swinnen (2009) document that horticultural exports from Africa to the EU increased strongly despite tightening standards over the past decade.

[11] I refer to Swinnen and Vandemoortele (2008, 2011); Swinnen et al. (2015) and Swinnen (2017) for more technical analysis and more details.

motives even if the initial standards were not introduced for protectionist reasons (Swinnen 2017).[12]

These differences in standards may even persist if the difference in consumer preference (or in implementation costs) is temporary. If producers in different countries have access to the same technology and face the same implementation costs, but there is a temporary difference in consumer preferences in one country, this may lead to long-term differences in standards: a so-called butterfly effect.

A well-documented case is how several food crises in the EU in the late 1990s had a huge impact on EU food safety and quality regulations, triggering much more stringent standards than before, and have contributed to the global spread of food standards—as reflected in, for example, Fig. 10.1 (see Swinnen et al. 2005, 2015 for details). Many people have argued that these shocks also shifted the public opinion in the EU against new technologies in general. For example, Paarlberg (2008) and Zilberman et al. argue that consumers on both sides of the Atlantic tend to dislike GM technology, but agribusiness lobbying has been much more pro-GM in the USA. In the longer run it may that as consumers live in different GM-food environments in the USA and the EU, they develop different preferences. Consumer attitudes with respect to biotechnology are likely to be endogenous. In countries where GM products are available consumer preferences may shift in favor of this technology, while inversely consumers may distrust GM technology more in countries where GM products have been banned.

10.7   Trade and Political Dynamics

Trade may reinforce this divergence. The reason is that producer preferences will change in a dynamic way once the standard is introduced. The standard will affect comparative advantages, and will thus in the longer run induce producers to support maintaining the standard in order to protect them from (cheaper) non-standard production. In this case, although the standards are introduced because of consumer demands,

---

[12] These arguments are related to studies on hysteresis in socio-economic behavior and policy. For example, Dixit (1989) shows that output price uncertainty leads to investment hysteresis for certain ranges of entry and exit costs. Path dependence in technical standards and technical lock-in by historical events can also be driven by network externalities, increasing returns to adoption, or learning by doing (Arthur 1989).

their persistence in the long run results from (a coalition of consumer and) producer demands. Hence, regulatory differences may be long-lasting if governments respond to pressures of domestic producers, creating hysteresis in standards (even if the initial cause of the difference is temporary).

Several empirical case studies document that there can be strong persistence of standards over time, and that the protectionist or welfare reducing effects of standards may increase over time. For example, Meloni and Swinnen (2013) show how stringent standards in the wine industry which were first set in France in response to pressure on wine growers in the early twentieth century further tightened over time in response to more "crises" in the wine sectors and later spread to the rest of Europe with integration of other wine producing countries in the EU. Meloni and Swinnen (2015, 2016) also document how the introduction of food standards in the mid-nineteenth century in response to the discovery by new scientific means of massive fraud and adulterations in food production led to different regulatory approaches in different countries. These regulations and standards persisted for a long time and influenced production processes and consumer preferences in the domestic industries. They show how, for example, in the case of the chocolate industry, these regulatory differences caused major trade conflicts later as the chocolate industries lobbied their governments to impose their own standards on foreign producers. Similarly, van Tongeren (2011) analyzes standards in the German and European beer markets and finds that centuries-old regulations still today have a major impact on the different evolutions of the German beer market. He shows how the 500-year-old German Purity Law was the reason for trade disputes in the late twentieth century.

In summary, dynamic political economy considerations may lead to persistence of this standard in the long run. Minor or even temporary differences in implementation costs or consumer preferences may lead to significantly different standards in the long run.

Does this mean that reversals in standards are not possible? Not necessarily. For example, Vogel (2003, p. 557) documents important historical shifts in the difference between consumer and environmental protection policies in the EU and USA: "[f]rom the 1960s through the mid 1980s American regulatory standards tended to be more stringent, comprehensive and innovative than in … the EU. However, since around 1990 … many important EU consumer and environmental regulations are now more precautionary than their American counterparts."

However, significant "shocks" to the political economy system may be required for such changes, that is, to move the political economy equilibrium to another equilibrium given the dynamic political and institutional constraints to overcome (Rausser et al. 2011). Shocks may come from both internal and external sources. An internal source is the sudden emergence of "crises". There are several examples how domestic crises have affected food standards. The first wave of modern public food safety and quality regulations were induced in the late nineteenth century by public outrages of consumers over the use of cheap and sometimes poisonous ingredients in food production (Meloni and Swinnen 2015, 2017). At the end of the twentieth century, the tightening public standards in food in the EU have followed food safety scandals in the late 1990s with consumers demanding better protection (McCluskey and Swinnen 2011). Also the introduction of various public regulations in China in the late 2000s followed the "milk scandal" where people died from consuming milk products with poisonous ingredients (Mo et al. 2012).

Another source of shocks is external. One example is the integration of countries with different standards through international agreements. This may either cause the removal of "inefficient standards" or the opposite: that inefficient standards are extended to other countries with international integration.

In summary, theory and historical evidence suggest that there is an important dynamic component to the political economy of food standards. Countries have introduced different standards to address consumer, producer, or environmental concerns. However, once these standards have been introduced, vested interests change after they made the investments. What was a cost for producers initially now becomes a potential instrument for market protection. International integration can both lead to the mitigation of inefficient standards and to a spread of such regulations, depending on the political equilibria.

References

Anders, S.M., and J.A. Caswell. 2009. Standards as Barriers Versus Standards as Catalysts: Assessing the Impact of HACCP Implementation on U.S. Seafood Imports. *American Journal of Agricultural Economics* 91 (2): 310–321.

Anderson, K., R. Damania, and L.A. Jackson. 2004. *Trade, Standards, and the Political Economy of Genetically Modified Food*, CEPR Discussion Papers 4526, C.E.P.R. Discussion Papers.

FOOD STANDARDS 183

Bacchetta, M., and C. Beverelli. 2012. Non-tariff Measures and the WTO, VoxEU. org, 31 July. http://www.voxeu.org/article/trade-barriers-beyond-tariffs-facts-and-challenges.

Bagwell, K., and R. Staiger. 2001. Domestic Policies, National Sovereignty and International Economic Institutions. *Quarterly Journal of Economics* 116 (2): 519–562.

Baldwin, R.E. 2000. Regulatory Protectionism, Developing Nations, and a Two-Tier World Trade System. In *Brookings Trade Forum*, ed. S. Collins and D. Rodrik, 237–293. Washington, DC: Brookings Institution Press.

Barrett, S. 1994. Strategic Environmental Policy and International Trade. *Journal of Public Economics* 54 (3): 325–338.

Barrett, C.B., and Y. Yang. 2001. Rational Incompatibility with International Product Standards. *Journal of International Economics* 54 (1): 171–191.

Beghin, J. 2013. *Nontariff Measures with Market Imperfections: Trade and Welfare Implications (Frontiers of Economics and Globalization, Volume 12)*. Bingley: Emerald.

Beghin, J., M. Maertens, and J. Swinnen. 2015. Non-Tariff Measures and Standards in Trade and Global Value Chains. *Annual Review of Resource Economics* 7: 425–450.

Boom, A. 1995. Asymmetric International Minimum Quality Standards and Vertical Differentiation. *The Journal of Industrial Economics* 43 (1): 101–119.

Brian Arthur, W. 1989. Competing Technologies, Increasing Returns, and Lock-In by Historical Events. *The Economic Journal* 99 (394): 116.

Chen, M.X., and A. Mattoo. 2008. Regionalism in Standards: Good or Bad for Trade? *Canadian Journal of Economics* 41 (3): 838–863.

Cook, D.C., and R.W. Fraser. 2008. Trade and Invasive Species Risk Mitigation: Reconciling WTO Compliance with Maximising the Gains from Trade. *Food Policy* 33 (2): 176–184.

Cooper, R., and W. Ross. 1985. Product Warranties and Double Moral Hazard. *RAND Journal of Economics* 16 (1): 103–113.

Copeland, B.R., and M.C. Taylor. 1995. Trade and Transboundary Pollution. *American Economic Review* 85 (4): 716–737.

Costa-Font, M., J.M. Gil, and W.B. Traill. 2008. Consumer Acceptance, Valuation of and Attitudes Towards Genetically Modified Food: Review and Implications for Food Policy. *Food Policy* 33: 99–111.

Costinot, A. 2008. A Comparative Institutional Analysis of Agreements on Product Standards. *Journal of International Economics* 75 (1): 197–213.

Crampes, C., and A. Hollander. 1995. Duopoly and Quality Standards. *European Economic Review* 39 (1): 71–82.

Curtis, K.R., J.J. McCluskey, and J. Swinnen. 2008. Differences in Global Risk Perceptions of Biotechnology and the Political Economy of the Media. *International Journal of Global Environmental Issues* 8 (1/2): 77–89.

184 J. SWINNEN

Dixit, Avinash. 1989. Entry and Exit Decisions Under Uncertainty. *Journal of Political Economy* 97 (3): 620–638.

Dries, L., T. Reardon, and J. Swinnen. 2004. The Rapid Rise of Supermarkets in Central and Eastern Europe: Implications for the Agrifood Sector and Rural Development. *Development Policy Review* 22 (5): 525–556.

Emons, Winand. 1988. Warranties, Moral Hazard, and the Lemons Problem. *Journal of Economic Theory* 46 (1): 16–33.

Fisher, R., and P. Serra. 2000. Standards and Protection. *Journal of International Economics* 52 (2): 377–400.

Grossman, G.M., and E. Helpman. 1994. Protection for Sale. *American Economic Review* 84 (4): 833–850.

Hensen, S., and J.S. Wilson, eds. 2005. *The WTO and Technical Barriers to Trade.* Cheltenham: Edward Elgar Publishing.

Hossain, F., B. Onyango, B. Schilling, W. Hallman, and A. Adelaja. 2003. Product Attributes, Consumer Benefits and Public Approval of Genetically Modified Foods. *International Journal of Consumer Studies* 27: 353–365.

Jeanneret, M., and T. Verdier. 1996. Standardization and Protection in a Vertical Differentiation Model. *European Journal of Political Economy* 12 (2): 253–271.

Kerr, W.A. 2009. Political Precaution, Pandemics and Protectionism. *The Estey Centre Journal of International Law and Trade Policy* 10 (2): 1.

Leland, H.E. 1979. Quacks, Lemons, and Licensing: A Theory of Minimum Quality Standards. *Journal of Political Economy* 87 (6): 1328–1346.

Li, Y., B. Xiong, and J. Beghin. 2017. The Political Economy of Food Standards Determination: International Evidence From Maximum Residue Limits. In *Nontariff Measures and International Trade*, ed. J. Beghin. Singapore: World Scientific Publishing.

Li, Yuan, and John C. Beghin. 2014. Protectionism Indices for Non-Tariff Measures: An Application to Maximum Residue Levels. *Food Policy* 45: 57–68.

Maertens, M., and J. Swinnen. 2007. Standards as Barriers and Catalysts for Trade and Poverty Reduction. *Journal of International Agricultural Trade and Development* 4 (1): 47–61.

———. 2009. Trade, Standards and Poverty: Evidence from Senegal. *World Development* 37 (1): 161–178.

Marette, S. 2014. *Non-Tariff Measures when Alternative Regulatory Tools can be Chosen.* Mimeo.

Marette, S., and J. Beghin. 2010. Are Standards Always Protectionist? *Review of International Economics* 18 (1): 179–192.

Maskus, K., and J.S. Wilson, eds. 2001. *Quantifying the Impact of Technical Barriers to Trade: Can It Be Done?* Ann Arbor: Michigan University Press.

McCluskey, J.J., and J. Swinnen. 2004. Political Economy of the Media and Consumer Perceptions of Biotechnology. *American Journal of Agricultural Economics* 8: 1230–1237.

FOOD STANDARDS   185

——. 2011 The Media and Food-Risk Perceptions: Science & Society Series on Food and Science. *EMBO Reports* 12 (7): 624–629.

McCluskey, Jill J., Kristine M. Grimsrud, Hiromi Ouchi, and Thomas I. Wahl. 2003. Consumer Response to Genetically Modified Food Products in Japan. *Agricultural and Resource Economics Review* 32 (02): 222–231.

McCullough, E., P. Pingali, and K. Stamoulis. 2008. *The Transformation of Agri-Food Systems: Globalization, Supply Chains and Smallholder Farmers*, 416. London: Earthscan Ltd..

McCluskey, Jill J., Nicholas Kalaitzandonakes, and Johan Swinnen. 2016. Media Coverage, Public Perceptions, and Consumer Behavior: Insights from New Food Technologies. *Annual Review of Resource Economics* 8 (1): 467–486.

Meloni, G., and J. Swinnen. 2013. The Political Economy of European Wine Regulations. *Journal of Wine Economics* 8 (3): 244–284.

——. 2015. Chocolate Regulations. In *The Economics of Chocolate*, ed. M.P. Squicciarini and J. Swinnen. Oxford: Oxford University Press.

——. 2016. *Bugs, Tariffs and Colonies: The Political Economy of the Wine Trade 1860–1970*.

——. 2017. Standards, Tariffs and Trade: The Rise and Fall of the Raisin Trade Between Greece and France in the Late 19th Century and the Definition of Wine.

Mo, D., J. Huang, X. Jia, H. Luan, S. Rozelle, and J. Swinnen. 2012. Checking into China's Cow Hotels: Have Policies Following the Milk Scandal Changed the Structure of the Dairy Sector? *Journal of Dairy Science* 95: 2282–2298.

Mussa, M., and S. Rosen. 1978. Monopoly and Product Quality. *Journal of Economic Theory* 18 (2): 301–317.

Paarlberg, R.L. 2001. *The Politics of Precaution: Genetically Modified Crops in Developing Countries*. Washington, DC: Intl Food Policy Res Inst.

Paarlberg, R. 2008. *Starved for Science. How Biotechnology Is Being Kept Out of Africa*. Cambridge, MA: Harvard University Press.

Rausser, G., J. Swinnen, and P. Zusman. 2011. *Political Power and Economic Policy: Theory, Analysis, and Empirical Applications*. Cambridge: Cambridge University Press.

Reardon, T., P.C. Timmer, C. Barrett, and J. Berdegué. 2003. The Rise of Supermarkets in Africa, Asia and Latin America. *American Journal of Agricultural Economics* 85 (5): 1140–1146.

Ronnen, U. 1991. Minimum Quality Standards, Fixed Costs, and Competition. *RAND Journal of Economics* 22 (4): 490–504.

Schleich, T. 1999. Environmental Quality with Endogenous Domestic and Trade Policies. *European Journal of Political Economy* 15 (1): 53–71.

Sheldon, I. 2012. North–South Trade and Standards: What Can General Equilibrium Analysis Tell Us? *World Trade Review* 11 (3): 376–389.

186   J. SWINNEN

Spence, M. 1976. Product Differentiation and Welfare. *American Economic Review* 66 (2): 407–414.

Sturm, D.M. 2006. Product Standards, Trade Disputes, and Protectionism. *Canadian Journal of Economics* 39 (2): 564–581.

Swinnen, Johan F.M., Jill McCluskey, and Nathalie Francken. 2005. Food Safety, the Media, and the Information Market. *Agricultural Economics* 32 (s1): 175–188.

Swinnen, J. 2017. Some Dynamic Aspects of food Standards. *American Journal of Agricultural Economics* 99 (2): 321–338.

Swinnen, J., and M. Maertens. 2007. Globalization, Privatization, and Vertical Coordination in Food Value Chains in Developing and Transition Countries. *Agricultural Economics* 37 (2): 89–102.

Swinnen, J., and T. Vandemoortele. 2008. The Political Economy of Nutrition and Health Standards in Food Markets. *Applied Economic Perspectives and Policy* 30 (3): 460–468.

———. 2009. Are Food Safety Standards Different From Other Food Standards? A Political Economy Perspective. *European Review of Agricultural Economics* 36 (4): 507–523.

———. 2011. Trade and the Political Economy of Food Standards. *Journal of Agricultural Economics* 62 (2): 259–280.

Swinnen, J., K. Deconinck, T. Vandemoortele, and A. Vandeplas, eds. 2015. *Quality Standards, Value Chains and International Development*. New York/ USA: Cambridge University Press.

Sykes, A. O. 1995. *Product Standards for Internationally Integrated Goods Markets*. Washington, DC: The Brookings Institution.

Thilmany, D.D., and C.B. Barrett. 1997. Regulatory Barriers in an Integrating World Food Market. *Review of Agricultural Economics* 19 (1): 91–107.

Tian, H. 2003. Eco-labelling Scheme, Environmental Protection, and Protectionism. *Canadian Journal of Economics* 36 (3): 608–633.

Tirole, J. 1988. *The Theory of Industrial Organization*. Cambridge, MA: MIT Press.

Valletti, T.M. 2000. Minimum Quality Standards Under Cournot Competition. *Journal of Regulatory Economics* 18 (3): 235–245.

Van Tongeren, F. 2011. Standards and International Trade Integration: A Historical Review of the German 'Reinheitsgebot. In *The Economics of Beer*, ed. J.F.M. Swinnen. Oxford: Oxford University Press.

Van Tongeren, F., J. Beghin, and S. Marette. 2009. *A Cost-Benefit Framework for the Assessment of Non-tariff Measures in Agro-Food Trade*.

Vogel, D. 1995. *Trading Up: Consumer and Environmental Regulation in a Global Economy*. Cambridge, MA: Harvard University Press.

———. 2003. The Hare and the Tortoise Revisited: The New Politics of Consumer and Environmental Regulation in Europe. *British Journal of Political Science* 33: 557–580.

Yeung, M.T., W.A. Kerr, B. Coomber, M. Lantz, and A. McConnell. 2017. *Declining International Cooperation on Pesticide Regulation: Frittering Away Food Security*. Cham: Springer.

CHAPTER 11

Public Investments in Agricultural and Food Research

11.1 Introduction

Another important policy area is the public investment of governments in research and development (R&D) of innovations in agriculture and food. Also in this policy area, government decisions affect efficiency and equity simultaneously and this will again influence the government's decisions.

Public investment in agricultural research is an important source of productivity growth. There have been significant increases in public R&D when economies have developed (see, e.g. Figs. 4.4 and 4.5 in Chap. 4), and there are important shifts in public R&D spending during economic development, with developing and emerging countries' share in global public R&D spending increasing—and China, India, and Brazil now out-spending the USA. However, despite these investments and high social rates of return to public agricultural research investments (PARI), many experts argue that there is significant underinvestment in research in both poor and rich countries (Alston 2018; Alston et al. 2009; Huffman and Evenson 1992; Pardey et al. 2016; Pardey and Smith 2017; Ruttan 1982).

The political economy question which is addressed in this chapter is obvious: why is there underinvestment in both rich and poor countries if these investments have such high social rates of returns?

© The Author(s) 2018
J. Swinnen, *The Political Economy of Agricultural and Food Policies*,
Palgrave Studies in Agricultural Economics and Food Policy,
https://doi.org/10.1057/978-1-137-50102-8_11

189

190   J. SWINNEN

11.2   Spillover Effects of Public Research

One political economy explanation of the underinvestment by governments is spillover effects (or externalities) in a policy environment where government research investments in one country (state) affects other countries (states). Research has both public and private good characteristics, as some of the benefits of research expenditures can be captured by specific groups while other results spill over to other groups or countries (Cornes et al. 1986). This property of research affects governments' incentives to invest in research (Khanna et al. 1994).

For example, if one country that produces grain invests in the development of improved grain varieties, grain producers and consumers in other countries can benefit from these R&D expenditures if the improved varieties come on the market. Spillover effects can thus induce free-riding behavior by governments.

This aspect has been emphasized by scholars which analyzed public R&D expenditures by state-level institutions in the USA (including the land grant universities) with spillover effects to other states (Rose-Ackerman and Evenson 1985; Huffman and Miranowski 1981). However it obviously also applies to the international spillovers of R&D and its outcomes. There can also be spillover effects between private sector research investments and government research investments which may lead to suboptimal public research investments (Ulrich et al. 1986).

Governments in one country or state will invest less than optimal since they pay for all the costs while part of the benefits are reaped by other countries (states) or a specific part of the private sector. Or, inversely, governments may think that they can reap (some of) the benefits from other countries or companies' investments without having to bear the (fill) costs of research investments.

11.3   Distributional Effects of Public Research Investment

A different political economy explanation draws on the distributional effects of research investments—similar in logic to the political economy of food standards (Chap. 10) and land reforms (Chap. 12). While society as a whole may gain from public research, the welfare of specific groups, such as consumers, producers, and other interest groups, such as input supply firms, may be differently affected by the research effects, and these

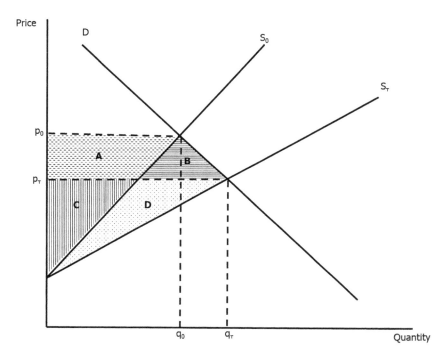

Fig. 11.1 Welfare and distributional effects of public research in a closed economy

interest groups may thus have different preferences for the level of research investments. Lobbying by these interest groups may then lead to suboptimal investment levels (Baland and Kotwal 1998; de Gorter et al. (1992); de Gorter and Zilberman (1990); Gardner (1989); Rausser (1982, 1992)).

To illustrate these distributional effects and show how they may differ between rich and poor countries and between open and closed markets it is useful to use a simple conceptual model of the impact of PARI. Figure 11.1 presents a graphical analysis of the impact of PARI which improves agricultural productivity in a closed economy.[1] D and S_0 represent the demand and supply curves, respectively. A market clearing price P_0 is paid by

---

[1] For a more complex model, with more inputs on consumer and producer effects, see Alston (2018).

consumers and received by producers. Domestic consumption and production are at q on the horizontal axis.

Now consider the effects of PARI which increases agricultural productivity and shifts the supply curve to S_τ. The market price falls to P_τ. Consumers benefit since they can consume more ($q_\tau > q_0$) and at a lower price ($P_\tau < P_0$). The increase in consumer surplus is area A + B. It is obvious from Fig. 11.1 that consumers always benefit from PARI in a closed economy.

The net effect on producers is less obvious because they are affected by two (opposing) effects: they benefit from lower costs due to increased productivity but they lose from declining prices. In Fig. 11.1 the net effect on producer surplus is area D – A (as the pre-research producer surplus was A + B and their post-research surplus is C + D). Whether D – A is positive or negative depends on the elasticity of the supply and demand functions. We will return to this below.

The general implication is that this example illustrates how research affects not just the aggregate welfare but also the distribution of income *within* an economy. Clearly in the case illustrated by Fig. 11.1, consumers will support a government when it proposes to invest in public research. Producers will be less supportive and may even oppose public spending if D is smaller than A. These distributional effects thus translate in heterogeneous preferences for research investments, and in a political system where interest groups can influence government's decisions, this will thus affect political decision-making.

Governments will balance the political costs and benefits of diverging from the interest groups' private optimum level of research. If some interest groups oppose social optimal investment in research because of income distribution effects, governments may underinvest in public research. De Gorter and Swinnen (1998) have shown that as negative income effects typically are a stronger driver of political actions (similar to the relative income effect in determining taxes and subsidies—see Chaps. 3, 4, 5 and 6), in general, with unequal income distributional effects, a government maximizing political support will underinvest in public research.

11.4   Economic Development and Research Investment

Economic development is likely to affect underinvestment in PARI because it will affect the distribution of the benefits from research investment. To understand this it is important to understand structural differences between rich and poor countries. Rich countries typically have more elastic supply curves for agriculture, because they have less production factor market constraints, better institutions, and so on. Another well-known structural difference between rich and poor countries is that demand for food is more price elastic in poor countries.

The effects as depicted in Fig. 11.1 are more representative of the situation in rich countries, with relatively inelastic demand. In this case the effect on producer income may well be negative (in Fig. 11.1 this is indeed the case with the gains D being smaller than the losses A, and thus D − A < 0).

Many experts such as Ruttan (1982) have argued that public investments in research have contributed to the dramatic increase in productivity of agriculture during the twentieth century, and to a long-term decline in agricultural prices, benefiting consumers and putting pressure on farm incomes. In the face of inelastic demand and the "technological treadmill" (Cochrane 1965), the relative decline in farm incomes and the ensuing hardship caused by the structural adjustment and outflow of labor was called the "farm problem" (Schultz 1953).

Also Gardner (1983, 2002) emphasized that significant public investments in public goods, including research, have contributed to the dramatic transformation of agriculture in the past century, characterized by an accelerated increase in output and total factor productivity, a decline in food prices, and in the number of farms. In countries such as the USA and the EU, the relative productivity of agriculture has sky-rocketed, resulting in an approximate 3% annual reduction in the number of farms and rural population migrating to urban areas. It has contributed to agriculture becoming a capital-intensive sector in industrial countries as the remaining farmers invested in mechanical, chemical, and biological capital, which have substituted for land and labor. This process has induced protests from farmers on the role of public research. Farmers have protested technological advances in agriculture induced by public and private research expenditures in these countries as they objected against the impact of the technological advances on prices and farm incomes (Rausser and Foster 1992). Empirical studies by, for example, Gardner (1989) and Oehmke and Yao (1990) indeed find that underinvestment occurs if farmers gain relatively less from research.

In developing countries, the effects of public research will be different as supply is typically more inelastic and demand more elastic in developing countries (Binswanger et al. 1985). In this perspective, Schultz (1953) distinguished between the "farm problem" in rich countries, where farmers benefit relatively less from technology with inelastic demand, from the "food problem" in developing countries with elastic demand. This implies that one would expect that in rich countries, research favors consumers, while in developing countries, agricultural producers (farmers) benefit relatively more from research.

Note that this implies that those groups who benefit most from PARI, and thus would be most likely to lobby the strongest, are also those who are politically the weakest. Chapter 4 explained why urban consumers are relatively more politically influential in developing countries and farmers more so in rich countries in terms of agricultural subsidies and taxes. As those who stand to benefit most from PARI have less politically influence both in rich and poor countries, one would therefore expect to observe underinvestment in both regions (de Gorter and Swinnen 1998; Swinnen et al. 2000).

11.5 Trade and the Impacts of Public Research

Trade will affect the distribution of benefits from PARI since it will affect the impact of PARI on prices. In the case of a small open economy, which is illustrated in Fig. 11.2, the world market price P_W determines the domestic price. Domestic consumption is q_0^D and supply is at q_0^S. If the country is a small open economy, that means that changes in domestic production or consumption will be too small to influence the world market price.

With prices determined by the world market, the impact of PARI will be very different: research shifts the domestic supply curve to S_τ and increases domestic production to q_τ^S. However since the domestic price does not change, consumption and consumer surplus will be unaffected. Producer surplus increases by area E + F, which is also the total welfare effect. Hence all the benefits of research go to producers in this case.

As in the closed economy case (Fig. 11.1), the gross welfare impact or research on society as a whole is positive.[2] In Fig. 11.1 it equals B + D; in Fig. 11.2 it is E + F. However, the distributional effects of PARI differ strongly between these cases: in the closed economy case with inelastic demand, consumers get most of the gains (Fig. 11.1), while in the open economy case, producers get all the gains (Fig. 11.2). While society as a whole gains in both cases, consumers and producers will have different

---

[2] To measure the net welfare effect, one has to take into account the tax costs to finance PARI.

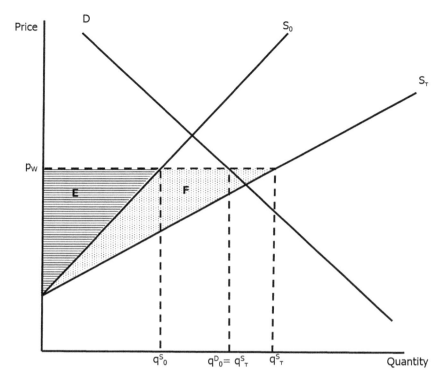

Fig. 11.2 Welfare and distributional effects of public research in a small open economy

preferences for PARI, dependent on how it affects their income. They will prefer the government to choose their private optimum level of PARI, and will negatively react to the government's choice if this diverges from their private optimum.

Finally, if the country is larger and changes in its domestic consumption and production affect the world market price, the impact would be mixed: production increases would cause a price decline. However note that in this case part of the benefits from research are "exported", that is, they go to foreign consumers. In this case foreign consumers would benefit from international spillover effects of domestic research expenditures. Since foreign consumers typically are not part of the constituency of domestic policy-makers, they are likely to discount these benefits from research in their decision-making.

11.6 Interactions with Other Policies

Another factor which has a major impact on the distributional effects of PARI, and thus on the political incentives for PARI, is the (potential) existence of other government policies, such as subsidies and taxes on farmers and consumers. The interactions between both policies may affect the political incentives to support or lobby for/against the other policy. For example, when PARI stimulates productivity growth it may increase market distortions caused by existing subsidy policies. Another example is that when prices are fixed by government regulations of markets, PARI may no longer lead to price reductions (since prices are fixed by politicians and not by the market). This means that consumers may benefit less and producers may benefit more from PARI, and this should affect their incentives to politically support or oppose more PARI investments. Chapter 13 will analyze these interaction effects in more detail.

References

Alston, J.M. 2018. Reflections on Agricultural R&D, Productivity, and the Data Constraint: Unfinished Business, Unsettled Issues. *American Journal of Agricultural Economics* 100 (2), 392–413.

Alston, J.M., M.A. Andersen, J.S. James, and P.G. Pardey. 2009. *Persistence Pays: US Agricultural Productivity Growth and the Benefits from Public R&D Spending (Vol. 34)*. New York: Springer Science & Business Media.

Baland, J.M., and A. Kotwal. 1998. The Political Economy of Underinvestment in Agriculture. *Journal of Development Economics* 55 (1): 233–247.

Binswanger, H., Y. Mundlak, M. Yang, and A. Bowers. 1985. *Estimation of Aggregate Agricultural Supply Response*. Washington, DC: World Bank Mimeo.

Cochrane, W.W. 1965. Some Observations of an Ex Economic Advisor: Or What I Learned in Washington. *Journal of Farm Economics* 47 (2): 447–461.

Cornes, R., C.F. Mason, and T. Sandler. 1986. The Commons and the Optimal Number of Firms. *The Quarterly Journal of Economics* 101 (3): 641–646.

de Gorter, H., and J. Swinnen. 1998. The Impact of Economic Development on Public Research and Commodity Policies in Agriculture. *Review of Development Economics* 2 (1): 41–60.

de Gorter, H., and D. Zilberman. 1990. On the Political Economy of Public Good inputs in Agriculture. *The American Journal of Agricultural Economics* 72: 131–137.

de Gorter, H., D.J. Nielson, and G.C. Rausser. 1992. Productive and Predatory Public Policies. *American Journal of Agricultural Economics* 74: 27–37.

Gardner, B.L. 1983. Efficient Redistribution Through Commodity Markets. *American Journal of Agricultural Economics* 65 (2): 225–234.

———. 1989. *Price Supports and Optimal Spending on Agricultural Research.* Department of Agricultural and Resource Economics. Working Paper 88-01, University of Maryland.

Gardner, B. 2002. *US Commodity Policies and Land Prices.* Government Policy and Farmland Markets. Washington DC: USDA-ERS, University of Maryland.

Huffman, W.E., and R.E. Evenson. 1992. Contributions of Public and Private Science and Technology to U.S. Agricultural Productivity. *American Journal of Agricultural Economics* 74: 751–756.

Huffman, W.E., and J.A. Miranowski. 1981. An Economic Analysis of Expenditures on Agricultural Experiment Station Research. *American Journal of Agricultural Economics* 63 (1): 104–118.

Khanna, J., W.E. Huffman, and T. Sandler. 1994. Agricultural Research Expenditures in the United States: A Public Goods Perspective. *The Review of Economics and Statistics* 76 (2): 267–277.

Oehmke, J.F., and X. Yao. 1990. A Policy Preference Function for Government Intervention in the US Wheat Market. *American Journal of Agricultural Economics* 72 (3): 631–640.

Pardey, P.G., and V.H. Smith. 2017. Waste Not, Want Not: Transactional Politics, Research and Development Funding, and the US Farm Bill. Report. American Enterprise Institute.

Pardey, P.G., C. Chan-Kang, S.P. Dehmer, and J.M. Beddow. 2016. Agricultural R&D is on the Move. *Nature* 537: 301–303.

Rausser, G.C. 1982. Political Economic Markets: PERTs and PESTs in Food and Agriculture. *American Journal of Agricultural Economics* 64 (5): 821–833.

———. 1992. Predatory Versus Productive Government: The Case of U.S. Agricultural Policies. *The Journal of Economic Perspectives* 6: 133–158.

Rausser, G.C., and W.E. Foster. 1992. Political Preference Functions and Public Policy Reform: Reply. *American Journal of Agricultural Economics* 74 (1): 227–230.

Rose-Ackerman, S., and R. Evenson. 1985. The Political Economy of Agricultural Research and Extension: Grants, Votes, and Reapportionment. *American Journal of Agricultural Economics* 67 (1): 1–14.

Ruttan, V.W. 1982. *Agricultural Research Policy.* Minneapolis: University of Minnesota Press.

Schultz, T.W. 1953. *The Economic Organization of Agriculture.* New York: McGraw Hill.

Swinnen, J.F.M., H. de Gorter, G.C. Rausser, and A. Banerjee. 2000. The Political Economy of Public Research Investment and Commodity Policies in Agriculture: An Empirical Study. *Agricultural Economics* 22 (2): 111–122.

Ulrich, A., H. Furtan, and A. Schmitz. 1986. Public and Private Returns from Joint Venture Research: An Example from Agriculture. *Quarterly Journal of Economics* 101 (1): 103–130.

CHAPTER 12

Land and Institutional Reforms

12.1 INTRODUCTION

There is a vast literature on the role of land rights and institutions for agricultural and economic development (see, e.g. Binswanger et al. 1995; Deininger and Feder 2001; Keefer and Knack 2002; Platteau 2000, for reviews). The creation of optimal land institutions attracted renewed attention in the 1990s because of its central role in the transition process in former Communist countries in East Asia, the former Soviet Union, and Eastern Europe (Lerman et al. 2004; Rozelle and Swinnen 2004), and more recently because of the large-scale land investments in developing countries (Deininger 2013; Jayne et al. 2014).

As with other policies we discussed earlier (in Chaps. 8, 9, 10 and 11), changes in land rights and other institutions have both equity and efficiency effects. Part of the literature focuses mostly on the efficiency aspects to explain differences and changes in land institutions as an endogenous response to changes in the external environment. For example, the emergence of private property rights is seen as an endogenous response to increased scarcity of land and the associated incentives for land-related investments (Boserup 1965) or to reduced risk to income and consumption (Feder and Deininger 1999).

© The Author(s) 2018   199
J. Swinnen, *The Political Economy of Agricultural and Food Policies*,
Palgrave Studies in Agricultural Economics and Food Policy,
https://doi.org/10.1057/978-1-137-50102-8_12

However, others question the hypothesis that changes in land institutions are efficiency-driven and argue that there is no assurance that an institution will come into being simply because it is more efficient than existing alternatives (Baland and Platteau 1998). Changes in land institutions also imply a redistribution of wealth and rents, and often of economic power and political influence. The emphasis on distributional aspects of institutional change underlies studies on the political economy of land reforms (de Janvry 1981; Swinnen 1999).

Bardhan (1989: 10–11) argues that the inherent link between efficiency and distributional issues brings together Marxist and neoclassical thinking on institutions and institutional change:

> [N]eoclassical institutional economists focus their attention on allocative efficiency-improving institutions, whereas Marxists often emphasize how institutions change or do not change depending on considerations of surplus appropriation of a dominant class. ... The emphasis on the effect of an institutional change on control of surplus by a particular class also suggests that the question of efficiency-improving institutional change cannot really be separated from that of redistributive institutional change.

In this perspective, it is not surprising that significant land rights reforms were often associated with changes in the political regime (Binswanger et al. 1995; de Janvry 1981; Hayami et al. 1990; Swinnen 1997a; de Janvry et al. 2001).

Historical cases, such as major political reforms in the early and late twentieth centuries in Europe and Asia, provide a "natural experiment" to study the formation and change of land institutions and their political economy. In this chapter I summarize insights on the political economy of land reforms from several of these "natural experiments". The first case is from the late nineteenth and early twentieth centuries when the combination of enhanced political rights for farmers and a dramatic rural crisis caused major changes in land rights and regulations in Western Europe.[1] The second is from China in the 1970s where the combination of widespread hunger in the countryside and the death of Mao induced major land reforms; the second from the collapse of the Communist political regimes in Eastern Europe and the Soviet Union triggered major land reforms in these countries in the 1990s.

---

[1] For studies on land reforms and their political economy in other regions and periods, see, for example, de Janvry (1981) and Binswanger et al. (1995).

12.2 Political Reforms and Land Reforms: Lessons from Early Twentieth-Century Western Europe

There is a remarkable diversity in land institutions among Western European countries which have been long-term market economies, which are geographically close, and which have been part of the same policy environment (the EU's Common Agricultural Policy) for many years. Figure 12.1 illustrates this diversity. In some countries, (such as Ireland) almost all farm land is owned by the farmers, while in others (such as Belgium and France) the vast majority of the land is not owned by the farmers but rented in. This puzzling observation triggered the obvious question: why? The answer, as in many cases discussed in this book, is a combination of efficiency and equity, or, in other words, of economics and politics.

12.2.1 *Efficiency of Land Rental and Sales Markets*

An economic (efficiency) explanation could be that these differences in land institutions reflect differences in local circumstances which affect the optimality of land buying (owning) versus renting (Deininger and Feder 2001). The sale of land is often considered superior to land rental because (a) land sales transfer full rights to the new user; (b) they are more likely

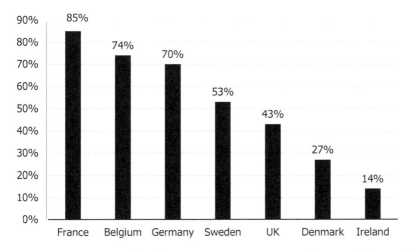

Fig. 12.1 Importance of land renting in Western Europe. (Source: Ciaian et al. (2015), based on FADN data)

to increase access to credit as owned land can be used for collateral purposes, and (c) they provide optimal incentives for investment by providing permanent security of rights (Binswanger et al. 1995). However, imperfections in input, product, capital, and insurance markets often prevent flexible adjustments of land use through land sales (Carter and Zimmerman 2000; de Janvry et al. 2001). Deininger (2003) argues that land rental markets can go a long way toward bringing the operational distribution of holdings closer to the optimum, given market imperfections. The potential of rental markets is (a) to allow more flexible adjustments of the land area used with relatively low transaction costs; (b) to require only a limited capital outlay, thereby leaving more liquidity available for productive investments rather than locking it all up in land; (c) to facilitate easy reallocation of land toward more efficient users than the current owners; and (d) to provide a stepping stone toward landownership by the landless. Several of these advantages are especially relevant when transaction costs for land sales are high and in conditions of uncertainty.

But rental markets have problems as well. There may be weak investment incentives without long-run security. It does not enhance access to credit because rented land cannot be used as collateral; and insecure property rights are not only a problem for sales markets, but also for rental markets (Macours et al. 2010; Skoufias 1995; Vranken et al. 2011).

Hence, a crucial element in the sales versus rental market choice is the trade-off between security of operation and liquidity. Many farms have both owned and rented land, and the proportion of such mixed land use increases with the size of the farm (Feenstra 1992). A minimum amount of owned land ensures security of operation and security for long-term investments while extending the farm by rented land allows capital otherwise invested in land to be used for investing in other productive assets. In a capital-intensive production system, with the possibility of using other assets as collateral, farms prefer to invest in new technology and farm-specific assets rather than tying up large sums of capital in land purchases. In this way, farms can combine tenure security (with their assets and long-term investments concentrated on owned land) on the one hand and flexibility in land allocation, and freeing up capital for other investments (by renting additional land rather than buying) on the other hand (Vranken and Swinnen 2006).

Let us now go back to "the puzzle": why do we observe such differences in rent/sale markets in market economies? The economic arguments above suggest that the optimality of land institutions will differ with differences in factor market imperfections, in particular credit markets, technology requirements, and security of operation. However, it is hard to imagine that these conditions differ so strongly between countries which are relatively similar in terms of economic development and which have been part of an integral agricultural market and policy for so long. This suggests that the answer to the puzzle must lay elsewhere.

12.2.2 A Political Economy Answer to the Puzzle

The short-term answer, it turns out, is politics, and more specifically government regulations of land markets which differ strongly among EU countries. The optimal mix of rented and owned land is affected by factors that affect the operational security. Government regulations which enhance tenant rights may stimulate both land renting (by improving security of property rights) and investments in rented land. In some European countries governments have introduced legislation to enhance tenant rights, for example, by guaranteeing a minimum length of rental contract of several years in order to guarantee tenants sufficient security of land operation. Regulations obliging landowners to compensate tenants for investments tenants made in land improvements enhance the right of first purchase, further enhancing the tenant's incentives to invest in rented land.

The more fundamental question now is: why are there such large differences in land regulations among these countries? To understand this, we need to go back in history, more particularly to the late nineteenth and early twentieth centuries when political reforms and agricultural crises lead to major land reforms and regulations, many of which have persisted until today.

12.2.3 Political Reforms in the Nineteenth and Twentieth Centuries and Land Tenure Reforms[2]

There was substantial variation among European countries in their land structure and the associated relations between those who owned the land and those who worked on the land, and many political changes affected this in earlier times—one obvious example is the French Revolution and the expansion of land registration and inheritance regulations to other countries with Napoleon's military expansion. Yet in many West European countries land was distributed unequally and ten-

---

[2] See Swinnen (2002) for more details.

ant farmers often had very weak rights. Their demand for improved tenure rights was reflected in *the three F's* ("Fair rents, Fixity of tenure, and Free sales") since landowners determined terms of setting the length of tenure, the rent, the use of the land (crop patterns), and captured land investments made by tenants.

These demands were not met in many countries since landlords dominated governments and tenants, farm workers and small farmers often had no voting rights. However this political-economic equilibrium changed with industrialization and democratization, in particular the distribution of voting rights to workers, small farmers, and tenants. For example, in England, voting reforms extended voting rights to workers, small farmers, and tenants and reduced the share of parliamentary seats occupied by large landowners from 60% before 1885 to 10% in 1920 (see Table 12.1).

Important (and effective) policy-induced improvements in tenants' situation (e.g. regulation of rents, compensation for tenant investments, enhanced security of tenure, etc.) emerged after tenants obtained voting rights which occurred in the late nineteenth and early twentieth centuries in many West European countries. This has been a necessary condition for the improvement of tenure rights, although not a sufficient condition.

Even with increased political power, policy changes which significantly benefited tenants and small farmers only arrived after crises situations worsened their living conditions. Strong declines in market prices for farm products (see Chap. 7) induced distress sales of land by small farmers in the late nineteenth and early twentieth centuries and again in the 1930s. These market developments triggered major social upheaval and political pressure from the tenants and small farmers for changes in the property

Table 12.1 Voting rights reforms and landowners' parliamentary power in England

	Voting Reform Act	Main Beneficiaries	Share of parliamentary seats by large landowners (%)
1832	I	Farm managers	
1867	II	Industrial workers	60%
1885	III	Farm workers and tenants	30%
1906			20%
1918	IV	Women	10%

Source: Swinnen (2002)

rights and tenure regime (Tracy 1989; Swinnen 2009). Hence, it was the *combination* of political reforms (improved political representation by tenants), and social upheaval (increasing political pressure) which resulted in policy reforms and new regulations giving tenants (and landless labor and small farmers) more security of operation and improved access to land.

12.2.4 Tenure Reform Patterns

However, there is more than one way to improve tenants' land rights. One can, in broad terms, distinguish two types of policy strategies to improve the situation of the tenants. The first strategy was to improve the rental conditions for the tenants through regulations, including better conditions in case of contract termination, such as compensation for land improvements and automatic rights for rent renewal and pre-emptive rights. The second strategy was to help the tenant become the owner of the land through government subsidies to buy the land (stimulating the demand for land) or through increased land and inheritance taxes (stimulating the supply of land).

The first strategy was followed in countries such as Belgium, France, and the Netherlands, where rent regulations were introduced which focused primarily on improving the tenure security for farmers.[3] These were not introduced all at once, but incremental increases throughout the twentieth century led to a situation where farmers no longer wanted/needed to purchase land since their tenure security was high, and they could use their capital for other investments. As a result, the share of land renting has remained almost constant over 150 years in Belgium (around 70%).

The second strategy, to help tenants become landowners, was followed by countries like Ireland and Denmark. There, the government set up state funds to purchase farms for poor tenants, and/or to subsidize the purchase of land by poor tenants, either directly or through regulating land sales prices, through subsidized loan conditions, or through tax benefits for purchasing land. This strategy caused a strong shift from land renting to ownership by farmers. The most dramatic impact occurred in

---

[3] Swinnen et al. (2016) calculated a "tenant protection index" (TPI) in land regulations and found that Belgium, France, and the Netherlands have the highest TPI in Europe. In these countries, rental contracts have minimum lengths and are automatically extended. Moreover, landowners can only get the land back for specific purposes. State land committees can intervene in regulated rental contracts and in rental setting.

Ireland where the debate for improved tenure security was interrelated with the independence struggle: it was a conflict between Catholic Irish tenants versus (mostly absentee) Protestant English landlords.[4] Almost 96% of all land was still rented in the late nineteenth century, and this share declined to 6% after independence in 1921.

In England, improvements in the situation of tenants followed from a mixed approach. The decline in political power of the large landlords,[5] resulted, first, in improved rights of tenants, such as the right to determine crop rotations and the right to determine purchases and sales of farm products, the right for compensation if they were to leave the land, and the creation of Land Tribunals for resolution of conflicts between landowners and tenants. The second major change was the increase of land and inheritance taxes and the shift of income taxes from tenants to landlords. In combination, these policy changes contributed (a) to better and more secure rights for tenants, and (b) to a decline of tenancy as landlords sold their land to tenants. As a result, the share of rented land has declined from 89% in 1910 to 43% now.

In summary, similar political pressures led to different regulations and land market situations in Western Europe. One could think of the different regulation-market combinations as different equilibriums in market economies. These equilibria have persisted for a long time despite their integration in an economic union and a common agricultural policy. Swinnen et al. (2015) find a positive correlation between an indicator of tenant protection regulations and the share of land rented by farms in Western Europe.[6]

[4] This additional factor made the conflict more extreme and violent. After 1876 falling agricultural prices induced a dramatic increase in violence. The extension of voting rights to farm workers and tenants in 1885 resulted in several land laws which allowed an increase in landownership of small farmers (Guinnane and Miller 1997). After Ireland became independent in 1921, virtually all land was transferred to small farmers. The share of leased land fell to 6% in 1930.

[5] Voting reforms extended voting rights to workers, small farmers, and tenants and reduced the share of parliamentary seats occupied by large landowners from 60% before 1885 to 10% in 1920.

[6] There have been adjustments in land regulations in recent decades because, while initially the tenure regulations enhanced the rights of tenants and their access to land, later on some of the distortionary impacts created perverse effects. In countries with extensive regulation of land rental contracts, landowners no longer wanted to rent land to farmers. Hence, overregulation led to the paradoxical outcome that land rental decreased. For example, in the Netherlands and France, land renting decreased substantially as a consequence of these tight

12.3 Political Changes and Institutional Reforms: Lessons from East Asia and Eastern Europe in the Late Twentieth Century

In the 1960s and 1970s many poor and middle-income countries, representing a large share of the world's rural population and poor, were heavily affected by state interventions. This was most extreme in the Communist world, spreading from Central Europe to East Asia, where the entire economic system was under direct control of the state. The lives of more than 1.5 billion people were directly controlled by Communist leaders. In most of these states, incentives were massively distorted. The leaders were committed to Communist ideology and designed their economies to be insulated from the market.

Under Communism, inefficient state farms and collective farms operated on state-controlled land.[7] The state made investments, set planting plans, purchased inputs through planning channels and remitted profits up through the ministerial system. Many of the collective farms were initially created by the forced integration of family farms into large farms.

By now, many of these countries have liberalized their (agricultural) economies, but not always their political regimes. The most dramatic set of reforms began toward the end of the 1970s and beginning of the 1980s when China embarked on its reform path by reforms of its farm institutions and land rights. Vietnam followed in the mid-1980s. The reforms in China and Vietnam have been heralded as lifting hundreds of millions of people out of dire poverty (World Bank 2000), as "the biggest antipoverty program the world has ever seen" (McMillan 2002: 94), and as having led to "the greatest increase in economic well-being within a 15-year period in all of history" (Fischer 1994: 131).

---

regulations. In response to these developments, France relaxed rental regulations which stimulated rental agreements again and renting increased significantly over the past decades from around 50% in 1980 to 75% in 2010. The Netherlands recently relaxed liberalized rental contracts.

[7] The farms were inefficient because, besides ownership incentive problems, monitoring farm workers was difficult and logistics often compounded the problems. Incentives were distorted both through price regulations and property rights control (Brada and King 1993; Brooks 1983; Mead 2000; Lin 1990; Putterman 1992).

208   J. SWINNEN

Countries in Central and Eastern Europe (CEE) and in the former Soviet Union (FSU) introduced a series of reforms in the 1990s.[8] However, both the choice of the reforms and their effects were quite different, causing a vigorous debate on the optimal reform choices (Dewatripont and Roland 1995; Sachs and Woo 1994). In this section I focus on *why* governments made different reform choices, that is, on the political economy.[9]

12.3.1   Leadership Change, Reforms, and Legitimacy of the Political System in China

The start of the reforms in China coincided with the political transition from Mao Zedong to Deng Xiaoping after Mao died in 1976. There was no dramatic overthrow of the Communist Party after Mao's death. Deng assumed power from within the system. The Communist Party was in control both before and after Deng's accession to the position of supreme leader. Moreover, while Deng had a number of bold ideas, he also was essentially committed to the same system that had been built during the previous three decades (Yang 1996).

Still, the beginning of the Reform Era is clearly marked by the political rise of Deng in the wake of Mao's death. Deng was attracted by the rapid growth that was transforming most of the rest of East Asia, and drew on a self-learned belief in incentives and technology. However, he was also very pragmatic. While Deng's name is inextricably linked to his first bold reform move—the household responsibility system (HRS) reforms which gave land rights (back) to individual farmers, decollectivized agricultural production, and replaced it with a system of household-based farming (Lin 1992)—it turns out that most of the move to household farming had already taken place by the time the HRS became official CP policy.[10]

---

[8] Also outside the Communist Bloc, in many African, Latin American, and South Asian countries, the state played an important role in the economy. There were many distortions in these countries as well and reform attempts in the 1980s and 1990s (see Swinnen et al. 2013 for a comparative study of the different models and reforms).

[9] Studies comparing the *effects* of the reforms include Macours and Swinnen (2002), Roland (2000), and Rozelle and Swinnen (2004).

[10] The HRS was the first step in a longer and broader reform process (McMillan and Naughton 1992; Sicular 1995). In the years afterwards, prices were administratively raised by officials in the planning bureau who retained control over the economy. It was not until property rights had been fully reformed in the mid-1980s that the leadership decided to begin to move to marketing and other reforms. The subsequent reforms increasingly allowed farmers to sell their output to private traders (Park et al. 2002). Entry by non-state entities

LAND AND INSTITUTIONAL REFORMS   209

Reforms started clandestinely in several regions in China, especially those regions that suffered heavily during the famine that followed the Great Leap Forward (Zhou 1996). In the temporary leadership vacuum that existed after Mao's death, both reinforced each other (McMillan 2002). The spread of the HRS system—across nearly a million brigades and more than ten million teams in less than five years—did not reflect careful planning but, instead, as one village official in China is quoted by McMillan (2002): *HRS spread like the flue*.[11] Within a few years, the larger collective farms completely broke up into small household farms.[12] The success of the HRS reforms in increasing output, reducing poverty, and maintaining social stability in China's countryside reinforced the positions of the pro-reform groups in Beijing. Inversely, the enhanced position of the pro-reform groups created the policy space that was necessary for the grassroots land reform initiatives to spread across rural China.

Paradoxically and ironically, the radical land and institutional reforms in China, which looked like moves away from Socialism, probably did more to consolidate the rule of the Communist Party than any other measures taken during this period (Oi 1989).[13] The changes directly affected more than 70% of the population, living in the rural areas. The rise in food production also increased food supplies to cities and took a lot of pressure off the government.[14]

and individuals was gradually allowed. Ultimately, competition forced the entire state-owned marketing system to be disbanded. It took 20 years to replace China's planned agricultural marketing system of the early 1980s by a system of competitive markets (Huang et al. 2004). Tariff reductions and trade liberalization finished the process (Huang et al. 2008). In the process taxation of Chinese farmers reduced strongly—see also Chap. 7.

[11] While several papers have pointed at the importance of (regional) experimentation in the economic reform process in China (Qian and Xu 1993; Qian et al. 1999), this appears to have been more important in the later stages of the reforms, for example, in market liberalization, in the implementation of fiscal reforms, and in the emergence of TVEs (Nyberg and Rozelle 1999; Zhang 2006). Experimenting with agricultural reforms was actually more important in the Soviet Union in the 1970s and 1980s (Radvanyi 1988; Van Atta 1993). See Swinnen and Rozelle (2006) for a more elaborate discussion on this.

[12] Doi Moi, Vietnam's reform program in the 1980s, closely followed China's strategy (Pingali and Xuan 1992; Pingali and Khiem 1995). Outside East Asia, a few countries distributed land rights to households on collective farms. For example, in moves that were even more radical than China, reformers in Albania and Armenia gave households almost complete, private ownership rights to their land (Cungu and Swinnen 1999; Lerman et al. 2004).

[13] Similar dynamics occurred in Vietnam (Wurfel 1993; Pingali and Xuan 1992).

[14] Once China had successfully implemented the land rights reform (as well as adjusted prices to reduce the implicit tax on farmers—see Chap. 7), liberalizing markets became less

210   J. SWINNEN

12.3.2   Economic Reforms and Political Collapse in Eastern Europe

The situation was very different in the Soviet Union and Eastern Europe in the late 1980s. Communist leaders had failed to substantially reform for decades.[15] The lack of significant reforms ultimately contributed to the fall of the Communist leadership. The collapse of the Communist regimes throughout Eastern Europe and the (former) Soviet Union in the early 1990s then triggered a bold series of reform policies—a "big bang". Within a short period of time, land and other property rights were privatized, prices and trade liberalized (Anderson and Swinnen 2008; Macours and Swinnen 2002).[16]

Once they lost power, the anti-Communist political forces that came to power were determined to get rid of the Communist system and to introduce political changes (introduce democracy) and economic changes (a market economy), which were to reinforce one another (Balcerowicz 1994). The ultimate political reform objective was not only economic efficiency in the short run, but also dynamic political objectives through how the post-transition governments can control governments and the economy in the future (Rausser et al. 1994; Rausser et al. 2011).[17]

The mixture of political and economic objectives was especially paramount in land and farm reforms. The reform of land rights was one of the most hotly disputed issues. The land reforms also had the objective to

imperative (Rozelle 1996). The early pricing changes (which were not done through markets, but by the planning bureaucracy) and HRS helped the reformers to meet their initial objectives of increased agricultural productivity, higher farm incomes, and food output (Sicular 1988; Lin 1992). The reforms fuelled economic growth and reduced concerns about food security. The legitimacy of leaders of being able to run a government that could raise the standard of living of its people was at least temporarily satisfied (Putterman 1993).

[15] Acemoglu and Robinson (2006, 2008) analyze under which conditions the (in)ability of existing governments to introduce sufficient redistribution through fiscal means will lead to or prevent revolutions which imply a redistribution of economic and political rights.

[16] Political changes were not equally strong in all countries. In several of them, such as Belarus, Turkmenistan, and Uzbekistan, there have been hardly any democratic reforms. In other countries, such as Russia, political freedoms have been cut back again. Swinnen and Heinegg (2002) show a positive relationship between political reforms and agricultural reforms.

[17] There are many examples of such mixed political and economic objectives such as Thatcher's privatization policies in the 1980s in the UK (Studlar et al. 1990) and nineteenth-century rural reforms in Western Europe to stop the growth of socialist influence (Craeybeckx 1973).

influence the political constellation, that is, the distribution of power and wealth in the post-transition period. The objectives of anti-Communist (or anti-Soviet) political parties were explicit in using the land reforms to break the rural power and organization structure of (former) Communist organizations (Lyons et al. 1994; Rabinowicz 1997; Swinnen 1997a).

Reforms were launched despite resistance by farm managers, workers, and local officials. Farm workers in Eastern Europe and the Soviet Union benefited from large government subsidies and high wages (OECD 1996). Despite low farm productivity, workers in the Soviet Union's state farms and collectives lived at standards of living far higher than those in China's rural sector. With overemployment and soft-budget constraints, many farm workers and farm managers opposed reforms. Reformers chose to push through as much of the reform agenda as possible at the time that they were (still) in charge—using their "window of opportunity." Hence, for both political and economic reasons, a comprehensive set of radical reforms were pursued. Since the previous reforms had failed to result in efficiency improvements with marginal and slow policy shifts, in the view of the reformers a more radical and broad-based reform approach was necessary.

A broad and encompassing reform strategy was also required for technical and administrative reasons. First, the more industrialized nature of the Soviet agricultural production system and the inefficiencies imbedded in the agro-food supply chain required an approach beyond the confines of farming sector (Johnson and Brooks 1983). Second, the more complicated technologies in Soviet agriculture and in Eastern Europe meant a more complex set of exchanges between a larger number and greater variety of firms, which required massive information to design an optimal sequence of policies (McMillan 2002). Third, unlike in China, agriculture in the Soviet Union and Eastern Europe was much less important in the economy, requiring a much broader reform agenda.

12.3.3   *Grassroots Pressure and Leadership Support for Reforms*

Radical institutional reforms under the Communist regimes could only occur when there was simultaneously strong grassroots support for the reforms and support at the top of the Communist Party (see Table 12.2). Reform failed in China in the 1960s because there was no support by the top leadership (Mao) for radical reforms demanded by households at the grassroots level. Reform failed in Russia in the 1970s because there was

212   J. SWINNEN

Table 12.2 Political and economic conditions for agricultural reforms under communism

		Grassroots pressure for agricultural reform	
		NO	YES
Support of top leadership for agricultural reform	NO	NO REFORM Example: USSR 1970s	NO REFORM Example: CHINA early 1960s
	YES	NO REFORM Example: USSR 1980s	REFORM Example: CHINA late 1970s & 1980s

Source: Swinnen and Rozelle (2006)

neither grassroots nor leadership support for radical changes. The distortions under Mao in China in the 1970s resembled much more the distortions under Stalin in the Soviet Union of the 1930s than the distortions in the Soviet Union in the 1970s (Wädekin 1990). As Mao, Stalin's desire to modernize fast and his commitment to heavy industry—and his distrust of the farming population—led to his policy to use his centrally controlled economic system to tax the countryside to finance industrial development.

Soviet agricultural policy, however, changed after World War II when the state began to reduce taxes on agriculture and to provide substantial assistance, both in terms of investment support and in terms of higher farm prices (see Table 4.2) (Gray 1990). A similar situation occurred in Central and Eastern Europe, countries in which farm workers lived relatively well due to large subsidies to overstaffed and inefficient farms (Liefert and Swinnen 2002). Agricultural reform failed in the 1980s in Russia because the reform proposals from the top of the Communist leadership (Gorbachev) were not supported at the grassroots level. Only in China at the end of the 1970s and the early 1980s was there a confluence of interests in favor of radical reforms at the top and at the grassroots, from both farm households and local officials. It took a dramatic political change to trigger fundamental reforms in Eastern Europe and the Soviet Union.

The support of officials for reforms in China was sustained by their personal interests as farm village leaders (Oi 1989) and later by reforms of the bureaucracy and by rural industrialization and fiscal reforms (Qian and

Weingast 1997).[18] These changes stimulated interest of bureaucrats in local economic growth. In the Soviet Union, little change took place in the bureaucracy (Shleifer 1997), and, since the interests of local officials were also here aligned with those of farm managers, the rational response of both was to resist, not support, reform. Frye and Shleifer (1997) refer to the different bureaucratic attitudes in implementing the reforms as the "grabbing hand" in Russia and the "helping hand" in China.

12.4   Historical Legacies and Land Reforms

While all (ex-) Communist countries introduced major land reform programs, it is intriguing that the way the land property rights were reformed differed very strongly among transition countries. Key choices in the land reform decisions were: (a) *who* should receive the land rights: people who are currently farming the land or others; (b) *what* types of rights are transferred: ownership rights, use rights, alienation rights, …; (c) *how* are land rights transferred: linked to specific plots of land or as entitlements to a certain amount of land. It turns out that countries made very different choices on these three questions.[19]

The household responsibility system (HRS) in *China* gave land use rights and the primary responsibilities for farming to the individual household. It allowed farmers to keep the residual output of their farms after paying their agricultural taxes and completing their mandatory delivery quotas. However, the collective did not disappear from land controls. Villages and the government retained legal ownership rights over land and controlled the entities that were charged with contracting land to the farmers and setting rules for land management. So households effectively received use rights and not ownership of the land.

The dominant land reform procedure in *Eastern Europe* was restitution of land to the former owners that had lost their land during the collectivization movement in the past (or their heirs). Typically land reform laws restituted land in the historical boundaries. If restitution in the original

---

[18] Deng Xiaoping imposed a mandatory retirement program in 1980, effectively removing the old guard and replacing them by younger and more pro-reform people (Lee 1991), and, in the mid-1980s, allowed bureaucrats to quit government positions and join business, which stimulated bureaucrat interest in economic growth and enterprise development (Li 1998).

[19] See Lerman et al. (2004) and Rozelle and Swinnen (2004) for more details on the characteristics of land reforms.

boundaries was not possible, former owners received rights to a plot of land of comparable size and quality. The restitution process did not just transfer use rights but complete ownership rights of the land. Land was now (again) privately owned by individuals.

In *Russia* and most of the former Soviet Union, in a first step, reformers transferred land from state ownership to ownership by the collective farms. In the second step, land was then given to the individuals that were living and working on the collective farms under the form of certificates of entitlement to land. Although the certificates frequently were called land shares, they were, in fact, 'paper shares' that did not establish a direct link between a specific plot of land and an individual.

Ideology and structural differences among the countries played a role in the choice of different approaches to land reform.[20] The latter determine the efficiency and distributional effects of the land reform options in various countries, and thereby the preferences of the affected interest groups, and the pressure they put on the leaders and governments.

12.4.1   Transfer Landownership or Use Rights?

The *choice to privatize land, or not,* was affected by historical and legal legacies of landownership, and by the ideology of the rulers. The still present memory of their history of private land rights provided a strong incentive for reformers in Eastern Europe to choose to privatize land. All of these countries had a history of private landownership and family farms before land was collectivized or nationalized and run as cooperatively managed or state farms. Proximity to the EU and the familiarity of the local population with the land systems in Western Europe reinforced this preference for private landownership.

In contrast, in Russia and Central Asia no such tradition existed. When Communist leaders nationalized the land, the land was often taken from large feudal estates where many rural households were employed as serfs. Although some serfs had individual use rights on family plots, all land belonged to the feudal landlords and most farming consisted of feudal sharecropping. In Central Asia, there was even less of a history of individual as it was dominated by migratory or semi-migratory pastoralism.

---

[20] For more details and wider country coverage see, for example, Swinnen and Rozelle (2006) and various chapters in Swinnen (1997a) for detailed analyses of the positions of the political parties in the land reform debates in various CEEs.

Much of the land in these countries was used and managed communally. In those regions, there was a popular preference that land should not be privately owned. The absence of a tradition in private farming was reinforced by the length of time since the onset of collectivization.

In China, the continuation of the Communist regime and its ideology played an important role. With land the most basic factor of production in agriculture in a Communist country, leaders believe that the state, or its representative, the collective, should have control over land.

12.4.2 Transfer Land to the Current Users or Previous Owners?

Restitution of farm land to former owners, many of whom were no longer active in agriculture, was vehemently opposed by farm managers. It was argued that the efficiency of farming would suffer due to a high incidence of tenancy and excessive fragmentation. Many economists and policy advisors also were opposed to restitution.[21]

Despite the objections, land restitution became the most common process of land reform in Eastern Europe. A key reason for the choice appears to be a combination of the "Historical Justice" argument, the pre-reform legal ownership structure, and strategic anti-Communist or nationalist ideology. "Historical Justice" was the argument of the former owners of the land—families and farmers who had lost their land during the Communist occupation.[22] The vast majority of these small- to medium-sized landowners at the time,[23] were very different from, for example, Russia where former owners were feudal landlords.

---

[21] Many economists, policy advisors, and politicians were wrong in their prediction that restitution would lead to an efficient fragmentation of farms. While the restitution process resulted in the fragmentation of ownership, for several reasons it did not lead to a fragmentation of farms. To the contrary, the nature of transaction costs in land markets actually contributed to a consolidation of land use (Mathijs and Swinnen 1998). Except in some of the poorer regions, the new landowners did not return to farming and primarily were interested in renting their land out. In most cases the new lessees were large-scale (now private) farms.

[22] In the Baltic countries, which were occupied and fully integrated in the Soviet Union after World War II, agricultural land was nationalized under the Soviet system, and 'Historical Justice" was reinforced by nationalistic feelings. Restitution was to disassociate themselves from their former Soviet colonizers (Rabinowicz 1997).

[23] In Central and Eastern Europe many large landowners (including institutions like the church) had lost most of their land in post-World War II land reforms, prior to the Soviet occupation (Swinnen 1999).

216   J. SWINNEN

Another factor was the legal ownership structure. In China and in the Soviet Union, all cultivated land was owned by the state (or the collective). However, in Eastern Europe, through the entire period of Communism, individuals were still the legal owners of most of the farm land. While these legal differences had little impact on the operation of the land in the Communist era, they affected land reform choices after liberalization.

Land restitution was also seen as a long-term anti-Communist strategy. Collective and state farm managers were appointees by the Communist Party, and farm workers had benefited heavily from extensive subsidies. That made them often supporters of the Communist regime, and collective farms were not only economic but also political organizations which dominated the rural areas and the votes. Taking the land from them and giving it to former owners was seen as a way of breaking the Communist Party's political control of the rural areas by anti-Communist parties which came to power in the early 1990s.[24]

In summary, the combination of these factors made restitution the common choice in Eastern Europe despite much opposition, also from economists (Swinnen 1999).

12.4.3   In-Kind Versus Share Distribution of Land?

Among those nations that did *not* restitute land, why did some choose to give land in specifically delineated plots (in-kind) to rural households and others decide to distribute land in shares to groups of farmers?

The distribution of land in specific and clearly delineated plots to farm workers or rural households made it easier for poor households and individuals to use that land for themselves and leave the large-scale farm to

---

[24] To overcome the resistance of farm managers and local officials, reform-minded governments in some cases tried to explicitly exclude them from the reform implementation process (Swinnen 1997a). For example, in Bulgaria, when reformers came in government in the early 1990s they brought in outsiders to chair local committees implementing land reform and farm restructuring (the so-called 'Liquidation Councils'). This design of the implementing institutions was explicitly designed to break local resistance to reform implementation by former Communist officials and farm managers who, had control until then, blocked local implementation of the reforms by the local institutions responsible for implementing the reforms (Swinnen 1997b). When the former Communists came back to power a year later, they 'liquidated the Liquidation Councils' and put the local managers and officials back in charge.

start a farm on their own if they wished to do so. Such direct access to land was particularly important for poor households to increase their food security, incomes, and assets. Poor households would therefore prefer in-kind distribution, ceteris paribus. These preferences were reinforced in labor-intensive farming systems—which are typical for the poorest countries. The benefits of farm individualization are higher and the costs lower with higher labor intensity.

Share distribution of land was more likely to stimulate the continuation of large farms and prevent fragmentation, as it made leaving the farms more difficult for households, in particular with farm managers hostile to the idea. Farm managers and employees with specific skills that were more valuable with the large farm organizations, generally opposed any policies that undermined the survival of the large farms. Farm managers also preferred share privatization over in-kind distribution, as it offered additional benefits to accumulate shares, and thus wealth, for themselves. They often tried to convince workers to trade land shares for employment guarantees. This resulted in a strong concentration of landownership within the farm management or with the farm managers themselves. Hence, paradoxically the land reform system which was designed to prevent individual private ownership of the land and the emergence of feudal-type estates has led to the strongest concentration of landownership in the entire transition world (Lerman et al. 2004; Sedik 1997).

While many other factors may have played a role, these arguments explain why in poor nations with labor-intensive technologies (e.g. China, Vietnam and Albania, Armenia, and Georgia) most land was distributed in-kind to rural households. In the richer and more capital-intensive farming countries, such as Russia, Ukraine, and Kazakhstan, most land was distributed as shares to groups of farmers.

12.5 Conclusions: Political Regime Change and Grassroots Pressure

Land institutions are crucial for economic development, but changes in land rights and institutions have both equity and efficiency effects. Distributional effects are an important reason why there may be strong resistance against efficiency-enhancing reforms. Changes in land institutions typically imply a redistribution of wealth and rents, and often of economic power and political influence.

This is an important reason why major changes in land institutions only occur with shocks to the political-economic equilibrium. Changes in political institutions may provide such shocks. In this chapter we reviewed insights from several "natural experiments" that occurred in the twentieth century where political changes contributed to important reforms of land and related institutions: major changes in land tenure regulations and inheritance rules which followed political reforms in Western Europe in the early twentieth century; the introduction of the household responsibility system that transformed Chinese agriculture in the 1980s; and the land reforms that followed the collapse of the Communist political regimes in Eastern Europe and the Soviet Union in the 1990s.

In all cases there was a major change in leadership or political institutions preceding the land reform. The most dramatic change was the collapse of the Communist regimes in Eastern Europe where an entire political system (one-party) was replaced by another (democracy). In the other cases there were important changes without a change in the system as such: in China one-party rule did not change but there was a leadership change; while in western Europe the extension of voter rights to poor farmers extended the democratic system to a larger part of the population.

The cases also indicate that in particular the combination between regime change and events which cause strong demand at the grassroots level for policy change (such as an income crisis) is needed to trigger important policy reforms. This was the case in China in the late 1970s where dramatic poverty and hunger (and an associated demand for reforms) combined with a leadership change that was supportive of such reforms. In Western Europe significant reforms of land institutions only came when price declines which caused rural poverty increases and social upheaval in the countryside (increasing demands for reforms) were combined with extended voting rights for poor tenants (increasing the reform supply, i.e. the governments' incentives to reform).

Political institutions and policy reform affect one another in a dynamic and bi-directional fashion: economic reforms affect the political regime as well. In China the dramatic success of the early economic reforms contributed to the legitimacy and the survival of the Communist Party and mitigated the pressures for further economic reforms. In the Soviet Union the opposite occurred: the failure of timid reforms contributed to the decline in legitimacy of the Communist Party, and once changes were possible, opponents tried to implement reforms which were intended both to reform the economic system and to change the future political regime.

The radical approach to restitute land rights to former landowners in many East European countries can also be interpreted within such framework. In several countries the objectives of anti-Communist (or anti-Soviet) political parties were explicit in using the land restitution policy to break the rural power and organization structure of (former) Communist organizations and to create a long-run political base for democratic and market-oriented governments and policies.

The historical and comparative analysis also learns that "reform" can mean a variety of things and that land reforms can be implemented in a variety of ways, with quite different effects. Also the choice of the nature of the land reform is important and has both equity and efficiency implications—and is thus subject to economic and political forces. This is illustrated by the variety of land regulations that have emerged and persisted in Western Europe and in the variety of land rights for farmers that have emerged in transition countries.

Finally, with land being such a fundamental factor in (rural) societies, a number of other factors play an important role in determining land reform decisions. This includes the history of land and its ownership in countries, ideology, geography, and the quality and cultural values associated with land and its use. They add to the complex set of factors that determine its political economy.

References

Acemoglu, D., and J.A. Robinson. 2006. *Economic Origins of Dictatorship and Democracy*. Cambridge: Cambridge University Press.

———. 2008. Persistence of Power, Elites and Institutions. *American Economic Review* 98 (1): 267–293.

Anderson, K., and J.F.M. Swinnen. 2008. *Distortions to Agricultural Incentives in Europe's Transition Economies*. Washington, DC: World Bank Publications.

Baland, J.M., and J.P. Platteau. 1998. Division of the Commons: A Partial Assessment of the New Institutional Economics of Land Rights. *American Journal of Agricultural Economics 80* (3): 644–650.

Balcerowicz, L. 1994. Common Fallacies in the Debate on the Transition to a Market Economy. *Economic Policy* 9 (19): 17–50.

Bardhan, P. 1989. The New Institutional Economics and Development Theory: A Brief Critical Assessment. *World Development 17* (9): 1389–1395.

220   J. SWINNEN

Binswanger, H., K. Deininger, and G. Feder. 1995. Power, Distortions, Revolt and Reform in Agricultural Land Relations. In *Handbook of Development Economics*, ed. C. Hollis and T.N. Srinivasan, vol. 3, 2659–2672. Amsterdam: Elsevier Publications.

Boserup, E. 1965. *The Condition of Agricultural Growth. The Economics of Agrarian Change Under Population Pressure*. London: Allan and Unwin.

Brada, J.C., and A.E. King. 1993. Is Private Farming More Efficient than Socialized Agriculture? *Economica* 60: 41–56.

Brooks, K. 1983. Productivity in Soviet Agriculture. In *Prospects for Soviet Agriculture in the 1980s*. Bloomington: Indiana University Press.

Carter, M.R., and F.J. Zimmerman. 2000. The Dynamic Cost and Persistence of Asset Inequality in an Agrarian Economy. *Journal of Development Economics 63* (2): 265–302.

Craeybeckx, J. 1973. De agrarische depressie van het einde der XIXe eeuw en de politieke strijd om de boeren I. *Belgisch Tijdschrift voor Nieuwste Geschiedenis* IV: 190–230.

Cungu, A., and J. Swinnen. 1999. Albania's Radical Agrarian Reform. *Economic Development and Cultural Change* 47 (3): 605–619.

Deininger, K.W. 2003. *Land Policies for Growth and Poverty Reduction*. Washington, DC: World Bank Publications.

Deininger, K. 2013. Global land Investments in the Bio Economy: Evidence and Policy Implications. *Agricultural Economics* 44 (s1): 115–127.

Deininger, K., and G. Feder. 2001. Land Institutions and Land Markets. *Handbook of Agricultural Economics 1*: 287–331.

Dewatripont, M., and G. Roland. 1995. The Design of Reform Packages Under Uncertainty. *The American Economic Review* 85: 1207–1223.

Feder, G., and K. Deininger. 1999. Land Institutions and Land Markets. World Bank Policy Research Working Paper No. 2014, Washington DC.

Feenstra, R.C. 1992. How Costly Is Protectionism? *The Journal of Economic Perspectives 6* (3): 159–178.

Fischer, S. 1994. Structural Factors in the Economic Reforms of China, Eastern Europe, and the Former Soviet Union. *Discussion Economic Policy* 9 (1): 131–135.

Frye, T., and A. Shleifer. 1997. The Invisible Hand and the Grabbing Hand. *American Economic Review* 87 (2): 354–358.

Gray, K.R., ed. 1990. *Soviet Agriculture: Comparative Perspectives*. Ames: Iowa State University Press.

Guinnane, T.W., and R.I. Miller. 1997. The Limits to Land Reform: The Land Acts in Ireland, 1870–1909. *Economic Development and Cultural Change 45* (3): 591–612.

Hayami, Y., M.A. Quisumbing, and L. Adriano. 1990. *Toward an Alternative Land Reform Paradigm: A Philippine Perspective*. Quezon City: Ateneo de Manila University Press.

LAND AND INSTITUTIONAL REFORMS 221

Huang, J., S. Rozelle, and M. Chang. 2004. The Nature of Distortions to Agricultural Incentives in China and Implications of WTO Accession. *World Bank Economic Review* 18 (1): 59–84.

Huang, J., Y. Liu, W. Martin, and S. Rozelle. 2008. Distortions to Agricultural Incentives in China. In *Distortions to Agricultural Incentives in Asia*, ed. K. Anderson and W. Masters. Washington, DC: World Bank Publications.

de Janvry, A. 1981. *The Agrarian Question and Reformism in Latin America*. Baltimore: Johns Hopkins University Press.

de Janvry, A., G. Gordillo, J.P. Platteau, and E. Sadoulet, eds. 2001. *Access to Land, Rural Poverty, and Public Action*. Oxford: Oxford University Press.

Jayne, T.S., J. Chamberlin, and D.D. Headey. 2014. Land Pressures, the Evolution of Farming Systems, and Development Strategies in Africa: A Synthesis. *Food Policy 48*: 1–17.

Johnson, D.G., and K.M. Brooks, eds. 1983. *Prospects for Soviet Agriculture in the 1980s*. Bloomington: Indiana University Press.

Keefer, P., and S. Knack. 2002. Polarization, Politics and Property Rights: Links Between Inequality and Growth. *Public Choice* 111 (1): 127–154.

Lee, H.Y. 1991. *From Revolutionary Cadres to Party Technocrats in Socialist China*. Berkeley: University of California Press.

Lerman, Z., C. Csaki, and G. Feder. 2004. *Agriculture in Transition: Land Policies and Evolving Farm Structures in Post-Soviet Countries*. Landham: Lexington Books.

Li, D.D. 1998. Changing Incentives of the Chinese Bureaucracy. *American Economic Review* 88 (2): 393–397.

Liefert, W.M., and J.F.M. Swinnen. 2002. *Changes in Agricultural Markets in Transition Economics*, Agricultural Economic Report 806. ERS, USDA.

Lin, J.Y. 1990. Collectivization and China's Agricultural Crisis in 1959–1961. *Journal of Political Economy 98* (6): 1228–1252.

———. 1992. Rural Reforms and Agricultural Growth in China. *American Economic Review* 82 (1): 34–51.

Lyons, R., G. Rausser, and L. Simon. 1994. Disruption and Continuity in Bulgaria's Agrarian Reform. In *Privatization of Agriculture in New Market Economies: Lessons from Bulgaria*, ed. A. Schmitz, K. Moulton, A. Buckwell, and S. Davidova, 87–117. Norwell: Kluwer Academic Publishers.

Macours, K., and J.F.M. Swinnen. 2002. Patterns of Agrarian Transition. *Economic Development and Cultural Change* 50 (2): 365–394.

Macours, K., A. De Janvry, and E. Sadoulet. 2010. Insecurity of Property Rights and Social Matching in the Tenancy Market. *European Economic Review 54* (7): 880–899.

Mathijs, E., and J. Swinnen. 1998. The Economics of Agricultural Decollectivization in East Central Europe and the Former Soviet Union. *Economic Development and Cultural Change* 47 (1): 1–26.

McMillan, J. 2002. *Reinventing the Bazaar. The Natural History of Markets.* New York: W. W. Norton & Company.

McMillan, J., and B. Naughton. 1992. How to Reform a Planned Economy: Lessons from China. *Oxford Review of Economic Policy* 8: 130–143.

Mead, R.W. 2000. China's Agricultural Reforms: The Importance of Private Plots. *China Economic Review* 11 (1): 54–78.

Nyberg, A., and S. Rozelle. 1999. *Accelerating Development in Rural China,* World Bank Monograph Series, Rural Development Division. Washington, DC: The World Bank.

OECD. 1996. *Agricultural Policies in Non-Member Countries.* Paris: Organization of Economic Cooperation and Development.

Oi, J. 1989. Market Reforms and Corruption in Rural China. *Studies in Comparative Communism* 22 (2/3): 221–233.

Park, A., H. Jin, S. Rozelle, and J. Huang. 2002. Market Emergence and Transition: Transition Costs, Arbitrage, and Autarky in China's Grain Market. *American Journal of Agricultural Economics* 84 (1): 67–82.

Pingali, P.L., and N.T. Khiem. 1995. *Rice Market Liberalization and Poverty in Vietnam,* Working Paper. International Food Policy Research Institute, Washington, DC.

Pingali, P.L., and V. Xuan. 1992. Vietnam: Decollectivization and Rice Productivity Growth. *Economic Development and Cultural Change* 40 (4): 697–718.

Platteau, J.P. 2000. *Institutions, Social Norms, and Economic Development.* Vol. 1. Mahwah: Psychology Press.

Putterman, L. 1992. Dualism and Reform in China. *Economic Development and Cultural Change* 40 (3): 467–493.

———. 1993. *Continuity and Change in China's Rural Development.* New York: Oxford University Press.

Qian, Y., and B.R. Weingast. 1997. Federalism as a Commitment to Preserving Market Incentives. *Journal of Economic Perspectives* 11 (4): 83–92.

Qian, Y., and C. Xu. 1993. Why China's Economic Reforms Differ: The M-form Hierarchy and Entry/Expansion of the Non-State Sector. *Economics of Transition* 1 (2): 135–170.

Qian, Y., G. Roland, and C. Xu. 1999. Why Is China Different from Eastern Europe? Perspectives from Organization Theory. *European Economic Review* 43 (4): 1085–1094.

Rabinowicz, E. 1997. The Political Economy of Land Reform in the Baltics. In *The Political Economy of Agrarian Reform in Central and Eastern Europe,* ed. J.F.M. Swinnen. Aldershot: Ashgate.

Radvanyi, J. 1988. The Experiments in Georgia, 1974–1984: Quest for a New Organization in the Soviet Agricultural System. In *Socialist Agriculture in Transition: Organizational Response to Failing Performance,* ed. J.C. Brada and K.-E. Wädekin, 110–124. Boulder: Westview Press.

Rausser, G.C., L.K. Simon, and K.T. van't Veld. 1994. *Political-Economic Processes and Collective Decision Making.* Berkeley: Department of Agricultural & Resource Economics, UCB.

Rausser, G.C., J.F.M. Swinnen, and P. Zusman. 2011. *Political Power and Endogenous Policy Formation.* Cambridge/New York: Cambridge University Press.

Roland, G. 2000. *Transition and Economics: Politics, Markets and Firms.* Cambridge: MIT Press.

Rozelle, S. 1996. Gradual Reform and Institutional Development: The Keys to Success of China's Rural Reforms. In *Reforming Asian Socialism: The Growth of Market Institutions,* ed. J. McMillan and B. Naughton, 197–220. Ann Arbor: The University of Michigan Press.

Rozelle, S., and J.F.M. Swinnen. 2004. Success and Failure of Reform: Insights from the Transition of Agriculture. *Journal of Economic Literature* 42 (2): 404–456.

Sachs, J.D., and W.-T. Woo. 1994. Structural Factors in the Economic Reforms of China, Eastern Europe and the Former Soviet Union. *Economic Policy* 9 (1): 101–145.

Sedik, D.J. 1997. Status of Agricultural Reforms in the NIS/B Countries in 1997. In *Situation and Outlook Series: Newly Independent States and the Baltics,* 4–9. Washington, DC: U.S. Department of Agri-culture, Economic Research Service.

Shleifer, A. 1997. Government in Transition. *European Economic Review* 41 (3–5): 385–410.

Sicular, T. 1988. Plan and Market in China's Agricultural Commerce. *Journal of Political Economy* 96 (2): 283–307.

———. 1995. Redefining State, Plan, and Market: China's Reforms in Agricultural Commerce. *China Quarterly* 144: 1020–1046.

Skoufias, E. 1995. Household Resources, Transaction Costs, and Adjustment Through Land Tenancy. *Land Economics* 7: 42–56.

Studlar, D.T., I. McAllister, and A. Ascui. 1990. Privatization and the British Electorate: Microeconomic Policies, Macroeconomic Evaluations, and Party Support. *American Journal of Political Science* 34 (4): 1077–1101.

Swinnen, J., ed. 1997a. *The Political Economy of Agrarian Reform in Central and Eastern Europe.* Aldershot: Ashgate.

———. 1997b. On Liquidation Councils, Flying Troikas and Orsov Cooperatives: The Political Economy of Agricultural Reform in Bulgaria. FAO Rome.

———. 1999. The Political Economy of Land Reform Choices in Central and Eastern Europe. *The Economics of Transition* 7 (3): 637–664.

———. 2002. Transition and Integration in Europe: Implications for Agricultural and Food Markets, Policy and Trade Agreements. *The World Economy* 25 (4): 481–501.

———. 2009. The Growth of Agricultural Protection in Europe in the 19th and 20th Centuries. *The World Economy* 32 (11): 1499–1537.

224   J. SWINNEN

Swinnen, J., and A. Heinegg. 2002. On the Political Economy of Land Reforms in the former Soviet Union. *Journal of International Development* 14 (7): 1019–1031.

Swinnen, J., and S. Rozelle. 2006. *From Marx and Mao to the Market: The Economics and Politics of Agricultural Transition*. Oxford: Oxford University Press.

Swinnen, J., L. Knops, and K. Van Herck. 2013. Food Price Volatility and EU Policies. In *Food Price Policy in an Era of Market Instability: A Political Economy Analysis*, ed. P. Pinstrup-Andersen. Oxford: Oxford University Press.

Swinnen, J., K. Deconinck, T. Vandemoortele, and A. Vandeplas, eds. 2015. *Quality Standards, Value Chains and International Development*. New York: Cambridge University Press.

Swinnen, J., K. Van Herck, and L. Vranken. 2016. The Diversity of Land Markets and Regulations in Europe, and (some of) Its Causes. *The Journal of Development Studies 52* (2): 186–205.

Tracy, M. 1989. *Government and Agriculture in Western Europe 1880–1988*. 3rd ed. New York: Harvester Wheatsheaf.

Van Atta, D. 1993. *The 'Farmer Threat': The Political Economy of Agrarian Reform in Post-Soviet Russia*. Boulder: Westview Press.

Vranken, L., and J. Swinnen. 2006. Land Rental Markets in Transition: Theory and Evidence from Hungary. *World Development 34* (3): 481–500.

Vranken, L., K. Macours, N. Noev, and J. Swinnen. 2011. Property Rights Imperfections and Asset Allocation: Co-ownership in Bulgaria. *Journal of Comparative Economics 39* (2): 159–175.

Wädekin, K.E. 1990. Determinants and Trends of Reform in Communist Agriculture: A Concluding Essay. In *Communist Agriculture: Farming in the Soviet Union and Eastern Europe*, 321–331. London/New York: Routledge.

World Bank. 2000. *World Development Report 2000/2001: Attacking Poverty*. Washington, DC: The World Bank.

Wurfel, D. 1993. Doi Moi in Comparative Perspective. In *Reinventing Vietnamese Socialism: Doi Moi in Comparative Perspective*, ed. W. Turley and M. Selden, 165–207. Boulder: Westview Press.

Yang, D. 1996. *Calamity and Reform in China: State, Rural Society, and Institutional Change Since the Great Leap Famine*. Stanford: Stanford University Press.

Zhang, X. 2006. Fiscal Decentralization and Political Centralization in China: Implications for Growth and Inequality. *Journal of Comparative Economics 34*: 713–726.

Zhou, K.X. 1996. *How the Farmers Changed China: Power of the People*. Boulder: Westview Press.

CHAPTER 13

Policy Interactions

13.1 Introduction

So far we have analyzed the political economy of various agricultural and food policies mostly in isolation, meaning that we analyzed them as if there were no other policies (or at least we mostly ignored the other policies). However, in reality, many public policies exist together and sometimes are implemented simultaneously.

The fact that multiple policies exist together or are implemented simultaneously does not influence the analyses of single policies as presented in the previous chapters as long as there are no interaction (effects) between the policies. However, if they do interact then the impacts of the policies may change, either economically or politically or both. For example, the economic impact of price support on markets is likely to be different if price support policies are accompanied by production limitations (quota) than if they are not. A different example is when two policies are introduced as part of a "policy package" whereby people who are hurt by one policy benefit from the other policy. The combination of both policies will affect the political reactions to either policy and thus the likelihood of its political feasibility. In the case of both examples, it is important to analyze the joint effect of the policies and their interactions.

These examples illustrate that the interactions between policies and their political economy can take several forms. One can distinguish between two types of policy interactions: "*economic* interaction effects" and "*political*

© The Author(s) 2018   225
J. Swinnen, *The Political Economy of Agricultural and Food Policies*,
Palgrave Studies in Agricultural Economics and Food Policy,
https://doi.org/10.1057/978-1-137-50102-8_13

interaction effects" (Swinnen and de Gorter 2002). Economic interaction effects (EIEs) arise where one policy affects the distributional and welfare effects of other policies (PIEs). Political interaction effects occur when the existence or introduction of one policy affects the political incentives of governments to introduce or change other policies.

13.2   Economic Interaction Effects

Economic interaction effects (EIEs) can be negative or positive. An example of positive EIE is when combined reforms reinforce the (beneficial) impacts of separate policy reforms. For example, in the reform strategies in China and Eastern Europe in the 1990s, land reforms and privatization strategies provided new opportunities and better incentives for farmers (see Chap. 12), while, at the same time, price and market policies that kept prices for farmers low were reduced or removed (see Chaps. 6 and 7). In these cases, the combination of both policy reforms further improved efficiency.

An example of negative EIEs is the interaction between public agricultural research (see Chap. 11) and policies that subsidize or tax farmers by regulating agricultural prices or production (see Chaps. 4, 5 and 6). The latter policies induce market distortions, and these distortions can be increased by public research investments. If agricultural research increases productivity, this will shift supply functions and thus cause an increase in the distortions of existing regulations. Some studies have argued that under some conditions, the increased distortions may outweigh the benefits from research and thus make the net effects of public research investments negative (Murphy et al. 1993; Alston et al. 1993). We will analyze these EIEs in greater detail.

13.3   Political Interaction Effects: Compensation

Probably the best-known example of PIEs is the use of distributional policies for compensation purposes. Compensation is an important element in the political economy of policy reform or public investment (Rausser et al. 2011; Anderson et al. 2013).[1] Reforms to a more efficient policy usually

---

[1] Trade policy reform and compensation have a long history in the economics literature, going back to the early analyses of Adam Smith and David Ricardo. A crucial element in the arguments on the optimality of free trade are that the gains of the winners of trade liberalization are more than sufficient to compensate the losers of reform, an issue which has clearly

imply gains for some groups and losses for others. Similarly, building a road may lead to major gains in rural development but may hurt those displaced by the construction of the road. If the gains outweigh the losses, it is socially optimal to implement the reforms or make the investment, since the gains of those who win are more than sufficient to compensate the losers.

In various chapters in this book we have analyzed specific cases where policies create winners and losers, for example, in land reforms (Chap. 12), in increased government investments in research (Chap. 11), in institutional reforms, and so on.[2] The introduction of socially optimal policies may thus hurt some groups in society. In those cases, distributional policies may have to be used to compensate those who are hurt, or benefit less—and thus oppose the policy reforms or public investments—in order to make the welfare-enhancing policies politically possible. While the distributional policies may cause distortions, in combination the package of both distributional and productive policies can increase overall welfare. Hence compensation is an essential element of the economics of policy reform (Rausser et al. 2011).

There are numerous empirical examples of "policy packages" that include compensation for certain groups. They are a traditional part of multi-annual agricultural policy decision-making in both the European Union and the USA.[3]

An important issue to which we return at the end of this chapter is under which conditions compensation schemes in policy reform are possible or effective in practical policy applications. Those who lose from reform may oppose the reforms if they expect that (full) compensation will

---

become highly relevant again in recent years with discussions on the gainers and losers from globalization.

[2] Trade policy reform and compensation have a long history in the economics literature, going back to the early analyses of Adam Smith and David Ricardo. A crucial element in the arguments on the optimality of free trade are that the gains of the winners of trade liberalization are more than sufficient to compensate the losers of reform. The study of trade policy reform and compensation includes many important contributions (e.g. Bhagwati 1971; Corden 1969; Heckscher 1949; Stolper and Samuelson 1941). In recent years there is a renewed interest in the role of compensation schemes in coping with trade liberalization adjustment, which has been stimulated by recent research on the nature of the structural changes that take place in an economy following liberalization (Kletzer 2004).

[3] Modeling such joint policy decisions is complex and the identification of equilibria may be difficult, in particular when decision-making institutions are modeled explicitly (see, e.g. Pokrivcak et al. 2006).

228   J. SWINNEN

not take place. The latter may be the case when governments lack the credibility to effectively provide compensation when the reform effects emerge (Acemoglu and Robinson 2006; Swinnen and de Gorter 2002), when governments only offer partial compensation to mitigate political opposition sufficient to get the reforms through (Foster and Rausser 1993), when local institutions prevent the creation of effective compensation schemes (Swinnen 1997), or when there is uncertainty on the effect of the reforms—and thus on who will be the losers and gainers of the reforms (Fernandez and Rodrik 1991).

13.4   An Illustration of EIEs and PIES

13.4.1   Interactions of Public Agricultural Research Investment and Commodity Policies

To illustrate the economic and political interactions between two policies more specifically, let us consider the case of interactions between public agricultural research investments (PARI—which we analyzed as a separate policy in Chap. 11) and commodity policies (such as subsidies, tariffs, etc.—which we analyzed as separate policies in Chaps. 4, 5 and 6). Figures 4.4 and 4.5 in Chap. 4 illustrate how public R&D investments and subsidies to agriculture (measured by the PSE or NRA indicators) have increased simultaneously with economic development.

I will analyze the interactions (EIEs and PIEs) between both public policies in four steps: first, I document EIEs; second, I discuss how political incentives will affect the EIEs by endogenizing the commodity policies; third I discuss how the politically optimal PARI will respond to commodity policies; and finally I consider the outcome when both of the policies are determined endogenously in a political economy framework.

13.4.2   EIEs with Fixed Commodity Policy

The EIE in this case arises because productivity increasing PARI affects the distortions and deadweight costs of a commodity policy. Alston et al. (1993), Murphy et al. (1993), Chambers and Lopez (1993), and Alston and Martin (1995) all study this "economic interaction effect" as the change in deadweight costs of commodity policy with a change in research funding.

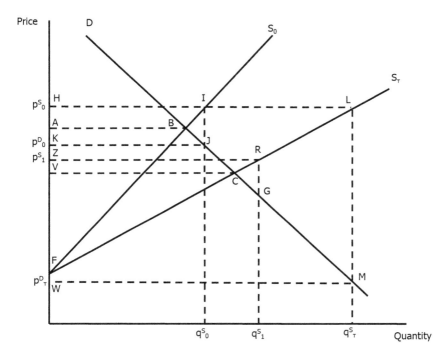

Fig. 13.1 Joint welfare and distributional effects of public research and price interventions in a closed economy

Figure 13.1 illustrates how PARI will affect the deadweight costs of a given commodity policy[4] when governments use the combination of a target price P_0^S which producers receive and payments to cover the difference with the market clearing price P_0^D paid by consumers, where D and S0 represent the demand and supply curve, respectively, in a closed economy. The net transfer to farmers is area HIBA, and the increase in consumer surplus is area ABJK. Taxpayer expenditures are area HIJK and social costs are area BIJ. PARI shifts the supply curve to S_r. With a fixed target price P_0^S, market prices fall to P_r^D and deadweight costs increase to area CLM.

---

[4] Alston, Edwards, and Freebairn compare the benefits from cost-reducing research in the presence of different commodity policies with the benefits from research under free-market conditions. This analysis is identical to calculating the impact of cost-reducing research on deadweight costs of existing commodity policies (Alston and Martin; Anania and McCalla).

230 J. SWINNEN

13.4.3 EIEs with Endogenous Commodity Policy

However, if we want to fully understand how PARI affects the impact of the commodity policy, we need to integrate the fact that the commodity policy itself is determined by political economy factors. In other words, holding the commodity policy fixed may not be a realistic assumption. We know from earlier chapters that governments respond to changes in the relative income position of producers or consumers by changing policies. How does this politically induced change affect the EIEs?

Figure 13.1 shows that besides the increase in deadweight costs, PARI has some important additional effects (1) on income distribution in the economy and (2) on income transfers caused by the commodity policy intervention.[5] With fixed target price P_0^S, producer surplus increases by area FIL and consumer surplus increases by area KJMW in Fig. 13.1. Net transfers to farmers (from area HIBA to HLCV) and costs to taxpayers (from area HIJK to HLMW) also increase. These PARI effects on income distribution and on the distributional effects of commodity policies are likely to have an impact on the level of commodity policy intervention set by the government. Political economy studies show that governments tend to protect farm incomes when farm incomes fall relative to incomes in the rest of the economy.

It is unlikely that governments will keep commodity policies fixed when the public research expenditures have important impacts on the income distribution in the economy. Many empirical and theoretical political economy studies show that governments respond to changes in relative incomes and policy distortions by adjusting commodity policies (see Chaps. 3, 4, 5, 6 and 7).

Therefore, in the example in Fig. 13.1, a PARI-induced increase in relative farm incomes is likely to cause a reduction of the target price. If the impact of research on farm incomes is large enough, the target price may be completely removed. In other cases, one should expect governments to lower the level of the intervention. A reduction in the commodity policy level will, in turn, reduce the impact of PARI on deadweight costs and thus increase the social benefits from research, compared with results of studies holding policy intervention levels fixed.

---

[5] Swinnen and de Gorter (1998) analyze the consequences of endogenizing commodity policies for the size and distribution of research benefits for different policies (target price with deficiency payments and import tariffs) and for three alternative decision-making models of government: (1) guaranteeing a minimum income, (2) maximizing a weighted utility function, and (3) maximizing political support.

To endogenize the commodity policies, one has to specify an objective function of the government setting the commodity policy level. Consider the case when the government's political incentives cause it to guarantee a minimum income for producers. With this objective, the government chooses its target price (in Fig. 13.1) such that producer surplus does not fall below minimum income. The sectoral minimum income is thus producer surplus HIF. With PARI, producer surplus increases to HLF and the government reduces the target price from P_0^S to P_1^S to secure the same minimum income HIF (= ZRF). As a consequence, deadweight costs will be CRG instead of the much larger CLM under the fixed target price assumption.

A key result is that with endogenous commodity policy model the impact of PARI on deadweight costs will always be less than under the exogenous commodity policy assumption. In Fig. 13.1 producer surplus increases by area FIL with the target price constant. However this will no longer be politically optimal after PARI. The post-PARI optimal target price will be lower, and so will the deadweight cost impact.

13.4.4   Politically Optimal PARI with Commodity Policy

In a complete political economy analysis we should not only consider the endogeneity of the commodity policy but also how PARI may change when commodity policies can be introduced or changed. The change in PARI results from changes in political incentives because of the (potential) presence of commodity policies, and is an example of a "political interaction effect" which emerges when changes in one policy affect the political support for the other policy, and so the political incentives for governments in determining the other policy.

This effect has been emphasized by, for example, de Gorter et al. (1992) arguing that commodity policies can play an important positive role in stimulating efficiency and growth if one considers them in an integrated political economy framework where they can play a role in mitigating opposition against efficiency increasing public investments. By providing a vehicle through which to compensate producers for unequal income effects from research expenditures, production subsidies may be necessary components of potentially Pareto-improving portfolios of policy instruments.[6]

---

[6] These results reinforce the conclusion that PARI and commodity policies are complementary because under general assumptions PARI reduces deadweight costs per unit of transfer (see Swinnen and de Gorter (1998) for an analysis with more cases).

232   J. SWINNEN

This "complementarity" of both policies depends on the structure of the economy but is shown to be likely under the conditions characterizing US agriculture (de Gorter et al. 1992, 1995; de Gorter and Zilberman 1990). Finally, the EIE will affect the PIE also. If policies used for compensation induce economic distortions (such as the price intervention with commodity policies we consider in Fig. 13.1) or involve transaction costs, then the compensation effect is mitigated. Only with non-distortionary compensation may a political support maximizing government invest in public research at the social optimum (de Gorter and Swinnen 1998).

13.4.5   *Economic Development and Endogenous Research and Commodity Policies*

To conclude, consider the political economy outcome when both PARI and commodity policies are jointly determined, taking into account all EIEs and PIEs.[7] Economic development affects this equilibrium policy combination because it affects the distribution of the benefits from research investment and political incentives and costs (see Chaps. 4 and 11). Typically, the richer the country, the more price inelastic is food demand and rich countries have relatively elastic supply curves for agriculture, while supply is more inelastic in developing countries (Binswanger et al. 1985). This implies that in rich countries research favors consumers, while in developing countries, agricultural producers benefit relatively more from research.

In a joint policy equilibrium, agricultural subsidization through commodity policy will be positively related with economic development for three reasons: (a) because farmers' political organization improves relative to that of consumers, inducing a relative increase in the farmers' power coefficient; (b) because relative incomes of farmers typically decline with development, inducing farmers to pressure governments for support; and (c) because farmers benefit increasingly less from research.

Consider the situation in rich countries where producers benefit less from research than consumers. The government then has political incentives to transfer income through commodity policy to farmers. In this way, the government responds to the differential income effects of research in

---

[7] The identification of the jointly determined political economy equilibrium requires a complex model. For a formal model and equilibrium and comparative statics derivations, see de Gorter and Swinnen (1998).

a similar manner as they do to (endowment) income gaps caused by structural changes. Commodity policy transfers are implemented to compensate groups (agricultural producers in this example) that benefit less from research. The situation in poor countries is opposite.

The impacts of development on the politically optimal research is not linear. At low levels of development, an increase in development will lead to more investment in research. In this case agricultural producers benefit more from research than consumers, while consumers have relatively more political influence (the "urban bias" effect). The government then has a political incentive to compensate consumers through commodity policies. This implies a tax on producers, as is typically the case in developing countries. If the economy grows, the producers' share of research benefits declines, and that of consumers increases. An increase in consumers' share of research benefits will increase their preference for more research. It also reduces the pressure for compensation through commodity policies, and hence the associated tax on producers and the deadweight costs. In combination, these factors induce an increase in the political optimal investment level because it reduces both the amount of compensation going to consumers through commodity policies (as consumers benefit more from research now) and the associated deadweight costs. Both factors reinforce each other causing research to go up.

In rich countries the effect is different. In this case farmers benefit less from research than consumers, but they have more political influence (the "development paradox"). In the political equilibrium producers will be compensated through commodity policies subsidizing farmers. If the economy grows, agriculture's share of research benefits further declines and the government will need to further increase compensation to farmers. This implies an increase in deadweight costs. In combination, these factors will reduce politically optimal research expenditures.

Empirical studies by Gardner (1989) and de Gorter et al. (1992) on US agriculture find that complementarity between productive and distortionary policies is indeed very strong: an increase in commodity price supports leads to more research than otherwise would have been the case. The empirical results (Swinnen et al. 2000) are consistent with the theoretical predictions here: structural changes in the economy have important effects on the incentives for politicians in government not only to subsidize or tax farmers but also to invest in public research. Furthermore, the analysis supports the hypotheses that the impact of development on government policies is not linear.

13.5 Institutions and Credible Compensation

An important problem with compensation is the credible implementation of such schemes. Those who lose from reforms may oppose the reforms if they expect that (full) compensation will not take place. This may occur when governments lack the credibility to effectively provide compensation for reforms (Swinnen and de Gorter 2002), when governments offer only partial compensation to mitigate political opposition to reforms (Foster and Rausser 1993), when local institutions prevent effective compensation schemes (Swinnen 1997), or when there is uncertainty regarding the effect of the reforms (Fernandez and Rodrik 1991).

Consider again the example of PARI. The analysis above ignores dynamic considerations. However; the benefits from current government investments in PARI will only materialize in the future. In contrast, compensation takes place at the time of decision-making, and hence there are potential problems of compensating for future effects.

An obvious problem in compensation is information: how to determine compensation if the future impact is not known with certainty? Fernandez and Rodrik (1991) explain that designing efficient compensation schemes is problematic when there is uncertainty on the effect of the policies—and thus on who will be the losers and gainers. This may prevent removing opposition to the policies. Foster and Rausser (1993) show how governments may strategically use specific policy instruments when the impacts are heterogenous and targeting is difficult. Using policy instruments such as price supports (instead of lump-sum transfers) may allow for self-targeting in compensation as it allows to compensate a minimal part of the opposing groups to sufficiently reduce political opposition at lower taxpayer cost.

However, even if the impact can be correctly assessed ex ante and well targeted compensation schemes can be designed, there is still a problem of government credibility in committing to future compensation. This problem originates from the fact that once the research investment has taken place, policy-makers have an incentive to change the compensation policy in a later period. In such case the government promise to compensate in the future is not credible and the policy is said to be time-inconsistent (Kydland and Prescott 1977).

Swinnen and de Gorter (2002) show that the dynamic effects of PARI create problems for compensation policies. The benefits from current research investments materialize in the future, while the taxation costs of the investment affect current incomes. In contrast, both costs and benefits of compensation policies occur in the same period. Therefore, a promise to compensate unequal research benefits between groups when the research affects incomes in the future is a time-inconsistent policy for a government maximizing political support in each period. Once the research investment has been made, the incentives for future governments to provide full compensation changes. However, if the government's promises for future compensation are not credible, then those who benefit less from research will maintain their opposition to more research investment. In this case, it will be politically optimal for the government to underinvest in research.

13.5.1 *Compensation, Enforcement, and Institutions*

This problem of enforcing compensation is not specific to agricultural or food policies. The inability of governments to credibly commit to compensate groups that are adversely affected is a prime cause of failures to implement aggregate welfare-improving policies. For example, Stiglitz (1998) argues that "the issue of commitment is especially important in establishing the compensations which are frequently associated with Pareto-improving policies". He explains how Pareto-improving policy proposals have failed because the government could not make a credible commitment that subsidies to compensate the groups that lost out with the policies would be continued: "The problem of commitment stems from the inherent nature of government itself. Government is the primary enforcer of contracts. ... There is no one however to guard the guardian. The government cannot make commitments because it has always the possibility of changing its mind, and earlier 'agreements' cannot be enforced" (pp. 9–10). *Similarly* Rodrik (1996, p. 37), *in trying to answer the question why* "if the problem with reform is that powerful groups get hurt by it ... can't policy makers come up with compensation schemes that remove the hurdle?", concludes that compensation, or the promise thereof, is not always an effective device to remove the distributional obstacle to reform, because if there will be an ex post majority in support of the reform's continuation—even in the absence of compensation—a promise to compensate losers ex post is not going to be credible. He argues that this may explain why many policies that would have been popular ex post are passed up ex ante.

An important question is therefore how to design desirable incentive constraints for policy-makers to bring the discretionary political equilibrium closer to the social optimum. Changing the incentives of politicians could involve the creation of institutions which make policy reversal more difficult and therefore enables policy-makers to make stronger commitments to future policies and, thus, enhance their credibility. This principle is

236   J. SWINNEN

emphasized in the macroeconomic policy literature (e.g. Rogoff 1985; Kotlikoff et al. 1988) and in studies on the political economy of policy reform (Rodrik 1996; Swinnen 1997; Stiglitz 1998). The classical example in the literature is to shift decision-making authority on monetary policy to independent central banks as credibility-enhancing institutions (Alesina 1989; Grilli et al. 1991; Giavazzi and Pagano 1988). Another example is international trade agreements like WTO and NAFTA which provide an enforcement mechanism imposing constraints on government trade and support policies in agriculture.

To illustrate how this could affect the benefits of agricultural research and consequently government investment, consider the situation in Fig. 11.1 (in Chap. 11) where producers are likely to lose from research and hence oppose research expenditures. Opening the economy to free trade increases the total demand elasticity (for a small economy this would mean going from the situation in Fig. 11.1 to the situation in Fig. 11.2), thereby reducing the price effect of research-induced shifts in the supply function and reducing producer opposition to technological advances. Baland and Kotwal (1998) have used this argument to explain why trade liberalization in developing countries may induce an increase in public investment in agriculture as it makes the terms of trade invariant to public investment.

However it should be pointed out that in other circumstances, the reverse can occur where international trade agreements may not allow governments to compensate, unless non-trade-distorting means are used. Because of this the compensation issue is inherently linked to the issue of policy instrument choice in compensation. Hence, economic distortions of compensation policies are not only an important issue in the perspective of the interaction between research and transfer policies, but also when considering their impact on optimal institutions to provide government credibility in compensation.

In summary, the inability of governments to credibly commit to compensate groups that are adversely affected is a prime cause of failures to implement aggregate welfare-improving policies. An important question is how to design mechanisms that constrain policy-makers to bring the discretionary political equilibrium closer to the social optimum. One way is the creation of institutions that make policy reversal more difficult to enhance the credibility of policy-makers to commit to future compensation. These institutions include international trade agreements, which impose constraints on government policies in agriculture and food.

REFERENCES

Acemoglu, D., and J.A. Robinson. 2006. *Economic Origins of Dictatorship and Democracy*. Cambridge/New York: Cambridge University Press.

Alesina, A. 1989. Politics and Business Cycles in Industrial Democracies. *Economic Policy* 4 (8): 55–98.

Alston, J.M., and W. Martin. 1995. Reversal of Fortune: Immiserizing Technical Change in Agriculture. *American Journal of Agricultural Economics* 77: 251–259.

Alston, J.M., C.A. Carter, and V.H. Smith. 1993. Rationalizing Agricultural Export Subsidies. *American Journal of Agricultural Economics* 75 (4): 1000–1009.

Anderson, K., G.C. Rausser, and J.F.M. Swinnen. 2013. Political Economy of Public Policies: Insights from Distortions to Agricultural and Food Markets. *Journal of Economic Literature* 51 (2): 423–477.

Baland, J.M., and A. Kotwal. 1998. The Political Economy of Underinvestment in Agriculture. *Journal of Development Economics* 55 (1): 233–247.

Bhagwati, J. 1971. Trade-diverting Customs Unions and Welfare-Improvement: A Clarification. *The Economic Journal* 81 (323): 580–587.

Binswanger, H., Y. Mundlak, M. Yang, and A. Bowers. 1985. *Estimation of Aggregate Agricultural Supply Response*. Washington, DC: World Bank mimeo.

Chambers, R.G., and R. Lopez. 1993. Public Investment and Real-Price Supports. *Journal of Public Economics* 52: 73–82.

Corden, W.M. 1969. Effective Protective Rates in the General Equilibrium Model: A Geometric Note. *Oxford Economic Papers* 21 (2): 135–141.

de Gorter, H., and J. Swinnen. 1998. The Impact of Economic Development on Public Research and Commodity Policies in Agriculture. *Review of Development Economics* 2 (1): 41–60.

de Gorter, H., and D. Zilberman. 1990. On the Political Economy of Public Good Inputs in Agriculture. *American Journal of Agricultural Economics* 72: 131–137.

de Gorter, H., D.J. Nielson, and G.C. Rausser. 1992. Productive and Predatory Public Policies. *American Journal of Agricultural Economics* 74: 27–37.

———. 1995. The Political Economy of Redistributive Policies and the Provision of Public Good in Agriculture. In *GATT Negotiations and the Political Economy of Policy Reform*, 85–106. Berlin: Springer-Verlag.

Fernandez, R., and D. Rodrik. 1991. Resistance to Reform: Status Quo Bias and the Presence of Individual Specific Uncertainty. *American Economic Review* 81: 1146–1155.

Foster, W.E., and G.C. Rausser. 1993. Price-distorting Compensation Serving the Consumer and Taxpayer Interest. *Public Choice* 77: 275–291.

238   J. SWINNEN

Gardner, B.L. 1989. Price Supports and Optimal Spending on Agricultural Research, Department of Agricultural and Resource Economics Working Paper 88-01. University of Maryland, April.

Giavazzi, F., and M. Pagano. 1988. The Advantage of Tying One's Hands: EMS Discipline and Central Bank Credibility. *European Economic Review* 32 (5): 1055–1075.

Grilli, V., D. Masciandaro, and G. Tabellini. 1991. Political and Monetary Institutions and Public Financial Policies in the Industrial Countries. *Economic Policy* 6 (13): 341–392.

Heckscher, E. 1949. The Effects of Foreign Trade on the Distribution of Income. In *Readings in the Theory of International Trade*, ed. Howard Ellis and Lloyd A. Matzier. Homewood: Irwin.

Kletzer, L.G. 2004. Trade-related Job Loss and Wage Insurance: A Synthetic Review. *Review of International Economics* 12 (5): 724–748.

Kotlikoff, L.J., T. Persson, and L.E. Svensson. 1988. Social Contracts as Assets: A Possible Solution to the Time-Consistency Problem. *The American Economic Review* 78: 662–677.

Kydland, F.E., and E.C. Prescott. 1977. Rules Rather than Discretion: The Inconsistency of Optimal Plans. *Journal of Political Economy* 85 (3): 473–491.

Murphy, J.A., W.H. Furtan, and A. Schmitz. 1993. The Gains from Agricultural Research Under Distorted Trade. *Journal of Public Economics* 51: 161–172.

Pokrivcak, J., C. Crombez, and J.F.M. Swinnen. 2006. The Status Quo Bias and Reform of the Common Agricultural Policy: Impact of Voting Rules, the European Commission, and External Changes. *European Review of Agricultural Economics* 33 (4): 562–590.

Rausser, G., J. Swinnen, and P. Zusman. 2011. *Political Power and Economic Policy: Theory, Analysis, and Empirical Applications*. Cambridge: Cambridge University Press.

Rodrik, D. 1996. Understanding Economic Policy Reform. *Journal of Economic Literature* 34 (1): 9–41.

Rogoff, K. 1985. The Optimal Degree of Commitment to an Intermediate Monetary Target. *The Quarterly Journal of Economics* 100 (4): 1169–1189.

Stiglitz, J.E. 1998. *Towards a New Paradigm for Development*. Geneva: United Nations Conference on Trade and Development.

Stolper, W.F., and P.A. Samuelson. 1941. Protection and Real Wages. *The Review of Economic Studies* 9 (1): 58–73.

Swinnen, J. 1997. Does Compensation for Disruptions Stimulate Reforms? The Case of Agrarian Reform in Central and Eastern Europe. *European Review of Agricultural Economics* 24 (2): 249–266.

Swinnen, J., and H. de Gorter. 1998. Endogenous Market Distortions and the Benefits from Research. *American Journal of Agricultural Economics* 80 (February): 107–115.

———. 2002. On Government Credibility, Compensation, and Under-Investment in Public Research. *European Review of Agricultural Economics* 29 (4): 501–522.

Swinnen, J.F., H. Gorter, G.C. Rausser, and A.N. Banerjee. 2000. The Political Economy of Public Research Investment and Commodity Policies in Agriculture: An Empirical Study. *Agricultural Economics* 22 (2): 111–122.

INDEX[1]

A

Acemoglu, D., 5, 38, 91n4, 210n15
Acemoglu–Robinson dynamic model, 39
ActionAid, 164n12
Adelman, I., 152
Africa, 6, 21n7, 47
  anti-trade bias, 93
  factors influencing policy choices, 46
  fertilizer subsidies in, 21n7
  horticultural exports, 179n10
  structural-adjustment programs, 54, 57, 101
Agrarian crisis of 1880s, 114n6
Agribusiness, 17n2, 24–26, 76, 77, 77n4, 102, 122, 124, 174, 180
Agricultural crisis, in Europe, 112–115
Agricultural policies, 5–7, 13–30, 87, 90, 98, 100, 101, 103–105, 225
  interactions (*see* Policy interactions)
  reforms, 109–131
  (*see also* specific entries)

Agricultural production in mid-twentieth century, growth of, 116–117
Agricultural subsidies, v, 5–7, 9, 20, 20n6, 21, 21n7, 26–29, 36–38, 40, 44, 47, 55–57, 69, 70, 74, 75, 78–80, 82, 88, 93, 109, 115, 118–126, 122n12, 153, 192, 194, 196, 205, 211, 212, 216, 226, 228, 231–233, 235
  reform, in rich countries, 102–105
  world's largest program, 128–131
Agricultural taxation reform and decline, in poor countries (1980–2010), 96–102
Albania, 47, 78, 78n5, 209n12, 217
Alston, J.M., xi, 191n1, 228, 229n4
American Farm Bureau Federation, *see* Farm Bureau
Anders, S.M., 179n10

---

[1] Note: Page numbers followed by 'n' refer to notes.

© The Author(s) 2018
J. Swinnen, *The Political Economy of Agricultural and Food Policies*,
Palgrave Studies in Agricultural Economics and Food Policy,
https://doi.org/10.1057/978-1-137-50102-8

241

242 INDEX

Anderson, K., xvi, 6, 40n4, 69n1, 70n2, 74n3, 109n2, 140, 163n11, 175n8
Andreoni, J., 155n5
Anti-standard coalitions of food standards, 176–177
Anti-trade bias, 87–90, 93, 96, 101, 105, 122
Armenia, 209n12, 217
Asset inequality, 38
Australia, 23, 102, 105
reforms in agricultural and food policies, 109n2

B
Bad News Hypothesis, 52, 157
Bagwell, K., 174n7
Baland, J.M., 236
Baldwin, R.E., 174n7
Bardhan, P., 200
Baron, D.P., 5
Barrett, C.B., x, 26, 142
BASF, 25, 26
Basic Food Law Regulation, 19n5
Bates, R.H., 46, 47
Bayer, 25
Becker, G., x, 4, 5
Beghin J., 170n2, 178, 179n10
Belarus, 210n16
Belgium, 18, 77, 80
agricultural crisis in late nineteenth century, 113, 113n4, 114
land tenure reforms, 205, 205n3
political land reforms, 201
political organization of formers, 116n9
Bellemare, M., 142
Bhagwati, J.N., 4
Binswanger, H., 152, 200n1
Biofuels, v, 26–27, 122, 125–126
policies, 137

Blanchard, E.J., 24, 53
Block, S., 46
Brazil, vi, 25, 98, 105n3
public investment in agricultural and food research, 189
Brinkman, H., 163
Briones Alonso, E., 17
Buchanan, J., 4
Bulgaria, 17n3
transfer of land ownership, 216n24
Bureaucracies and institutions, 45–46

C
Cadot, O., 50
Calculus of Consent, The, 4
Canada, 20, 25, 124
CAP, *see* Common Agricultural Policy
Caswell, J.A., 179n10
CEE, *see* Central and Eastern Europe
Central and Eastern Europe (CEE), 208
transfer of land ownership, 215n23
Central Committee of the Communist Party of China, 129
CETA, *see* Comprehensive Economic and Trade Agreement
Chambers, R.G., 228
Chemical companies, 25
Chen, M.X., 126n16, 129, 131, 174n7
Chicago school of political economy, 4
China, xv, xvi, 6, 19, 25, 47, 54, 56, 78–80, 79n5, 98, 100, 104, 105, 105n3, 109, 217
food price volatility, 138, 142–145
food standards, 182
Great Leap Forward, 209
household responsibility system, 213
land and institutional reforms, 200, 207
land reforms, 208–209
leadership change, 208–209

milk scandal (2000), 182
policy interactions, 226
policy reforms, 109
political changes, grassroots
    pressure, and agricultural
    reform, 126–128
political regime change, 218
political system, legitimacy of,
    208–209
public investment in agricultural and
    food research, 189
transfer of land ownership, 216
world's largest agricultural subsidy
    program, 128–131
Ciaian, P., xi, 21
Clinton, B., 124
CNN factor, 157
Coase, R.H., 4, 40, 41
Co-decision, 55n11
Cold War, 163
Collective action, 48
    costs, 76
    theory, 76
Commodity policies
    economic development and
        endogenous research and,
        232–233
    economic interaction effects with
        endogenous, 230–231
    economic interaction effects with
        fixed, 228–229
    interaction with public agricultural
        research investments, 228
    politically optimal PARI with,
        231–232
Common Agricultural Policy (CAP),
    v, 22, 28, 54, 55, 89n2, 93, 103,
    110, 117–118, 201
Communication
    costs, 102, 163
    incentives, 155–156
    infrastructure, 50, 75, 100

networks, 48
policy, 151, 154, 155, 158
price effects on poverty and food
    security, 154–155
Communism, 207, 216
    political and economic conditions
        for agricultural reforms, 212
Communist Party of China
    Central Committee, 129
Compensation, 36, 91, 115n7,
    204–206, 226–228, 235, 237
    credible, institutions and, 234–236
Comprehensive Economic and Trade
    Agreement (CETA), 170
Conconi, P., 42n6
Conservation Reserve Program (CRP),
    22, 124
Consumer–farmer coalitions, 28–29
Convergence, 29n15, 170
Convergence of agricultural
    taxation and subsidization,
    see Development paradox
Corden, W.M., 41
Corn-ethanol program, 29n15
Corn Laws, 110, 112
Costinot, A., 174n7
Countercyclical payments, 123, 124
Countercyclical policies, 37, 37n3, 39
Crimean War, 112
Crop insurance
    payments, 126
    policy, 122
    program, 27–28, 125–126
    subsidies, 14, 30
CRP, *see* Conservation Reserve
    Program
Cuellar, M., 29

D
Deadweight costs, 40–41
Deconinck, K., xi

244 INDEX

De Gorter, H., xi, xvi, xix, 5n2,
36, 36n1, 40n4, 70n2, 74n3,
111, 124, 124n14, 137n1,
192, 230n5, 231, 232n7,
233, 234
Deininger, K.W., 202
De Janvry, A., x, 152n1, 200n1
Demeke, M., 138
Democratization and agricultural
policies, 43–44
Deng Xiaoping, 127, 208, 213n18
Department of Health and Human
Services, USA, 29
Development paradox, 5, 69–82,
95–105, 129
agricultural subsidies reform in rich
countries and, 102–105
agricultural taxation reform and
decline in poor countries,
96–102
development and policy
combinations and, 79–82
economic growth, restructuring,
and political incentives and,
71–79
Development policy priorities,
159–162
Dewan, T., 5n3
Distortions and food price volatility,
balancing, 142
Distortions-volatility (DV),
142, 145, 147
Distributional effects of public
research investment, 190–192
Dixit, Avinash, 180n12
Doha Round, 164n12
Doi Moi, 209n12
Downs, A., x, 4, 5, 50, 74
Dust Bowl era, 22, 120, 124
Dutt, P., 38, 46
DV, see Distortions-volatility

E
East Asia
political changes and institutional
reforms, 207–213
Eastern Europe, 118
economic reforms and political
collapse in, 210–211
land reforms in, 213
policy interactions, 226
political changes and institutional
reforms, 207–213
EC, see European Commission
Economic development
and research investment,
192–194 (see also
Development paradox)
Economic growth, see Development
paradox
Economic interaction effects (EIEs),
82, 226
with endogenous commodity policy,
230–231
with fixed commodity policy,
228–229
Economic reforms, in Eastern Europe,
210–211
Economic structure, 39–40, 71,
78, 79, 109
Economic Theory of Democracy, An,
x, 4, 50
Edwards, G.W., 229n4
EEP, see Export Enhancement
Program
EFSA, see European Food Safety
Authority
EIEs, see Economic interaction effects
Eisensee, T., 157n8
Empirics, 5, 8, 9, 13, 20, 74n3, 77,
89n2, 100, 101
See also Policy choices, factors
influencing

Endogenous commodity policy,
   economic interaction effects with,
   230–231
Endogenous price, 153n2
England, *see* United Kingdom (UK)
English–French trade agreement
   (1860), 112
Equity effects, of food standards,
   171–174
EU, *see* European Union
Europe, 6, 19, 28, 54, 70, 78, 78n5,
   102, 103, 120
   agricultural crisis of late nineteenth
      century, 112–115
   agricultural production in
      mid-twentieth century,
      growth of, 116–117
   food standards, 181
   free trade in, 112
   land and institutional reforms, 200
   Perfect Storm, 118–119
   policy reforms, 110–119
European Commission (EC), x, 18n4,
   27n14, 45
European Food Safety Authority
   (EFSA), 19n5
European Union (EU), 17, 18n4,
   19n5, 20, 22–25, 23n9, 25n11,
   27, 27n14, 28, 37n3, 45, 54, 121
   Commission, 28
   Common Agricultural Policy, 110,
      117–118, 201
   on food standards, 179–182, 179n10
   on policy interactions, 227
   political economy, 203
   public investment in agricultural and
      food research, 193
   reforms in agricultural and
      production policies, 110
Exogenous price, 153n2
Export Enhancement Program (EEP),
   123, 124

F
FAIR Act, 124
Fair land rents, 114n6
Fair rents, 204
Falcon, W., xi
Fan, S., 137
FAO, *see* Food and Agricultural
   Organization
Farm Bills, 28, 29, 119
   emergence of, 119–122
   political coalitions in, 122–123
Farm Bureau, 120, 121
Farmers' Alliance, 114n6
Farm subsidies, *see* Agricultural
   subsidies
FCIP, *see* Federal Crop Insurance
   Program
FDI, *see* Foreign direct investment
Federal Crop Insurance Program
   (FCIP), 28, 125
Ferejohn, J.A., 5
Fernandez, R., 234
Feudal systems, 114
Finland
   agricultural crisis in late nineteenth
      century, 113n4, 114
Fischler, F., 118
Fixed commodity policies, economic
   interaction effects with, 228–229
Fixity of land tenure, 114n6, 204
Food advocacy groups, 13
Food aid, 26, 121, 123
Food Aid After Fifty Years, 26
Food and Agricultural Organization
   (FAO), 161, 164n12
Food crisis, 151–165
Food policies, xvi, 3, 6–9, 35, 39, 41,
   46, 52–57, 69, 71, 76, 79, 87,
   89, 95, 102, 103, 154, 164, 225
   development policy priorities and,
      159–162
   interactions (*see* Policy interactions)

246 INDEX

Food policies (*cont.*)
  reforms, 109–131
  See also Agricultural policies
Food politics, with volatility, 145–147
Food price, 152–154
  bad news or good policies, 162–165
  basic principles of, 152–154
  communication incentives and,
    155–156
  effects on poverty and food security,
    154–155
  funding and, 159–162
  mass media and, 156–159
  social media and, 156–159
Food price volatility, 137–147
  and distortions, balancing, 142
  empirical observations, 142–145
  politics with, 145–147
  price stabilization, benefits
    and costs of, 139–142
Food regulations, 19n5, 115, 226
Food security, price effects on, 154–155
Food stamp program, 123
Food standards, 169–182
  efficiency and equity effects, 171–174
  government decision-making on, 175
  media, 176
  persistence of, 179–180
  pro-standard and anti-standard
    coalitions, 176–177
  trade and, 177–179
  trade and power dynamics, 180–182
Foreign direct investment (FDI), 169n1
Former Soviet Union (FSU), 208
Foster, W.E., 91
France, ix, 18, 47, 49
  agricultural crisis in late nineteenth
    century, 112–114, 113n4
  land tenure reforms, 205, 205n3
  political land reforms, 201
  political organization of formers,
    116n9
Francken, N., 157n7

Francois, J.F., 49
Freebairn, J.W., 229n4
Free sales, 114n6, 204
Free trade, in Europe, 112
French–German trade agreement
  (1862), 112
Freund, C., 37
Frye, T., 213
FSU, *see* Former Soviet Union
Funding, 151, 156, 156n6, 228
  donor, 159–162, 164

G
Garcia, A.F., 44, 74n3
Gardner, B.L., 40n4, 74n3, 109n2,
    152n1, 163n11, 193, 233
GATT, 56, 103–105, 103n2
Gawande, K., 49, 74n3, 77n4
GDP, *see* Gross domestic product
Genetically modified organisms (GMOs),
    24–26, 174, 175, 177, 180
George, H., 4n1
Georgia, 217
Germany, 18, 49
  agricultural crisis in late nineteenth
    century, 112, 113n4
  free trade, 112
  National Socialist
    (Nazi) Party, 116n9
  political organization of farmers,
    116n9
Getting Prices Right, 152
Ghana, 46
Global Food Crisis Response
  Program, 161
Global food price spikes, vii, 18, 27,
    38, 52, 89, 125, 137–139, 151,
    154, 155, 163–165
GMOs, *see* Genetically modified
  organisms
Gorbachev, G., 212
Governance structure, 6n3, 70, 77, 97

INDEX 247

Government decision-making,
  on food standards, 175
Graber, E., xi
Graff, G.D., 25
Grassroots pressure, and agricultural
  reform, 126–128
Great Depression, 120
Great Leap Forward, 127, 128, 209
Great Recession, 123
Green box, 93, 105
Gross domestic product (GDP), 113n4
Grossman, G.M., 5, 6n3, 146n3, 175
Guariso, A., 158, 160

H
Haggard, S., 57, 101
Hayami, Y., 40n4, 109n2, 163n11
Headey, D.D., 155n4
Heady, D., 137
Heinegg, A., 210n16
Heinz, M., 52, 157n9
Helpman, E., 5, 6n3, 146n3, 175
Hendrix, C., 163
Hensen, S., 174n7
*High Level Forum for a Better
  Functioning Food Supply
  Chain*, 18n4
"Historical Justice" argument, 215,
  215n22
Historical legacies, and land reforms,
  213–217
History, 3, 8, 17, 19, 22, 26, 29, 30,
  77, 79, 88, 89, 92, 169, 179
  policy reforms in, 128–131
Hoekman, B., 49, 74n3, 77n4
Homestead Act, 119, 119n10
Household responsibility system
  (HRS), 127, 128, 208, 209, 213
Hoxha, E., 47, 78
HRS, *see* Household responsibility
  system

Huang, J., xi, 126n16, 129, 131
Hunger, 18, 23, 110, 126, 151, 154,
  159, 161, 162, 164, 200, 218

I
IFPRI, *see* International Food Policy
  Research Institute
Ignowski, L., xi
IMF, *see* International Monetary Fund
Import tariffs, 15–16
Income distribution, 15, 35–39, 71,
  192, 230
India, xvi, 98
  public investment in agricultural and
  food research, 189
Inequality and ideology, 38–39
Information costs, 74–76
In-kind *vs.* share distribution of land,
  216–217
Institutional reforms, 118, 199–219
  East Asia, 207–213
  Eastern Europe, 207–213
  grassroots pressure and leadership
  support for, 211–213
  political, 118
Institutions, 4, 5, 8, 9, 23, 25, 57, 77,
  91, 121, 153, 176, 190, 193, 228
  and credible compensation, 234–236
Insulation of domestic markets, 38,
  41, 43, 46, 138, 139, 207
International Food Policy Research
  Institute (IFPRI), 164n12
International institutions, 54–57,
  92–93
International Monetary Fund (IMF),
  93, 101
International organizations, 7, 23, 57,
  156n6, 157, 163, 164
Ireland
  land tenure reforms, 206n4
  political land reforms, 201

248 INDEX

Ivanova, N., 17n3
Ivory Coast, 46

J
Japan, v, 121
Jevons, W.S., 4n1

K
Kahneman, D., 37n2
Kazakhstan, 217
Kennedy, J.F., 29, 123
Kenya, 46
Kerr, W.A., 175
Kim, J. S., 157n8
Kono, D.Y., 42n6, 53
Kotwal, A., 236
Krueger, A.O., 4, 5, 69, 109n2

L
La Ferrara, E., 49
Land owners, 80, 122, 203–205
Land reforms, 199–219
China, 209
historical legacies and, 213–217
Western Europe, 201–206
Land rental, in Western Europe,
201–203
Land restitution, 216
Land rights, 199
Land tenure reforms
patterns of, 205–206
in Western Europe, 203–206
Latin America, 54, 57, 101
Lawrence, S., xi
Leadership, 127, 129
change, 54, 208–209, 218
support for institutional reforms,
211–213
Lecossois, E., xi
Lerman, Z., 213n19

Liquidation Councils, 216n24
Loan rates, 120, 121
Lobbying, 3, 13, 14, 15n1, 17,
17n2, 19n5, 20, 22, 24–28, 30,
36, 37, 43, 46, 49, 51, 53, 56,
75–77, 90, 102, 114, 117, 120,
123–126, 171, 174, 175, 180,
191, 194, 196
Logic of Collective Action, The,
x, 4, 48
López, R.A., 49, 74n3, 77n4,
129n19, 228

M
McCluskey, J.J., xvi, 52, 74, 177
McGuire, M.C., 42
Macours, K, 208n9
Maertens, M., 170n2, 179n10
Magee, S.P., 53
Malthus, T., 4n1
Mao Zedong, 47, 78, 79, 127, 208,
209, 211, 212
Market imperfection, 139
Market organizations, 89n2
Marshall, A., 4n1
Martin, W.J., 140, 155n4, 228
Marx, K., 4n1
Marxists, 200
Maskus, K., 179n10
Mason, Nicole M., 21n7
Mass media, 50–52, 51n9, 156–159
Masters, W.A., 44, 74n3
Mathijs, E., xi
Matschke, X., 74n3
Mattoo, A., 174n7
Maxwell, D., 26
Maystadt, J.F., 163
Media, 6, 9, 74, 75, 100–101
bias, 51n9
and food standards, 176–177
mass, 156–159
social, 156–159
Mellor, J., 152
Meloni, G., xi, 181

INDEX 249

Middle East and Northern Africa, 163
Mill, J.S., 3, 4n1
Millennium Development Goals, 129n18
Mitchell, D., 137n1
Mitchell, M., 91
Mitra, D., 38, 46
Monsanto, 25
Moro, A., 91
Morrell Act, 119n10
Mueller, D.C., 6n3
Mullainathan, S., 155n5
Munk, K.J., 41
Murphy, J.A., 228

N
NAFTA, *see* North American Free Trade Agreement
Nakasone, E., 100n1
National Farmers' Union, 121
Naylor, R., xi
Netherlands, the
  agricultural crisis in late nineteenth century, 113, 113n4, 114
  land tenure reforms, 205, 205n3
Neuberger, A., xi
Newbery, D., 141
New Deal, 120
New Zealand, 54, 102, 105
  reforms in agricultural and food policies, 109n2
NGOs, *see* Non-governmental organizations
Nominal Rates of Assistance (NRAs), 69, 87–89, 95–98, 100–104, 110, 111, 117, 119, 121–123, 125, 130, 228
Non-governmental organizations (NGOs), 23n9, 26, 26n12, 164n12, 174
Non-tariff barriers (NTBs), 88n1
Non-tariff measures (NTMs), 177–179

North American Free Trade Agreement (NAFTA), 56
North, D., 4
NRAs, *see* Nominal Rates of Assistance
NTBs, *see* Non-tariff barriers
NTMs, *see* Non-tariff measures
Number One Document, 129

O
Oberholzer-Gee, R., 52
Obfuscation argument, 53
Obfuscation perspective, 91
ODA, *see* Overseas Development Aid
OECD, *see* Organisation for Economic Co-operation and Development
Oehmke, J.F., 193
Olper, A., xi, 43, 44, 47, 52, 74n3, 78, 100, 101
Olper, P., 38
Olson, M., x, 4, 5, 42, 48, 76, 163n11
Orden, D., xi, 56, 104, 120n11, 122, 124
Organisation for Economic Co-operation and Development (OECD), 23n9, 110n3, 121, 164n12
O'Rourke, K., 42n6
Overseas Development Aid (ODA), 160, 161
Over-standardization, 175
Oxfam, 161, 164n12
Özden, C., 37

P
Paarlberg, R.L., 175, 180
Pakistan, 17
  food price volatility, 144, 145
PARI, *see* Public agricultural research investments
Payne, A.A., 155n5
Peltzman, S., 4

250 INDEX

Perfect Storm, 137
Persson, T., 5, 6n3
PIEs, *see* Political interaction effects
Pieters, H., xi, 44, 142, 145
Pirzio-Biroli, J., 45
Pokrivcak, J., xi, 45
Poland, 104
Policy choices, factors influencing,
35–57
crises, 53–54
deadweight costs and transaction
costs, 40–41
economic structure, 39–40
ideology, 46–47
income distribution, 35–39
information, 50–53
International institutions, 54–57
political institutions, 41–46
political organization, 48–50
Policy communication, 151, 154,
155, 158
Policy instrument choice, 14, 15n1,
30, 40, 53, 104, 236
political economy of, 89–92
trade and International institutions
and, 92–93
Policy interactions, 225–236
economic interaction effects, 226,
228–231
institutions and credible
compensation, 234–236
political interaction effects,
226–228, 231–232
Policy organizations (POs), 155–157
Policy package, 225, 227
Policy reforms, 6, 93, 101–105,
109–131, 226, 226n1, 227,
227n2, 236
in China, 126–131
in Europe, 110–119
persistence and, 123–125
in USA, 119–126

Political changes, and agricultural
reform, 126–128
Political coalitions
in agricultural and food policies,
13–30
in Farm Bills, 122–123
value chains and, 14–29
Political collapse, in Eastern Europe,
210–211
Political economy, 4–9
food price volatility and, 137–147
food standards, 171, 174, 176, 177,
179–182
land and institutional reforms, 200
origin of, 4n1
(*see also* specific entries)
policy implications, 225, 226, 228,
230–232, 236
Western Europe, 203
Political factors, 48
Political institutional equilibria, 53
Political institutional reforms, 118
Political institutions, 4, 9, 41–46, 77,
102, 111, 218
Political interaction effects (PIEs), 82,
226–228
Political organization, 48–50, 76–77,
216, 232
Political precaution, and food
standards, 171
Political reforms, 77–79, 100–101
Western Europe, 201–206
Political regimes, 42–43
change, grassroots pressure and,
217–224
Political system, in China, 208–209
Politics of Precaution, The, 175
POs, *see* Policy organizations
Poverty, 9, 23, 114, 126, 129, 151,
158, 161, 162, 164, 165, 207,
209, 218
price effects on, 154–155

INDEX 251

Power dynamics, trade and, 180–182
Price stabilization, 120, 146
  benefits and costs of, 139–142
  distortions from, 140
Principles of Economics, 4n1
Private property rights, 199
Producer Support Estimate (PSE),
  105, 105n3, 110n3, 115, 121,
  125, 129, 130, 228
Pro-standard coalitions of food
  standards, 176–177
PSE, *see* Producer Support Estimate
Public agricultural research
  investments (PARI), 189,
  191, 192, 194–196, 194n2,
  229–232, 231n6
  interaction with commodity
    policies, 228
  politically optimal, with commodity
    policies, 232
Public investment, in agricultural and
  food research, 189–196
  distributional effects, 190–192
  economic development and research
    investment, 192–194
  interactions with other policies, 196
  spillover effects, 190
  trade and impacts, 194–195

Q
Quasi-rents, 37

R
Raimondi, V., 43, 74n3
R&D, *see* Research and development
Rationally ignorant voter, 50
  See also Information costs
Rausser, G.C., xix, 5n3, 40n4, 41n5,
  46n8, 74n3, 91
Relative income and loss aversion, 36–38

Relative income effect, 90
Renewable Energy Directive (2009),
  EC, 27n14
Renewable Fuel Standard (RFS),
  125n15
Research and development (R&D),
  189, 190
Retailers, 17, 18, 174
Revenue motive, of public policy, 90
RFS, *see* Renewable Fuels Standard
Ricardo, D., 3, 4n1, 226n1, 227n2
Robinson, J.A., 5, 38, 91n4, 210n15
Rodrik, D., 234, 235
Roland, G., 208n9
Romania, 104
Roosevelt, Franklin D., 120
  New Deal and, 120
Rozelle, S., xi, 208n9, 209n11,
  213n19, 214n20
Russia, *see* Soviet Union
Ruttan, V.W., 193

S
Sadoulet, E., 152n1
SAF, *see* Societé des Agriculteurs de
  France
Sales markets, in Western Europe,
  201–203
San Nong, 129
SAPs, *see* Structural-adjustment
  programs
Schultz, T.W., 152, 193
SFP, *see* Single farm payments system
Shepsle, K.A., 5n3
Shleifer, A., 155n5, 213
Single farm payments (SFP) system, 119
Smith, A., 3, 4n1, 112, 226n1, 227n2
SNAP, *see* Supplemental Nutrition
  Assistance Program
Social media, 156–159
Social welfare maximizing (SWM), 142

252 INDEX

Societé des Agriculteurs de France (SAF), 116n9
Society of the Land for the People, 114n6
Soviet Union, 6, 47, 54, 56, 78, 79, 103, 104, 112, 210n16, 217
  agricultural reforms, 209n11
  land reforms in, 214
  political regime change, 218
  transfer of land ownership, 215n22, 216
Spillover effects of public research, 190
SPS, 169, 170
Staiger, R., 174n7
Stalin, J., 47, 78, 212
Stigler, G.J., 4, 5
Stiglitz, J.E., 141, 235
Strömberg, D., 52, 100, 157n8
Structural-adjustment programs (SAPs), 23, 57
  and policy conditionality, 101
Sub-Saharan Africa, 101
Supermarket revolution, 169n1
Supplemental Nutrition Assistance Program (SNAP), 29, 122, 123
Supply Chain Initiative, 18n4
Sweden, 54
  reforms in agricultural and food policies, 109n2
Swinnen, J.F.M., vi, vii, xvii, 5n2, 17, 17n3, 23n9, 26n12, 36, 38–40, 40n4, 44, 45, 52, 56, 70n2, 74, 74n3, 77, 100, 101, 105, 111, 116n8, 124n14, 138, 142, 145, 155, 156, 157n7, 157n9, 170n2, 175n8, 179n10, 179n11, 181, 192, 203n2, 205n3, 206, 208n9, 209n11, 210n16, 213n19, 214n20, 230n5, 232n7, 234
SWM, *see* Social welfare maximizing
Synthetic control method, 44

T
Tabellini, G., 5, 6n3
Tanzania, 46
Taxation, v, 3, 5, 6, 9, 15, 69, 70, 74, 78, 79, 87, 88, 90–93, 96–102, 126, 127, 129, 131, 137, 162, 192, 194, 196, 205, 206, 212, 213, 233, 234
Taylor, A.M., 42n6
Technological treadmill, 193
Tenant protection index (TPI), 205n3
Thatcher, M.
  privatization policies, 210n17
Theories, 5, 8, 13, 76, 77, 100, 101, 123
Theory of Economic Regulation, The, 4
Theory of Political Economy, The, 4n1
Timmer, C.P., 138, 152
Total Support Estimate (TSE), 110n3
Tovar, P., 37, 37n2
TPI, *see* Tenant protection index
Tracy, M., 47
Trade
  bias (*see* Anti-trade bias)
  and food standards, 177–179
  and power dynamics, 180–182
Transaction costs, 40–41
Transatlantic Trade and Investment Partnership (TTIP), 170
Transfer of land ownership, 214–215
Transfer of land to current users or previous owners, 215–216
Treaty of Nice, 118
TSE, *see* Total Support Estimate
Tsur, Y., 36n1
TTIP, *see* Transatlantic Trade and Investment Partnership
Tullock, G., 4
Turkmenistan, 210n16
Turnovsky, S.J., 141
Tversky, A., 37n2

INDEX 253

U

Ukraine, 217
Under-standardization, 175
United Kingdom (UK), 18, 49, 210n17
  agricultural crisis in late nineteenth
    century, 113, 113n4, 114
  Corn Laws, 110, 112
  landowners' parliamentary
    power, 204
  land tenure reforms, 206
  voting rights reforms, 204
United States (USA), v, vi, 20, 23–29,
    25n11, 37n3, 56, 104, 112, 122
  biofuels, 125–126
  biofuels legislation, 27n13
  crop insurance, 125–126
  Farm Bills (*see* Farm Bills)
  on food standards, 179–181,
    179n10
  persistence and policy reforms,
    123–125
  on policy interactions, 227, 233
  policy reforms in, 119–126
  public investment in agricultural and
    food research, 189, 190, 193
  reforms in agricultural and
    production policies, 110
URAA, *see* Uruguay Round
    Agreement on Agriculture
"Urban bias" effect, 233
Uruguay Round Agreement on
    Agriculture (URAA), 23, 56, 57,
    103, 104
Uruguay Round of GATT, 124
USA, *see* United States
Uzbekistan, 210n16

V

Value chains, 9, 14–29, 164, 169
  consumer–farmer coalitions, 28–29

consumers and, 17–19
crop insurance and, 27–28
environmental concerns and, 22–23
food, feed, fuel and, 26–27
food aid and, 26
globalization, and new international
    coalitions, 24
GM regulations and agribusiness
    and, 24–26
international interests and, 23
landowners and, 19–21
Van Belle, D. A., 157n8
Vandemoortele, T., xi, 175n8, 179n11
Van Herck, K., xi
Van Tongeren, F., 181
Vatn, A., 41
Vietnam, 209n13, 217
  Doi Moi, 209n12
  policy reforms, 126n16
Vogel, D., 181
Voter information paradox, 53
Voting reforms, 206n5

W

Waldfogel, J., 52
War on Poverty, 123
Weingast, B.R., 6n3
Western Europe, 112, 115, 116
  land rental and sales markets in,
    201–203
  land tenure reforms in, 203–206
  political and land reforms in, 201–206
  political economy, 203
Whittman, D., 6n3
Williamson, J., 57, 101
Williamson, O., 4
Willmann, G., 53
Wilson, J.S., 174n7, 179n10
World Bank, ix, x, 5, 6, 23n9, 69,
    93, 101, 161, 164n12

254 INDEX

World Trade Organization (WTO),
  vii, xvi, 55–57, 55n10, 88n1,
  92, 93, 118, 131, 141, 169,
  170, 174
  policy reforms and, 103–105
World War I, 115, 117, 119
Wright, 137n1
WTO, *see* World Trade Organization

Y
Yang, D., 128
Yao, X., 193
Yeung, M.T., 175

Z
Zilberman, D., x, 180

CPSIA information can be obtained
at www.ICGtesting.com
Printed in the USA
LVHW04*1241280518
578670LV00011B/734/P